John Charles G. Mexborough

Half round the old World

Being some Account of a Tour in Russia, the Caucasus, Persia, and Turkey

John Charles G. Mexborough

Half round the Old World

Being some Account of a Tour in Russia, the Caucasus, Persia, and Turkey

ISBN/EAN: 9783743316294

Manufactured in Europe, USA, Canada, Australia, Japa

Cover: Foto ©ninafisch / pixelio.de

Manufactured and distributed by brebook publishing software (www.brebook.com)

John Charles G. Mexborough

Half round the old World

HALF ROUND THE OLD WORLD.

BEING

SOME ACCOUNT OF A TOUR IN RUSSIA, THE CAUCASUS, PERSIA, AND TURKEY, 1865—66.

BY

VISCOUNT POLLINGTON, M.A., F.R.G.S.

London:
EDWARD MOXON & CO., DOVER STREET, W.
1867.

PREFACE.

THE following pages are an almost exact transcription of a diary, kept during the interval between August and April 1865-66. Thus the present and past tenses have been used indifferently, as we thought the one or the other served the sense best. We have added no after-thoughts; no descriptions of the origin of peoples, or of the former state of places, have been laboriously culled from the pages of encyclopædias. Under these circumstances, profoundly scientific disquisitions must not be expected. We preferred leaving the statements as they were written down day by day, only occasionally slightly arranging their order.

The names of places and persons are in almost every instance spelt phonetically.

THE AUTHOR.

London, *January*, 1867.

HALF ROUND THE OLD WORLD.

CHAPTER I.

ON the 14th of July in the year of grace 1865 we (editorial We!) started from London by the L. C. and D. Railway. This may appear a somewhat unimportant fact, but we had for our fellow-traveller an old lady who insisted to her companion that all hotels throughout the inhabited globe called "The Chatham" belonged to this company! Having booked our luggage through, we hardly expected to have to pay any duty on our saddle, but a certain sum was charged for the privilege of having that useful article conveyed through Prussia. Besides our saddle, we had also, previously to starting, invested in a most useful travelling dressing-case, calculated to hold nothing in the smallest possible space. Some one made the observation that in Prussia the difference between the several classes of carriages on the railway apparently is, that the first-class only hold six upon velvet and the second-class eight upon leather; the third-class as many as it will hold, upon wood, and the fourth, as many as can stand upon their feet. Stopping in Hanover just enough time to admire the splendid Linden-Allée we had often toddled in before, we proceeded to Berlin, that enlightened capital, and of course walked into the " Thiergarten," so called because there are no animals there except horses, " lionnes," and an occasional muzzled dog. As the heat was intense, we found the Seltzer-water emporiums very useful, and entered every one we could find to quench our thirst (they are distributed at perhaps every fifty yards in Berlin). Wandering about the museum, we overheard a pimply-faced cicerone in the picture gallery talking in extremely bad French to an imbecile French family; the remark we were most struck by, was his observing, of the famous Correggio—almost the gem of the gallery—Io and Jupiter, that it was " de l'école du Titien!" Again we went, as the great King of Prussia might say, into " Mon musée pour m'amuser!" Leaving for Dantzick, in company with two Russian ladies and one ditto gentleman, we were asked by one of them, on crossing the frontier into Prussian Poland, whether the partition of Poland dated from the " Guerre d'Italie!"— got into a charmingly old-fashioned hotel, the " Englisches Haus," immensely deep and very narrow, with no carpets in the rooms: such ruinous old houses with pointed gables. Booksellers appear to flourish here. This being considered in England a seaport town, we were not surprised to hear that the sea is four miles off; went into the largest church in the place, and should be considerably puzzled to say whether it was Protestant or Catholic. The grotesque wood carvings, belonging to a period when art was in swaddling clothes, deserve notice, and some pictures painted before the Flood, also. The changes that one's name goes through in hotel books are perfectly appalling; we have had the felicity of seeing ourselves printed and published in various gazettes as Minston,

Miryton, and once as Miss John. The town swarms with soldiers; there are many fine Allées outside affording a grateful shade in hot weather. The Bourse is well worth a visit, but we leave the descriptive portions to our Murray. The Jews walk about in their long gabardines, *vide* Mr. C. Kean when on the Rialto. At a village, rejoicing in the melodious name of Wierzoboloff, we reached the Russian frontier, where a revolver we had with us was confiscated. However, we got it back at St. Petersburg. Our passports were examined three times, the Russian authorities probably taking us for a " dirty conspirator." Reached St. Petersburg in due course, and got into a drosky, remarked that the people all were impressed with the idea that everyone must speak Russian fluently, not at all our case. After an ineffectual search for Miss Benson's establishment, we were obliged to put up at an hotel where they very considerately only charged us about £2 10*s*. for one night's lodging. In the morning we transported ourselves and effects to the English Quay, Miss Benson's, a wonderful view on the Neva. Truly we found

St. Petersburg, a "city of magnificent distances." Every house appears to choose what style of pavement it will have before its door, and lays it (the pavement) down accordingly, thus causing a variety which, as is well known, is always charming—wood, iron, M'Adam, stone, every kind appears to be represented, even india-rubber, and the "tout ensemble" is horrible! Admired the statue of Peter the Great on horseback and the Admiralty place—the horse is rearing and trampling on a snake!—why? Orthodox passers-by of Isaac's Cathedral cross themselves no end of times, on the head, breast, two shoulders, and stomach. Went with the Chargé d'Affaires to the "Hermitage:" magnificent dark marble caryatid negroes in front; we went first upstairs, but words would fail to express the magnificence of the rooms; we then went on into the first floor, and saw some Roman antiquities, including a shepherd with a very senile expression, and a stupendous greenish marble vase in Siberian jasper, some twelve feet long by five broad, on a fine pedestal of the same material. The Kertsch room contains some beautiful gold ornaments. My future travelling companion, Captain W——, arrived from Stockholm. The block of granite on which stands the statue of Peter I. suggested thoughts of how pleasant it must be to have an unlimited quantity of serfs who must work and of subjects who must pay for you. It is the largest block in Europe, we believe. At the Hermitage the floors are of marble, excepting where parquet is used. There is an immense collection of drawings, the greater portion carefully sealed up in cupboards, to allow of easier inspection presumably. An order is required before gaining admittance. One printed on a Russian rouble note and handed to the porter is as good as any. Vases of fabulous size, in green jasper, malachite, and lapis lazuli, stand about in reckless profusion. Those of the delicate rose and deep purple Siberian marble struck our fancy most. Peter the Great's collection of bric-à-brac is interesting. We entered the private theatre, which has a very deep stage; the auditorium consists of red velvet stalls arranged in a semicircle, so that all the spectators can see every part of the stage. For the Tsar there is a most uncomfortable straight-backed chair—penalty of greatness as much as being occasionally shot at. One hundred and eighty-eight of the best pictures in the gallery came from the Walpole collection at Houghton Hall, including four delightful Murillos. A "St. George" by Raphael once belonged to Charles I. of England, art-patron and martyr. The largest picture Sir J. Reynolds ever painted, "Infant Hercules strangling serpents," is also here, rather washy, however; G. Kneller and Thos. Jones are also represented. The collection of Intaglios is remarkably complete. After this we indulged in some "quass," bought in the street, a liquid of a yellow colour, somewhat like very sour lemonade.

On the 30th we entered Isaac's Cathedral to witness a Greek service, where all the congregation stand, and perpetually keep bowing like the Chinese porcelain figures. The singing of the concealed choir is, however, very impressive. Of course we went, by rail, to old Peterhoff palace, where we observed copies of the two Athletæ of the Vatican, by Canova, gorgeously gilt, spouting water at each other—rather a "come down" in the world. The Russian wodki, their brandy, we thought extremely nasty, but the black bread, like pumpernickel, excellent.

Next day we chartered a wild Irishman, who could hardly talk English, owing in a great measure to frequent imbibitions of wodki, but who called himself a commissioner, and visited the small house that Peter I. built himself, for himself, and very well too. An outer roofing is now over it, to preserve the priceless relic; a quantity of things manufactured by his own august hands lie about. The dining-room is converted into a chapel, having a lot of mould candles stored here for use in it. We remarked to W—— that these were some of the candles Peter moulded, whereupon our friend the Irishman turned round and explained that they were not. We also visited the Museum of Natural History, and observed some pickled babies, on the ground floor; on the second, the Mammoth found in the ice of Siberia is the most interesting object. There are also many stuffed animals, and minerals not stuffed), with a good many fleas of preternatural size, which are not contented to remain, but cling to one on going home. Saw a man being carried off to prison by a member of the police; his (the man's) hands were tied behind his back. We naturally went to see the largest ball-room in the world, that in the Torrida Palace, but it is mean, whitewashed, and with tawdry silver paper decorations. At a dinner, at a restaurant in Russian fashion, with Zakuska (Caviar and bitters) before, heard a story of C—— C——. When minister of America here, he gave a grand ball, to which archdukes came without their duchesses. When supper was announced, C—— C—— clapped one grand duke on the back, and said, "Come and have some *lunch* in American fashion." Consternation of duke!

On the 1st of August we dined with one of the attachés on an island in the Neva, and afterwards drove out in a barouche appertaining to the Spanish embassy, to see the illuminations in honour of the new Tsarewitch, who had taken the oath of allegiance to the Emperor to-day. The whole island was studded with places of amusement, and the concourse of mujicks and others was enormous; we had to join a string of carriages miles in length, and were continually at a standstill. The Summer theatre there was remarkably prettily illuminated with lamps, forming green, red, and white wreaths round the pilasters outside. There were fireworks going on, of which we only caught an occasional glimpse, through the trees, or when rockets shot up into the clear summer air. The various branches of the Neva wander about the island in an eccentric manner, and we were continually coming upon boat houses belonging to various clubs, and all well illuminated, especially the Russian national one, which had raised a very tall mast in front, supported by four ropes, along which all manner of coloured lamps were suspended; spasmodic Bengal fires kept illuminating distant vistas, and a long row of trees by the waterside was hung with lamps for more than a mile. The cold wind was the only drawback.

Next night we drove to Petrovskoe, another island, to an establishment called the "mineral waters," on account of there being none naturally there, but supplies from the different springs of Europe are kept in stock—none, however, from Bath ! There are gardens and a theatre, on which Swiss singers, English niggers, German ventriloquists, and French actors perform—anything but "native talent." There are lengthy intervals allowed for promenading in the garden, when the company bears a close resemblance to that to be observed at Cremorne. The last entertainment was termed " L'Africaine, a burlesque," possibly because not a particle of the music of the opera was introduced into it. We visited the palace of Tsarkoe Seloe by rail: a large, straggling building, in which, amongst other things we admired, or wondered at, a room pannelled with amber. Wandering about the fine gardens we came to some sham ruins, where was also a model mast for the little archdukes to play at sailors upon, and a netting underneath to catch them when falling off. Missing our way we dittoed (?) the train and thus being in for the penny we thought we would " go in for the pound," so took a train going to

Paulowsky, a summer garden with a concert-room, built as a speculation by the railway company, where for the small charge of nothing (excepting the railway ticket), you hear Strauss, John Strauss of Vienna; a military band played in the intervals of S.'s music, but remarkably badly—perhaps to act as a foil to his band. Coming back, W—— told us of an old house-keeper of his, who, upon his observing that he had seen a great many pretty faces lately, said "Ah! sir, it is very easy for them as has no work to do to be pretty!" Receipt for good looks:—Do nothing. Some of us ought to be very handsome! With a written order we entered the Winter Palace. Pictures of the battles of the Russian army are very numerous. Balaklava figures in a dark room, but full justice is done to the gallantry of the charge. The first Duke of Wellington's portrait is included in a collection of portraits of generals. The Crown jewels are kept in an upper room, with two old soldiers as their guardians.

On the 7th we started for Moscow, which we reached in twenty hours. At one of the stations, bells with agreeable voices are made. Plenty of stoppages for the purpose of eating.

One of our first visits was to the Kremlin. We took off our hats in passing beneath the sacred doorway and image, and then stood on the terrace, almost overpowered by the sight that met our eyes. A panorama is always difficult to describe, more especially such an one: more churches than in Rome, and most of them in the quaint Byzantine style. The river Moskau flowing in front; on the right the new Church of St. Saviour—an addition to the 380 (?) already existing, as if those were not enough. On the left and in front, innumerable silver, and gold, and green cupolas, and the green roofs of the houses; further, a dim range of mountains; nearer, the quaint Pegu, Ravenna, Chinese, Indian pagoda-like, picturesque, grotesque St. Basil Church, with others in the same, but not quite so barbarous style, quite bewilder the spectator. The great bell of Moscow lies on the terrace in front of the Ivan Tower, which we ascended, to be only more bewildered by the extent and marvellous character of the view.

Mr. Billo, our host, is a most obliging man. We found that no luggage is transported free on the Petersburg-Moscow line; but this is obviated by taking as much as possible into the carriages, which are tolerably comfortable—now, we believe, very good indeed. Writing of railways reminds us of a story of W——'s, which we insert here, though having nothing to do with our journey, but for want of a better place:— Once, on getting to Calais, W—— wanted to enter a first-class carriage, in which there were only two occupants, lying curled up, apparently fast asleep; the opposite seats covered with small bags, &c. He addressed each sleeping form in English and French, to know whether those seats were occupied, and getting no answer, he turned round to a friend at the door, observing, " It's no use, the old beggars won't answer." Sudden uprising of one of the bundles, crying out in great ire, " Beggars ! sir, who do you call beggars? No more a beggar than you are. I'm a *reel* gentleman, sir, and that's more than you are."

Having had almost all our hair cut off, it now

stands on our heads like the quills upon the fretful porcupine—Shakespeare. After breakfast *at the fork* we walked again to the Kremlin, which we discovered to be a portion of the town entirely consecrated to palaces and churches, and surrounded by a high wall. We entered the palace, which we should describe—but are not all these things written in Murray?—and afterwards saw the robes of the "Papas," the superintending priest keeping us waiting until he had got himself up in his best suit of silk, and accepting afterwards a small remuneration with thanks; we likewise saw the original cruse full of Jerusalem oil, which hath not failed yet.

Next day drove out to the Simonoff Monastery by a desperate road, passing countless churches, many of them having on their cupolas gilt crosses with crescents at the bottom of them, a curious mixture of Oriental and Occidental religious symbols; of coursé, the crescent is said to refer to the Virgin. The omnibuses appear uncomfortable; they are covered, and the seat at right angles to the driver, drawn by four horses abreast.

The monastery is on a low hill out of the town, and the bell-tower affords a fine view of Moscow. We had some difficulty in getting up, but at last seized on a monk who was walking about in a thick serge dress, with ditto round hat-cap, this about six inches high. He unlocked the door for us; presently the bellringer came up and received our offering, it being "infra dig." for the monk to do so, though we have little doubt he would not have refused a contribution. We entered an "old curiosity shop," where there were several "soi-disant" Italian and French pictures, but almost all without exception repainted, if ever painted before! After dinner we walked out to see the water-tower built by Peter the Great to resemble a ship. It requires to be told this previously, in order to find a resemblance between this building and anything that ever floated. It consists of a fine tall spire, rising from the midst of an oblong Gothic and Renaissance sort of building, which forms an archway. We had an interview with the friend of a prospective servant for our tour, but the friend seemed too great a swell, and required all his expenses calculated on a princely scale. We observed that the natives do not stare at one much. We went to the treasury in the Kremlin, where many magnificent things are to be seen. Here the "Constitution" of Poland lies buried in a small black box, not unlike a coffin: Resurgat! Downstairs some splendid carriages, one a gift of Queen Elizabeth, which shows English workmanship in a very good light. The ironwork is like the Venetian. Out to the Romanoff house. The rooms about six feet high, doors four feet, beds very small, windows in proportion; altogether like a large wax-doll house. We visited the common market for fruit and bread, crowded with filthy people very picturesque. Why does cleanliness seem incompatible with the picturesque? Drunkenness seems very prevalent in the town; we saw one man perfectly drunk going through the ceremony of crossing himself in the most imperturbable manner, only swaying violently to and fro; another was walking behind a water-barrel, singing and turning the imaginary handle of this supposititious barrel-organ. On the 11th we set out for the Troitza monastery, founded by Saint Sergius; we had a card to a monk who formerly was a colonel and a count, though that did not stand in the way of his accepting a trifling present. We visited the bakehouse; all the bread is blessed, and fashioned into round little loaves of the shape of a "devil on two sticks" with a thick waist. We drank some holy water, coming out of a fountain in the shape of a cross, in the yard, surrounded by lay and clerical tombs, and it was as nasty as any impure water would be. In the chapel of the Assumption some of the pictures of the Virgin are literally incrusted with emeralds as large as bantams' eggs. Returning, we went next day to the museum, a fine Doric sort of building, with cobwebs spun all over the door: no admittance except on business, and no one had any business there. Four of us then determined on a regular Russian dinner in a regular Russian restaurant. The waiters all wore white nightshirt overalls; we began with orange bitters, black bread, salt smoked fish, and caviare. Then six cups were placed on the table, each containing a different drink: four soups, two cold—one rejoicing in a name like Backvineyard, the other in Ochrowska, apparently milk with cucumber in small slices—and two hot, Onka and Solianca, a Polish preparation, both containing the famous Sterlet of the Volga. This fish tastes somewhat like well-fed eel: isinglass patties with the latter; excellent chicken cutlets with buckwheat, Crimean sherry, champagne, and claret, the latter nasty, the second bad gooseberry, but the brown sherry very palateable. After many other dishes, some very strong yellow tea, without milk and in diminutive cups, finished up the whole. This, of course, was some "caravan tea," and tasted to us very like good cowslip ditto. On the 13th we went to what our companion, the author of Murray's handbook, uneuphoniously called the Louse Market, where (dirty) merchants most do congregate on a Sunday morning. The articles exposed for sale are all second-hand here. We then went to the Church of the Christening, on the Kremlin, where we heard one of the bulls of Basan roaring the service; and afterwards watched a procession outside. This being a religious one all the populace took off their hats while it was passing, an excellent opportunity, as it was very raw weather, for catching cold, of which we both availed ourselves. We are sorry to say that we seldom have seen a more disreputable lot than the priests who took part in the ceremony. They never cut their hair or shave, and all these looked as if from time immemorial no water had ever profaned the dirt upon their faces. The procession descended to the river Morskau, when our friend the Bull blessed the water—we hope to the increase of its cleanliness. Small temples on rafts were prepared for him at intervals on the water. It is said that the town covers as much ground as Paris did, we suppose before the octroi was removed further out. Since the Ukase of the 1st of July smoking is permitted in the streets of St. Petersburg and Moscow. Walking out in a pouring shower of rain, in order to prove our waterproof for our tour, we entered the inner Boulevards of Moscow, and presently came upon a large pool of the most fetid water we ever had the pleasure of smelling. Yet there are some boats upon it, just as if it would not act like the Stymphalian lake on everybody's olfactory nerves. When in the stilly night we have fallen into sweet slumber we are generally awakened by a watchman making a hideous noise with a sort of rattle, that sounds like two of Christy's Minstrels' most infatuated " Bones " playing against time and each other. Probably the reason of making this noise is to afford any possible burglar timely notice of the watchman's approach—a purpose for which the now exploded shiny hats of our policemen were originally invented. The company at our hotel dinner is composed of several nationalities—as, two Swiss, one Frenchman, one American, three Germans, four Italians, one Irishman, and three Englishmen dined here. Our host says he will not have any more Russians in his house since a Russian colonel stole his watch!

On the 15th we remarked a primitive " Punch and Judy" in the streets, no scenery, no cover to the box, and the principal performer's legs were very apparent underneath. Our friend lost his way, and forgetting the name of his hotel, was unable to ask for further information until he remembered it had something to do with a ghost, Gostinska being the vernacular (here) for an hotel. We had now, through the kindness of our Chargé d'Affaires at St. Petersburg, obtained letters of introduction, and our Padarojna, or posting order for six horses, for our route from Petrovskoi, on the Caspian, to the Persian frontier, together with a Russian passport (useful), in German, French, and Russian, and a Persian visa (useless). The Padarojna is a piece of paper for which a somewhat high charge is made, which goes, however, we believe, to the keeping up of the post-houses; it is necessary, having to be shown at every station in order to establish a right to horses. There are three degrees of them: we obtained the second. The first is only given to government couriers, and the third everyone must have to travel at all by post. Each class takes precedence of the other; so that a government courier coming up to a post-house, while a person having the second class

Padarojna was having his horses harnessed, would have them taken away for his benefit as the bearer of the first class order, and the other in return could take the horses destined for a third class order. We eventually found that three horses were quite enough for our use. And now, before plunging into wilder districts, we must premise that we do not hold ourselves responsible for the orthography of any places or things mentioned hereinafter, that being entirely phonetic, nor for the opinions expressed by any of our correspondents!

Just as we were getting into our droskies to go off to the station, an Italian arrived, who spoke Russian, and offered his services as a courier. Thinking that perhaps we should not have such a chance again, we engaged him to come and catch us up at Nijni. We travelled in a saloon-carriage, with an unlighted stove in the middle: although in August, the night was very cold. During the night, as we had just closed our eyes, one of our fellow-travellers, thinking us asleep, pointed at us and remarked to a companion, in German, "There, that is the way descriptions of travel are written; the English go abroad, see the country in this way" (he must have met with Brown, Jones, and Robinson, in Belgium!) "and then write about a country being so poor; and their countrymen read and believe!" We regret, for his sake, that we have not much to say about land traversed in a railway, though this appeared to us well-wooded and with much corn at intervals. After twelve hours we arrived at Nijni Novgorod, where we bade good-bye to railways, but not to steam, for a good distance. We drove off to the Nikita Egoroff Hotel in two droskies, and must, we suppose, attempt to describe what we saw, though the task is a difficult one. For about a mile we drove along a row of one-storied wooden houses, excepting a few stuccoed, on the banks of the Oka. Every one of these houses had its whole front taken up by a shop. Then crossing a wooden bridge, crowded with mujicks of the lowest class, we passed a singular church of Italian Byzantine nondescript architecture, above which rose a steep hill on which is the permanent town. The banks of the Oka were literally covered with bales of merchandise lying about, and the traffic along there was very great. We then ascended a deep ravine, crowned on the one side by the Kremlin, and on the other by miscellaneous houses. Our hotel we discovered to be right at the top of the ravine, opposite the Kremlin. Owing to the continuance of the fair we had telegraphed for rooms, which we accordingly found prepared for us. The hotel resembled a dirty South Italian one in domestic economy. After breakfast we walked to the steamboat office to secure our places. We found it situated on the highest brow of the hill, with a most lovely, nearly natural terrace in front. At the foot of the hill ran the broad Volga, here some 1600 miles from the Caspian Sea, covered with small steamboats and merchant ships of every description. The opposite bank seemed perfectly flat as far as the eye could see, the view only broken by an occasional church with log-huts around it. A little to the right again the scene is totally changed; the busy fair is before us, with the town on both banks of the Oka and Volga. The horizon on the left is bounded by the same chain, on a mountain link of which we are at present standing. We found our inn rather far from the fair, (a two-mile walk,) to which of course we next turned our steps. Seven wooden bridges cross the river during fair time, and the banks are used as quays for disembarkation of merchandise at every available point. Crossing one of these bridges, we wandered about an inextricable labyrinth of one-storied wooden shops. However, on nearer acquaintance we found that they were all arranged according to a specific plan, with the governor's house in the centre. The commerce appears to be mostly wholesale. Under the governor's house are the precious marble, and nicknack shops, which of course have the greatest amount of attraction for the small purchaser. Here Siberian jasper, malachite, rock crystal, &c., may be purchased to any extent, as well as the delightful Circassian belts and daggers. A band of twelve tuneless violins played under the centre arcade, two of which intersect each other here. Perhaps altogether the effect produced upon us by the fair was not so great as we could have anticipated, since the mixture of different nations was not very striking; two or three Chinese being the only natives not be seen any day in St. Petersburg. Tartars there were in abundance, but the war with Bokhara had prevented any of that nation arriving this season. However, the sight is well worth coming from St. Petersburg to see.

CHAPTER II.

ON the 18th of August we started in a Russian built steamer down the river for Astrachan. Grazzini, our new servant, arrived just in time. We found the vibration of the engines something considerable. The deck is given up to the third-class passengers, who have the privilege of roaming all over it. The first-class is at the bows instead of near the steerage as in most boats: perhaps an advantage, as the smoke coming out of the funnel discharges countless blacks, the fuel being wood.

We quote verbatim from our diary: 3 P.M. There are two passenger steamers in front of us which we shall overtake directly. The banks are not more than twenty feet high, pretty well wooded, but the trees are small, and especially willows; the river light dirty chocolate colour; the day very rainy; the banks are sandy. We have adopted the fashion of wearing a thick cotton band round the waist, a practice that we adhered to during our travels, except when staying in any place. The boat we are in belongs to an English company, that of the "Volga." The feeding is according to bill of fare, at every hour. There are several Circassians on board, no doubt glad to return to their native mountains. Our fellow passengers consist in five ladies and three gentlemen, all Greeks. Whilst quietly reading in our cabin, which, of three berths, we have all to ourselves, we heard a crashing scooping noise, as if the bottom of the ship was coming off. Although we only drew two feet four inches of water we had stuck on a sandbank. We, however, by the help of an anchor let drop further down the river, soon got off. The channel is buoyed, but we had steered too far left. It must be confessed that at first the effect of pulling at this anchor was not to move the boat but rather the anchor itself. However, after re-dropping the anchor higher up, we got off. During our stoppage several small tugs, with their heavy ships after them, passed us scornfully. We were then about an hour from Nijni, of which we can still see the bold headland, as the range on which the town stands forms a projection there, and then slopes away from the river. Some wretched hens, in a large wooden coop on deck, are being continually fed on rye-bread soaked in water. Now the banks are varied by occasional old red sandstone rocks, and brushwood up the slopes; sometimes a verdant field or a village appears on the top, as the right bank is now some 100 feet high. The " Bints," W——'s favourite depreciatory term for ladies, being we believe Arabic for women, have taken up the whole of the deck cabin, so to smoke we are obliged to face the driving rain. Two stout mujicks are steering on the captain's quarterdeck (we believe that to be the correct nautical term). Our captain is a young man, a Russian. Herds of pigs are clambering about the banks, which are now really sometimes picturesque. On trying to go to bed the steward was astonished at a demand for water and towels, and utterly flabbergasted on being asked for sheets and bed-gear. He said such a thing had never occurred in the memory of the oldest passenger. So we were reduced to sleep on a narrow sofa, with a greatcoat for bedding and coverlet. We grounded twice during the night, and arrived at Kasan six hours and a half late, on the 19th. Here the Kasanka flows into the Volga. It is a flourishing commercial town, as almost all the trade with China passes through it. Soundings were continually taken with a long pole during our passage down. Here we changed into another larger and English built boat. We rather objected to the arrangement of the cabin deck, being strewn with the filthy bedding of the third class, but were told that they (the third class) were the chief source of profit to the company. The water melons are already very good here, but imported from the south. Our captain is a most gentlemanly Dalmatian, speaking five languages, besides his own, fluently and well. He told us that whilst running a cargo from Kertch, during the Crimean war, his ship was captured and burnt by the Allies, and he himself placed on the nearest shore. After wandering about for some time he took to his present occupation. The river is frozen up from about the middle of October to April, during a portion of which time a large trade is carried on on the ice by means of sledges. The left bank for almost the whole length of our sail was as flat as a pancake. The boat we are in was sailed into the Volga, all the way from England, by water, through the canals that connect the Neva with this river. The reason given for the bad accommodation on board as regards bedding was that the Russian passengers would all kleptomaniarize (?) it; and therefore the company confine themselves as much as possible to fixtures. The deck is crowded with mujicks in their greasy sheepskin cloaks, lined at the border with black Astrachan wool. We also have a dwarf on board, and a man with two large pots of leeches, which keep us in bodily fear. Though a river steamer the cabins here have the stereotyped nasty sea-boat smell about them. And now, whilst the banks are flat and uninteresting on both sides, and we are steaming some 1200 miles due south, we turn for a moment to the letters of Lord Royston, written

at the beginning of this century, to see what he thought of the river then. He went down in a small boat early in the season, with an interpreter and a companion, all well armed, and remarks:—
" In general I have been much gratified both with the opportunities of inspecting the inhabitants, and also with the beauty of the scenery; the right bank being in general very mountainous and well wooded. * * * The number of fish of all species which inhabit the Volga is amazing, but the superstitious prejudices of the Russian peasants prevent their making use of several sorts. I offered ' some fish resembling chad ' to our boat's crew; they refused them, alleging as a reason that all those fish were insane and swam round and round, and that if they eat them they would become insane too!" At the present day upwards of 10,000 boats are employed in fishing. The stations at which we stop are, almost all of them, simply a collection of log-huts. We are going at the rate of sixteen miles an hour. The captain is very amusing, and tells us long stories; he informed us that lately he had a Persian as third-

class passenger on board, and happening to get into conversation with him, the Persian had told him that at the time when the three (?) Italian gentlemen were travelling in Bokhara he also was there on business. The Italians were seized and thrown into prison. One day the Emir of Bokhara, his particular friend, sent for him, and asked his advice about these foreigners—where Italy was, and whether it was governed by a great emperor? According to his own account the Persian answered that the Emperor of Italy was a most powerful potentate, and that his (the Emir's) captives were chiefs of the greatest importance in their own country. He then asked him what he should do with them, as their execution had been decided upon. Our Persian advised him to let them go, or he would get into trouble; whereupon, the Emir, in a great rage, told him he had not asked him his opinion to receive such an answer as that. Then our Persian, " Well, if you kill them I shall kill myself, and that will get you into trouble with the Shah, the Emperor, and the Tsar all at the same time." The proof of the truth of the foregoing is that the Italians were discharged plus their heads!

On the third day we pass the picturesque portion of the Volga, such as it is! The hills are high and rocky on the right bank and very well wooded; on the left at some distance a well forested ridge of mountains may be seen. At Samara we stopped to take in wood, which lies ready piled on the pier, and was brought on board in baskets on women's heads. We walked on shore to look about us, and found a small fair going on in the immediate vicinity of the river. There were a quantity of shabby log-booths in rows, one row being consecrated to eating and drinking. The crowd of dirty people was so dense that we had to force our way, elbowing coats well stocked with every species of vermin. The noise created by the crowd, and they themselves, constituted a small pandemonium; the echo here is remarkable, and the boat's whistle was prolonged on shore indefinitely with a most musical effect. The town lay on the slope of a hill, with streets intersecting at right angles, and at the top of each street you can see down into the plain where a sluggish river "drags its slow length along," therein resembling the celebrated wounded snake. The dust was intense, but the greater part of the pavement is better than that of St. Petersburg, the trottoirs all of wooden planks; shops seemed scarce, all the trade going on in the log-huts below. The greater part of the houses appear unfurnished or burnt out, and the rest of stucco. In the winter it is said to be the residence of many converted Calmucks. We passed many large barges, called schkootes, laden with cotton from Bokhara and Persia, and being tugged up the river. Our ship is called the Tsarewna or Princess, and this is a most loyal company, for their others, three large passenger ships, are respectively christened Tsar (which we passed), Tsarina, and Tsarewitch. The captain informed us that a nice Englishman had been a passenger on this boat two years ago! This boat is considered (by her captain) the best on the river; there is a rival company, but *this* one considers *that* a bad one. Reading a book referring to the tour in Persia, we are about to make, we came upon a passage where mention is made of some "*mountains which had receded about ten miles from the sea.*" We read on, anxiously expecting to hear of some "*rivers taking up their beds and walking,*" but did not find the page. Apropos of literature for the British public, an officer in India drew a sketch, which he forwarded to an illustrated London paper. Some time after he was surprised to see his sketch in the paper, but with the addition of a whole forest of palm trees. On remonstrating with the proprietors, he was told that palm trees were necessary to make the aforesaid public realise the idea of India, and that they would not stand it without them!

Late on the third day we passed a village, (on the top of a sort of broad cliff,) composed entirely of little log-huts, even the Church being of wood, with two windmills crowning the whole, as we found to be usually the case. The village, extending almost half-a-mile, had a very striking appearance. On the fourth day we came to a pier, consisting of a boat moored in the midst of the stream, the current being too shallow to admit of an approach to the bank. Numerous sandbanks now make their appearance in the river: on most of them a quantity of pelicans. Enormous swallows are flying about. We have some of the Persian insect powder with us. It is made from a herb that grows about Erivan, and no biting insects (are supposed to) come near it, probably on account of its smell, which their nerves can feel, but ours cannot. Took in wood again at Saratoff. Our three days' sail consumes as much wood as would suffice to warm three rooms during an entire Russian winter—statistical! The first thing we remarked at Saratoff was the inscription on an alehouse, Voksal, (the Russians, like the present writer, spell all foreign names phonetically). The town lies on the slope of a hill and is said to contain 80,000 inhabitants. We saw at least fifteen churches. The streets are broad and boast of some tolerable shops. The dust lies about three inches deep, and indeed on approaching the town the whole view was obscured by clouds of it.

There are several fine stuccoed houses, but the town is very straggling. The river in summer is here more than two miles wide. Amongst our passengers were a Swede and a Norwegian; the latter we saw again at Tiflis, where he entered upon a business. We found the words of command, as "stop," "back her," &c., obtaining as much on this Russian boat as on those of all other nationalities. Fifth day—the south wind is the coldest we have ever experienced from that quarter. One of the men, dressed as a Circassian, who is on board, turns out to be a pure Russian; but it having been the habit of the Russian colonists in the Caucasus to adopt that dress for greater safety during the war of independence, he had retained it ever since. We passed many large rafts floating lazily down the river; their proprietors though, to all outward appearance, sunk in the lowest depths of poverty, are often possessed of a thousand pounds sterling a year. It is their custom to leave their homes in spring, directly the ice breaks up, to build a large raft which is loaded with as much wood as it will carry, and to start off from high up the stream. The master takes four or five men with him, three of whom he keeps solely for the purpose of singing to him. When the raft arrives at any village he moors it to the shore, gets out surrounded by these men, who wear red bands round their hats, and walks into the village to make the best bargain he can for his wood. If the terms do not suit him he returns to his raft and floats on to another more lavish village, until all is sold, when he returns to his home by land to begin again another spring. From Tsaritzin a railway runs to the Don, but passenger trains only start twice a week. Our Greek fellow-travellers, of whom two couples were newly married, and between whom a continual hugging and kissing in the face of all mankind had been going on, got out here to go to Taganrog, where they had extensive possessions. As they would not catch the Don steamer for about a week, we must hope they liked their enforced residence at some dirty little village. Some of their party were standing on shore as we came back from a walk into the uninteresting little town, and one of them observed, either thinking we did not understand French, or, more probably as we had neglected their acquaintance, throwing a Parthian shot at us, "Ils ont decha (sic) vu la ville!" alluding, we presume, to the reported celerity with which the British tourist views objects of interest. Half our passengers got out here. Many of the barges going up carried large quantities of watermelons on deck. We observed that our sailors viewed these edibles and their proprietors with most savage glances, and found out that, as it was their custom to take a supply back from Astrachan, where they grew in profusion, to do a little private trade, they justly considered these large quantities as calculated to flood and ruin the market. Below Tsaritzin the banks are studded by neat little villages built by German colonists. Now both banks are low and scantily covered with willows. The wide Steppes are before us.

On the sixth and last day we got to Yenitaieff, a town built on a rather higher sandbank than usual. We entered a branch of the Volga not broader than the Thames above London. We should strongly advise all future travellers to buy their quilts and other bedding at Nijni Novgorod before going on board, as, if they intend travelling further south, they must get them anyhow at Astrachan. We found that a great deal of land up the river seems wasted, and might be turned to better account than lying fallow, especially on the right bank; though it must be admitted that the spring floods, which sometimes extend seven miles either way, would seriously impede agricultural pursuits, except on the raised lands. The German colony of Sarepta is composed of Moravian brethren, and is one of the neatest towns on the Volga. The colonists originally came from Saxony. About mid-day we passed a Kalmuck encampment, and here we saw the first string of camels winding its way along. Numerous herds about. The conical roofed huts have a quaint appearance. We afterwards visited an encampment from Astrachan, where we can add more. They acknowledge a native prince, who lives near the principal temple, about eighty miles north of Astrachan. We have just passed this on the bank of the river. It is of stucco, and like a Chinese pagoda, with a sort of Grecian colonnade running from each wing and ending in two other smaller pagodas. The centre one has five semi-circular roofed verandah terraces; the other two, three each. The palace is a moderate sized wooden house in excellent repair, with two verandahs one above the other, and another smaller one in the centre higher up. During the summer the princess lives in two or three tents like those of her subjects, but of stouter material. The roofs of the cottages are covered with camel's hair felt. The round body of tent is wattled with cane, and also covered with felt. They possess vast numbers of horses, being all excellent horsemen. Each hut pays a capitation tax of a half imperial per annum (about 16s.) to the prince, who thereby obtains a revenue of about 50,000 roubles a year, say £2,500. We took in one passenger, a woman, who was dressed much as ordinary European women—perhaps not the last Mdme. Elise fashion, but civilised. The more valuable animals during the night-time are penned into an enclosure of willow branches stuffed up with mud, which stood before many of the huts. The left bank of the Volga is inhabited by the Kalmucks, the right by the Cossacks of the Volga. In the Russian army these Cossacks wear yellow facings; those of the Don red, and those of the Ural blue. During the spring the stench coming from the remains of the fish that are boiled down into oil here renders the passage in a steamer almost impossible. We did not come in for any of it. On arriving at Astrachan, our courteous captain accompanied us on shore, thus exempting us from the formality of exhibiting our passports, which were demanded of the other passengers. The first hotel was called "Table d'Hôte," the proprietor evidently fancying *that* an important French city, where nothing acceptable in the shape of lodging being forthcoming, we went on to the "Paris," called the "Russia Hotel" in Murray, which we found too filthy, and trudged on back to an hotel (save the mark !) called "Odessa," where we were fortunate enough to find two rooms to suit us. They were dirty, and swarmed with black beetles, but whereas there were no beds in the other two pothouses, here we found two bedsteads without sheets; we however managed to get one a-piece after a time. The appearance of the town from the river is very uninviting. It is built on one of the thirty or forty branches into which the Volga divides itself at its mouth, but is some thirty miles from the Caspian. With the exception of the Kremlin it lies quite flat, all the country around being on the same dead level, and very sandy. Grapes and water-melons grow very luxuriantly all around. Quantities of boats lay outside in the river, their owners fishing with handlines; and the throng of small cargo-boats heavily laden with watermelons, converts almost the whole watersurface into one moving market. These melons, of great size and excellent quality, are sold for a penny a-piece and under. Indigo barges are preparing to start for Nijni. Our inn is on the quay, with the fruit market close by, and just opposite a colony of smithies, the whole rendering the place anything but quiet. The town is, with the exception of the Government houses, entirely built of wood; the streets are thronged, and intensely dusty and ill-kept; the trottoir, such as it is, of wood. The bazaar is tolerably built, the outside arcade of the square is devoted to linen and cotton goods, and only extends on two sides, the other two having regular shops out on the street. The interior courtyard is filled up with booths, principally of Astrachan fur cap manufacturers and leather-stall keepers. We walked into the Kremlin, and found the Russian army in white undress, being exercised; the goose-step was the strategic movement under consideration, and one soldier after the other would advance gravely from his squad to march about fifty paces forwards, keeping himself as bolt upright as possible, and taking rather longer steps then nature intended, thus imparting a " hoppy " motion to his body. As each soldier approached the squad that had just undergone the same operation, he burst out laughing, his comrades beginning to chaff him; indeed the discipline seemed rather relaxed, an uncommon fault in the Russian army, where the slightest inattention on the part of a soldier is generally punished by a kicking and pummelling on the spot from the commanding-officer. We entered the chief church, and thought the Ikonastas very magnificent. It reached quite up to the roof—some 150 feet, and was entirely gorgeously gilt, excepting where the delicately painted pictures came in. The door of the sanctuary was of worked silver, and the side pillars carved to resemble vine-trees with golden grapes. The massive pillars in the church were, however, rather spoilt, by a kind of well executed scagliola.

Having presented our letter of introduction to the governor, he kindly invited us to dinner. We found him a most enlightened Russian; a disciple of free trade—when not pressed to extremes, and a Liberal-Conservative of the best school: rather inclining towards true Conservatism. The revenues of the town are small, though the inhabitants number 50,000, and double that number in summer, when the surrounding populations flock in to join in the fisheries. After dinner at 4 P.M., our host called out the firemen of the town, to prove to us their discipline and readiness. Their organization is certainly admirable, for in less than half an hour from the time of despatching one foot messenger (a soldier) to the four watch-towers to raise the red flag in each quarter of the town, the whole brigade was galloping past before the window. In this case, as all four divisions came together, they assembled before tower No. 1, until all were got together. The chief of the police, their direct superintendent, rode first. Then an outrider to clear the way, and an engine with a red flag with one black ball on it,—the number of black balls marking the division. Two water barrels on carriages, and thick felt coverings, to be thrown over buildings near a fire, attended each engine. After again assembling in the square in front of the government house (a square, by the way, really deserving that distinctive London appellation, as there was an enclosure in the centre of it fenced off by iron railings and containing a few trees), they galloped past in service trim. The thin Tartar horses were forced off at full speed, and the drivers shouted with all their might.

the little boys also adding to the general excitement. The Governor told us, amongst other things, that on the promulgation of the Ukase abolishing serfdom throughout Russia, the 3000 serfs on his estate, when informed that for the future they would have a certain quantity of land for their own and pay rent for it, wished, as formerly, to till his land for him, and be kept by him, rather than have a property of their own. They were quite satisfied with their condition, and could not be brought to see the benefits accruing to them from paying rent and keeping themselves—very much the case with the slaves of the South American States. He gave us some excellent sparkling Moselle, which is called the Emperor Alexander's Champagne, as that monarch first introduced it into Moscow. The district under the government of Astrachan is about the size of France, and the position hardly an enviable one in a pecuniary point of view, the salary being £1000 per annum, besides a sum of 20 per cent. on any great profit accruing to the Government from improvements—no great thing in a country where all improvements progress so slowly. There is no society, and the advent of two "distinguished foreigners" like ourselves was quite an event. The residency is a large incongruous building, but the reception rooms are very well parqueted, and there is a good view from the—well, cockloft above. The sturgeon fishery forms part of the state revenue, but much poaching is carried on. The revenue from all sources flowing into the provincial exchequer from 1860 to 1865 was only 60,000 roubles in those five years—£8000. We almost fancy there must be some error in the calculation, but so we were informed. On departing, our host presented us each with his photograph and a lithographed view of the cathedral. We have to stop here a week as the Caspian boats only start twice a month. We went out fishing one day, down the river, turning off into a small branch of it; and fish of all sizes were rising in the most tempting manner, but we found them too uncivilised to comprehend the advantages of English flies; so having caught one roach, we cut him up, and found that his kind voraciously seized on his mangled remains—much as the human species. On rowing home we were attacked by perfect swarms of musquitos. The native hooks and lines are of the coarsest nature. We found our companion in a great state of mind, as we had taken the key of our rooms with us by mistake. The thermometer was at 82° Fah. in the shade, and anything you please in the sun. The boats navigating the Caspian are heavy Dutch-looking galiots. We made a perfect hecatomb of cockroaches the first night, and then had our room thoroughly washed out; but we find that it still boasts of a small but interesting collection of spiders and earwigs—indeed, most of the insect kingdom are well represented in it, excepting those that black beetles devour. It is papered white and blue, and the window curtains are green and red to match. The streets are lighted with petroleum or naphtha, which is imported from Bakoo,* down south, where are the natural springs of that useful

---

* Bakoo is situated on the western shore of the Caspian, in Persian territory. The naphtha is collected by sinking deep pits into which it flows.

but explosive material. On getting up this morning (26th), we found that a large colony of small red ants had discovered it to be more convenient and economical to inhabit my sponge than to build a residence of their own: we immediately served them with a notice of ejectment—into water. The resources of the place, as regards amusement, are limited, and we went on board to smoke cigarettes with our Volga captain, who rejoiced in the classic name of Soupuk. We of course endeavoured to obtain some Astrachan lamb-skins, but found that no easy matter. No one has the least idea as to how long it takes to get to Petrovskoi, our next destination. It is said that "once upon a time" the Caspian covered the soil on which now stands Astrachan. This being simply sand, cultivation of anything requiring a richer soil is utterly out of the question. The way in which every person at the hotel bows to us since our dinner with the Governor is remarkable: he and the chief of the police, with perhaps two rich merchants, are the only inhabitants that are at all respected here; nine-tenths of the population have never heard of a Tsar, and the other tenth do not know his name. The new regime of censorship in newspapers admits of abuse of any local administration, but all praise of an individual Governor is strictly prohibited, as all good must (?) flow from the Tsar himself; thus the incentive of public approbation is taken from the Governor at any distance from the capital, and in winter it takes twenty-four days to communicate with St. Petersburg, only very important messages being transmitted by the telegraph, which is now completed for the entire distance. The principle of religious toleration is carried out to its fullest extent in this town—as indeed it is throughout the Russian empire; no proselytism is, however, allowed. The Catholic Church is represented in all its many branches, a Greek, Armenian, Lutheran, and Roman Church existing. The Jews have their synagogue, the Persians their mosque, and the Kalmucks their temple, as well as the Russian schismatics. The secret police acts independently of the Governor, under direct orders from the capital. We forgot to mention, that after dinner, when our host arose he crossed himself in front of one of the eternal holy pictures that was hanging on the wall, and then shook hands with us, thanking us for having dined with him. Now we thought we were summarily dismissed, until he asked us out on the balcony to smoke. We had some white wine grown in the neighbourhood—a little sweet, but capable of great improvement. Much good but wild snipe shooting may be got around the town, and indeed further down the river. All sorts of wild-fowl abound in the reed jungle.

We found about 5 P.M. the best time to enter the Bazaar, especially on Saturdays, when the place is crowded with buyers and sellers. The curly lambskins, of which the best come from unborn lambs, are mostly brought from Bokhara. All the shops are shut on Sunday, and the women walk about attired in every gaudy colour imaginable, with a white veil over head and shoulders. The bakers carry about their whole stock-in-trade on their heads and boards six feet long by two broad. We took a walk down the river; the Admiralty buildings soon caused us to make a circuit to get back to it: we found a green on which the greater proportion of the juvenile population were flying elementary kites; beyond this was the last resting-place for decayed ships, which were being broken up for fuel; most of them had their stern grotesquely carved in arabesque foliage, and a lion and two eyes generally painted on them. Then followed a row of huts some three miles in length. Rain set in and did not appear inclined to set out again. We observed that all the dogs, of which there are large numbers about, seem afflicted with the mange—not wonderful, as they wander about all day and all night, unfed and uncared for: almost all have wounds upon their ears—scars gained in honourable (or the reverse) combat with their species, of which amusement they seem very fond. Sunflower seeds are sold as a delicacy in all fruit shops. After returning, we were constantly attracted to the window by loud shouts, and then we would see two drunken men, one running after the other and hitting out *with rounded arms*, tumbling down occasionally in missing aim; a ring of people would gradually gather around them, and then the combatants would take off their coats and hit out more wildly than before, but without any very fatal results. The "Don Champagne" is not so very bad—sweet, and tasting a little of perry; and some of the white wine tastes like raspberries. During our dinner at the hotel, two violin players of Paganinistic propensities, but not execution, struck up variations upon Scotch reels, in our honour. On the S.W. wall of the Kremlin there is a sheet of marble, marking the altitude to which the Volga rose in 1857; as well as we could make out, it is fully thirty feet above the present level of the river, and must have submerged all the houses in the neighbourhood. The Volga is navigable for some 1800 miles from Tver to this place. The roads here get into a beastly state after any rains.

The Governor has a scheme for the increase of the carrying trade of Russia, which certainly has the merit of novelty, if not of easy feasibility, and that would attract the attention of English speculators:—It is, that all English goods destined for the Persian market should be securely packed and sealed up at the English custom-houses, and then proceed by sea to St. Petersburg, thence to go by railway (or indeed canal) and steamer or sailing vessel down the Volga to this place; they (the goods) should be admitted into Russia free from all dues, the increased traffic enabling her to recoup herself; then, here the seals should be examined and if found intact, the goods be sent on to Persia in Russian ships, to be landed at Resht on the Persian shore of the Caspian. It is a scheme which, if approved of by the Russian Government, would certainly have many chances of success, the carriage being so much less expensive all the way by water, and the time occupied much shorter than by Turkey, or to Busheer, the general plan.

28th. Strolling out into the town we found a small river, about two miles on the S.E., crossed by several rope ferry-boats, and a little higher up by a wooden bridge. A quantity of log huts, and then orchards as far as we could see, each surrounded by a wooden paling and with a platform raised about twenty-four feet from the ground in the centre; on each of these stood a boy, placed there to scare away any birds that might damage the fruit; some of them had slings, out of which they periodically darted stones at the offending bipeds, whilst others sprung a very huge rattle, which answered the same purpose with perhaps less muscular exertion. The Governor having kindly placed a small steamer at our disposal, we started one morning in company with a Russian staff-officer, who spoke French and explained what was going on, and a Kalmuck interpreter, to see the huts and temple of the Kalmucks, about five miles up the river on the right bank. The steamer got to within twelve feet of the shore, so we stepped into a small boat just pushed out to us, and emerging stood in the midst of the settlement. We entered one of the round huts, and found it rather smoky, but extraordinarily clean and comfortable: there is a round opening at the top to allow of the escape of smoke, and a piece of felt to draw over it in case of any heavy storm coming on. The physiognomies are certainly not traced in the direct lines of beauty—at least according to English tastes: they are of a dark copper colour, with no nose to speak *of*, but plenty of mouth to speak *with*. We then went into the temple. In an ante-room containing a bed, most probably that of the guardian, through the open doors of which we could see into the inner temple, we found six priests sitting cross-legged—three on each side of a small carpet; they had taken off their yellow morocco shoes, and laid their hats beside them; these were flat, octagonal and of a thick woollen material, red or yellow. Before each group of three lay a spittoon; before one of them a conch shell, another had a pair of cymbals, another a bell, and a fourth a sort of drum on a stand; they were dressed in yellow, with scarlet shawls over their shoulders, and were reciting their prayers in a continuous and monotonous tone, looking exceedingly sleepy. One of them was turning a circular praying machine, the prayer being written on it, and every turn, like roasting coffee, constituting a prayer—yellow prayers on a red ground. The recitative sounded somewhat like " ding-dong, jolly gong," repeated very fast; then a bell was rung, then another recitative, " Day Oh, Amen !"

repeated over and over again: lastly, an intoned prayer.

The priests sometimes folded their hands in the attitude of Christian adoration; sometimes the prayer was accompanied by all the instruments going at one time, but still keeping a sort of barbarous rhythm. We believe the religion varies very little from that of Thibet, Llamas, &c. After the conclusion of prayer we were allowed to enter the inner temple, which was small and not above nine feet in height; long brocaded scarves were suspended from the ceiling, and bundles of prayers lay on a platform in one corner, a circular table in the centre, with lamps burning in little tin vessels; in other cups, oil, water, salt,—the principal gifts of the Deity to mankind,—lay in succession all round, and flowers of tin representing nature's gifts; in centre of north wall, an idol holding a box with eight compartments, in each a cross-legged brass deity, and several others near; on the wall were hanging chintz prints of idols in Chinese style; one was curious, representing in the centre the Grand Llama, and on either side, below, a sort of heaven and the other place, with, above, various mansions of the blessed. The priests then gave us their greater service, blowing an enormous horn that sounded like a herd of enraged bulls, beating some most sonorous hollow cymbals, blowing in a conch shell, and playing on the shrillest sort of flute we had ever heard: all this at once. The din began softly, and then went on crescendo, until it again diminished, each prayer lasting only two minutes, probably from the exhaustion of the officiating priests. The ritual was beautifully written in white and gold letters on a black ground. We forgot to say that the salt was done up into white paper cones, and on some of the wheat lay a pastile of incense. Five hundred thousand persons profess this religion in the province of Astrachan. As in some other religious denominations, the common people cannot understand the services, as they are all in Thibetian language. The priests seemed very devout and impressed with what they were about, perhaps owing to their somnolent condition. On rising they bowed down thrice before the inner temple with their foreheads against the door, and each before entering rapped his forehead against the lintel. The worshippers who attended bowed down to the ground outside the temple, crossing their arms upon their breasts, and laying a small offering, of the value of a farthing, on the threshold. The temple itself is square, facing the cardinal points of the compass. On the table lay besides, a small silver teapot-looking thing, in which, we were told, water and oil were sometimes mixed and partaken of as a sacrament by good believers; on it stood some peacocks' feathers; around the table were stands supporting what looked like huge Chinese shoes of tinsel, and beside them a round, high, tapering cap, what for we know not, unless to keep flies off sacred things: a few copecks (the small Russian copper coin) lay before the principal idol, inviting others to join them. The priests came down to see us off, and looked very grand in their bright coloured dresses, long tunics even covering their feet.* The Governor paid us a visit

---

* Our Volga captain's idea of their religion was, the idolatrous worship of the ashes of their deceased rulers and priests turned into statuettes!

in full uniform and stars, and we parted with regret from a charming conversationalist. The common people feed their horses on melons during the season,—not entirely, of course!

On the 30th we went on board a barge, built for the purpose of passenger conveyance, and towed by a small tug, as, owing to the shallowness of the mouth of the Volga, the sea steamers cannot come up to Astrachan. These boats only start once a fortnight, and there are only four of them altogether on the Caspian. Almost all the passengers are wearing the conical Astrachan wool caps, the old fashion for Persians, and they all set-to playing cards on deck for copper stakes. The banks are perfectly flat, occasionally covered with reeds. The steerage on deck is partially reserved for 1st and 2nd class passengers. A gang of dirty cadets usurped part of it, but most of them were turned out. The absence of noise from engines, or smell from ditto on board the barge is very charming. As we near the mouth the jungle gets thicker and thicker on both banks, excepting where a space is cleared, to allow of huge sturgeon nets being dried there. It is a perfect paradise for the sportsman; swarming with herons and water-fowl of every species. The river at its estuary can hardly be seen across, so broad is it. About thirty miles out we changed into the sea steamer; luckily, it was a perfect calm. We pass some war screw steamers, which had been transported hither from the Black Sea, after the Crimean war.

We find that now there is one day missing in our diary. Alas! the calm was only a deception; in the morning we were rudely awakened by water dashing into our face; this was the rolling sea coming in through our open window; the wind had risen during the night, and we were in for a bad passage. Happily, the steward spoke French and Italian, so we were able to explain ourselves to him tolerably. We remained in our berth all day. At last on the 1st, we sighted Petrovskoi about 10 A.M., eighteen hours late; we then tossed about at anchor for two hours before a boat put out to us. The sea was going down, but the sailors on shore were such cowards that they durst not come out, though not more than 300 yards separated us from the shore. At length, after a struggle, we got in and luckily all our luggage was also tossed on board. We were several times nearly swamped from the overcrowding of the boat, but soon found ourselves on the shoulders of some men, to be carried to the beach. We found the proprietor of a sort of inn waiting for customers, on shore: we closed with him, and got two very dirty rooms and a decent breakfast.

The town seems well to do enough; substantial wood houses, with some in brick. A bluff hill rises behind it. A rough semicircular jetty is in course of construction; the stones being quarried from the rocks near the sea, loaded on cars, and allowed to run down an iron tramway to the extremity of the pier, which as yet, though extending some 150 yards into the sea, affords very little protection to ships even as small as our steamer. A dozen small fishing boats rested under its lee, but it protects only from south and, partially, west winds. The rocks around are of puddingstone, a shingly beach, the water is very little salt, cockles the chief shells. We called on the Governor, whom we found a jolly, fat man, talking French. He generally lives at Temichanshura, whither we are going, but came here as to a watering place for his children. He is a Georgian, in the Russian army. He kindly wrote a letter to his secretary at Temichanshura for us, and sketched out our route through the Caucasus. We found his house to be on the brow of the hill above the town. Above rose the fort, which seems of considerable extent.

We had a great hunt after the post-house, and got on to the highest ledge of the hill, whence we could see the mountains in the interior, looking stern and rugged, and frowning on the plain of no great extent which lay betwixt us: many villages scattered about. The postman we found, with an order on his coat, looking very dirty but tolerably amiable, especially after being soothed by the gift of a cigar. In the yard stood three "Telegas," the instruments of torture in which we were to proceed on the morrow. They are on four wheels, entirely of wood, and looking like a flat-bottomed boat cut down at both ends and square at the bows and stern, resting on two shafts over the wheels, without the slightest vestige of a spring.

In the early morning before starting we bathed in the green waters of the Caspian. My companion found the fish so tame that he caught a large one in his hand, and bore it home in triumph to his breakfast. We did not discover his fishing grounds. Of course, as we are no longer upon it, the sea has returned to a state of tranquillity. Our telegas (we were yet new to our work, and therefore had taken two with six horses) came to the door for us, and after loading our baggage and our servant into one of them, we started off in the other. We first proceeded along a low spur of the Caucasus, ourselves on the plain whence the Caspian had evidently retired ages ago. The dark rough stone of the mountains, occasionally wooded with stunted brushwood, was very picturesque. On the roadside we observed several little animals resembling the Norwegian Leming. All about grew plentifully yellow flowers, of the nature of our hollyhocks, and many-coloured butterflies fluttered gaily in the brilliant sunlight; on our right, behind us, lay the Caspian, perfectly calm, as if in our derision. Many Troikas (another name for our vehicle, from their being drawn by three horses abreast) passed us; the "rule of the road" being the same as in England. Most of these contained Russian officials. An occasional horseman, dressed in full Circassian costume, with the six cartridge cases, looking like 'Panpipes on each breast, his ornamental sword at his belt, and a rifle slung behind him, would also ride past us, every now and then.

In two hours we reached Kunperkalieff, where we changed horses, first producing our padarojna to the postmaster. Just before reaching this, we passed a high hill composed of yellow sand, which stood out in bold relief against the intense blue sky; and the cemetery. The inhabitants being Mohammedans, the tombs were the perpendicular flat stones, some six feet high, crowned with a high round knob, supposed to represent the turban, or here, perhaps, the Circassian helmet. One of these was brilliantly painted in white, red, and blue, and all had some verses of the Koran sculptured in high relief upon them. Three stones, probably the memorials of chieftains, stood apart from the vulgar crowd, and many were scattered along the road.

The village is built on a perfectly flat mountain overhanging a ravine, where flows a small stream which we afterwards continually forded and re-forded. The houses were all of one story, bricks composed solely of clayey mud being used, and then more mud plastered on. The roofs, flat of course, as usual. The banks of the stream were well cultivated, the chief crops being Indian corn and melons. We witnessed some of the process of thrashing out the corn in Eastern fashion : two unmuzzled oxen drawing heavy logs of wood, perfectly flat beneath, upon which the driver was seated to add weight, over the corn; indeed, a perfect wheat-sledge. Then it was winnowed by throwing the corn and chaff into the air in wooden shovels, when the wind blows away the chaff, leaving only the grains; however, this process is always imperfect.

We were now in the government circle of Daghestan,* the Thubal of the Jews, and Sarmatia Asiatica of the Ancients, " Land of Mountains." After skirting our little stream on both sides for some time we came to a plateau surrounded by most picturesque and wild-looking hills.

We passed a village, Kumuk, where the chief house was built on an isolated rock in the centre. The appearance of the village, all of mud, with a sort of open colonnade in front of each house, the interior wall being painted, in general, red, reminded us, we know not why, of Medina Sidonia, in Andalusia. Thence, over a horrible road, evidently made solely by being driven upon, we reached an elevation from which we saw Temichanshura stretched

---

* It is said to contain 180,000 inhabitants, and 9,196 square miles.

out before us. The large church, painted red and green, standing out from all the houses, and the only one visible, gave the town somewhat the appearance of a Swiss village. A mud wall surrounds the whole town. In the plain a few canvas tents were scattered about.

On entering the town by one of the gates, our first care was to look out for lodgings, when just as we were on the point of concluding a bargain, a fine-looking Circassian soldier came up and told us that rooms had been prepared for us in a government house, our arrival having been already announced. We accordingly left our lodging-house keeper disconsolate, and were presently installed in some rooms which had been left in exactly the same condition as when the last occupant left them: coats on the wall, books on the table, and even a box of "capsules" lying about. We had the run of four apartments, including a moderate-sized ball-room. The politeness of all was extreme. Monsieur Sergieff, the *locum tenens*, being unfortunately laid up, another Circassian officer called upon us, to know if we had everything we wanted. We obtained our food from the so-called, "club," an establishment of the officers in garrison here.

The day after our arrival we walked out of the town to the top of a hill on the S.W., whence we obtained a splendid view of the surrounding country. On our way we walked through a cemetery, not over-well kept. Dwarf oak constituted the principal vegetation. On the S. rose the higher range of the Caucasus; on the plain before us lay the town, forming an all but perfect parallelogram, the deficiency being at the north-eastern extremity, where it is built into a triangle. Though to all appearance perfectly level from our point of view, this is raised considerably above the stream that we had followed for five hours from our horse-changing place. The church stands in the centre, and there is a large square with arcaded shops in front of it. The roofs present a most variegated appearance. All the government houses are painted green, and the others either brown or red. On the S. a few huts are built outside the wall of circumvallation, one side of which consists entirely of low barracks. Many trees and poplars planted along some of the streets give the town a cheerful aspect. We found that our pedometer, which is quite insensible to the progress of an ordinary civilized carriage, advanced seven miles during yesterday's jolting.

On the Sunday we found the open-air market at the S.E. of the town thickly attended, the staple commodity being gossip. A perfect hurricane blowing. In the afternoon we paid a visit to the adjutant, who is the other occupant of the large house we are in. As he spoke no known language, we conversed by means of Grazzini our servant, who engrossed almost all the talk to himself, and was compelled to sit down and partake of tea, the obligatory accompaniment of every visit to a Russian.

On the 5th of September, after a good deal of preparation in the way of fastening our luggage to our horses' backs, we started for Kutishi, at half-past nine, A.M. Our cavalcade consisted of ourselves and fourteen Lesghians, given to us as an escort, not on account of any danger, as the country is thoroughly trodden down and pacified, but as a guard of honour. They were dressed in white caftans (a bastard species of frock coat), tall white Astrachan hats, somewhat resembling, excepting in colour, the familiar bearskin of the British grenadier, and red capotes hung down over their shoulders. Their little wiry horses were very ill kept, but capital goers. The set would have driven an English officer into desperation, such was their slovenliness; but, notwithstanding, their appearance smacked strongly of wild romantic guerilla warfare. We marched through the town with an advanced guard of three " guerrilleros " abreast. Next the commanding officer, the same who had apprized us of our prepared lodgings, then our two selves. The rest of the escort, our servant, and the baggage, bringing up the rear. Immediately upon starting our escort set up a wild sort of war song, which had the effect of bringing out most of the population, who gazed with wonder at our costumes, not being accustomed to any others but national dress or Russian uniforms. We are bound to state that our "get-up" might have created an equal sensation in St. James's-street! These songs continued at intervals during the march. One much resembled free variations on "Buffalo Gals," and in another, rather melodious one, the name of Schamyl was constantly repeated. We are now in his country, and were told that the events attending his last defence and capture were being sung by these fellows, who, on the whole, were rather inclined (as "de droit") to sympathise with their gallant countryman. Our baggage caused us numerous detentions, having a propensity to slip off the Cossack saddles of the post horses. The first portion of the journey lay over some monotonous black hills. The women we saw, wore those garments that a hen-pecked husband is said to make over to his wife. Some of the younger ones were pretty, with dark black eyes and hair guiltless of the disfiguring "auricomous fluid."

In about four hours we reached Zengutai, where a mosque is the principal place of worship. We found that the commanding officer, who seemed in a disconsolate state, (as well he might be, having only himself to command,) spoke French, and with the characteristic openhandedness of the soldier had prepared a sumptuous dinner for us. Leaving our host we passed through Zengutai the lesser, and soon plunged into the most romantic solitudes. Leaving the road, (a bridle path, as we did not follow the circuitous carriage-way,) we gained a grassy peak, whence we obtained a magnificent panoramic view. We saw all the country we had traversed, on the one hand; the cultivated fields on the plain spreading out before us in well-marked lines, like so many vari-coloured ribbons. On the left the Caspian Sea formed the boundary in the far distance. Before us lay a dim blue line of mountains, and behind us some picturesquely escarped mountains hemmed-in our view.

Shortly after descending and regaining our bridle path, we came upon a man with a species of flageolet, whereupon our escort dismounted, and two of them began to dance to a very shrill tune, much resembling portions of a hornpipe. The duo suggested reminiscences of the negro "break down" and the gipsies' dance. The non-dancers clapped their hands to the tune. Their cheers were the regular " Hurrah" so well known in the United Kingdom. After crossing an alternation of hills and plains we reached Urmah, when our baggage-horses were, after a considerable delay, changed. The houses here were all built of limestone, that material being here more easily obtainable than mud. The roofs all flat, and as Urmah is built on the steep slope of a hill, one house directly above the other, persons walking in the upper streets appeared to be parading the roofs of the houses below them. In this favoured spot the fuel consists almost entirely of dried cow-dung. We hence continued on by the light of the full moon, which permitted a delightfully hazy and indistinct view of the scenery. The lofty but not yet snow-capped hills had not a vestige of brushwood upon them. We now passed several places where our narrow path led along the sides of steep ravines, where "one false step would have been destruction." This phrase, or its equivalents, is used by every traveller in every mountainous district, so we may as well employ it also, though not to the purpose! We did not reach Kutishi till nigh 10·30 P.M., but we found here also our arrival foreseen, and the Commandant waiting for us. He could not speak any language of ours, but the doctor of the military post spoke a little German. In the kindest manner, he insisted on placing his bed and sitting-room at our disposal.

We had thus ridden forty-eight miles, at a jog-trot, on our first day, and were very glad of the English saddles we had conveyed with us. Here we met an artist-officer, who was commissioned by the Grand-Duke Michael (the governor-general of the Caucasus) to execute for him drawings of all the principal spots rendered famous by Schamyl's heroic defence. We were fortunate enough to see those already finished. During the latter portion of our ride we had to put on our greatcoats; the evening and the elevation combining to render the temperature rather cool. The sitting-room was hung all over with beautifully-worked fowling-pieces. Our escort, or one or two of them, were continually dashing out of their ranks at full gallop, in front of us, to show off their horsemanship by executing the renowned " tour de force" of picking up a small object from the ground without dismounting, whilst at full gallop: unfortunately, the failures quite counterbalanced the successes achieved. Our servant has a very vague nation of geography. He is continually asking us why such and such a thing is done in " Persia," as if we were already there. Along our road we observed many little square towers of observation, now no longer of any use. Innumerable dogs who, silent during the day, render night hideous by their incessant barking, greeted us on our arrival. The last office of our pedometer was to mark the jolting of the telega, for we lost it during a gallop on the grass.

All the officers in these parts appear to be princes.

Early next morning we started again; we saw many eagles floating in the air high above our heads. The rocks about appeared to be of some alluvial deposit, with quantities of fossils cropping out; and further on many stone boulders lay around, as circular as if just hewn for the cannon of a Byzantine emperor. Shortly before reaching Hadjel Machi, we passed an orchard of apple and cherry trees. Some twenty file of soldiers presented arms to us as we marched in. The carriage road was very good; two excellent stone bridges. Here we noticed that the women wore morocco slippers turned up at the toes, and a head frontal embroidered in gold, the device resembling Arabic letters. An ornamental drinking fountain, with the crescent on the top, stood in the village. A redoubt on a height commanding it. We now rode through the wildest scenery imaginable, lofty mountains, rising sheer above us, or descending straight below us, according as our route led at the foot, or higher up them, our road led us zigzagging up and down, till we got on to the side of a deep ravine, which could not have been more than a hundred yards across. On the side opposite to us we saw some rocks resembling pillars, as though the entrance to some great half-ruined Egyptian Temple. We halted for luncheon about 2 P.M., just past some blasting operations that were being carried on in order to widen the road. The Tartar bread, baked in flat loaves about one and a-half foot round and one inch thick, was very nasty. The red wine here somewhat resembled sour Valdepeñas, the flavour of the skins in which both are preserved being very perceptible in each. Soon after emerging from the narrow portion of the pass, we descried " Gounib " towering above us in front. This mountain, isolated on all sides, and only accessible (to the ordinary being) on one, was the scene of Schamyl's supreme defence and of his capture. We began to ascend it just as it was getting dark, by a winding road, and in one hour, at 7·30 P.M., reached our halting place—the adjutant's house. We passed through the military village, on a small plain upon the mountain itself.

A battalion is always quartered here. We found everything ready for us, and after our night's rest we made an excursion on horseback round the place. Riding up a ravine for about an hour, we reached Schamyl's village and last dwelling-place in Daghestan. Here he, with a band of 600 devoted followers, held the whole force of the Russian empire at bay for three months! Our guide, a Lesghian in the Russian service, who had assisted at the capture of the place—on which side he did not inform us, though probably on the Russian—was of opinion that if he ever should appear again in this country a revolt would immediately break out, notwithstanding the numbers of the Russian army, which, practically, would render any such an attempt abortive. The heroic struggle of Right against Might must always command the respect and admiration of all those who have nothing to lose by espousing such a cause. The name of Schamyl will go down to posterity as that of a brave patriot. It is quite apart from the question to argue that the country has benefited by Russian rule: that is easily admitted, but the right and justice of a people defending their ancient faith, their freedom, and their chief is indefeasible. The village is in ruins, and the rank weeds grow on the stone houses. An English farm-labourer would turn up his nose at Schamyl's house, which differed in no respect, excepting its comparatively larger size, from the others. On one side of an inner court-yard are the apartments of his three wives; his own occupy two storys.

About a quarter of a mile lower down the hill is shown the spot where Prince Bariatinsky sat on a flat stone to await the arrival of Schamyl, after his surrender in his own house. Some birch of stunted growth are planted around, and near, a few willows, the greater number weeping for their lord's ill fate. The Lesghian chief is now located in the interior of Russia, and, in all other respects but the loss of his freedom—an irreparable one to such a spirit as his—is much better off than when a chief in his own country. We saw these spots on the sixth anniversary of his capture. Continuing our ride for another hour, we arrived at the spot where the Russian soldiers climbed up the, to all appearance, perpendicular rock, thus taking the unsuspecting Schamyl in the rear. The feat performed here seems barely possible, but one soldier having gained the summit let down a rope to his comrades, and thus they contrived to clamber up. Hence the view extended as far as the eye could see, in an endless succession of mountain ranges of the greatest variety of form. Turning off to the West we ascended the highest part of "Gounib." On the very summit some "Forget-me-nots" were growing, forming an appropriate memorial for preservation. White misty clouds obscured our view from hence, so after halting for a short time, allowing our horses to crop the luxuriant grass around, we commenced our descent, skirting round the edge of the mountain for some eight miles, until we got into our old path again. The flora is very pretty, though there is hardly any flower here that does not grow in English fields. On the plateau, upon which stands the military village, we saw some soldiers drilling. Many of them are encamped in tents. The native population is very small, almost all their houses having been pulled down by the conquerors for greater security. On returning, we were informed that, the general being absent and the colonel ill, the officer in command was waiting to receive us at dinner; so we went down to the barracks and introduced ourselves to him and his wife. She spoke French, and indulged us with "Ah! che la morte" on a piano which had not been tuned for two years, and, considering the circumstances, was very good, not more than half the notes being utterly ruined. We talked and looked at each other, (the lady much admiring W.'s knickerbockers,) and smoked, our hostess joining us, for two hours and a-half, when we had supper, which is generally taken "heavy" at about 10 P.M. This included toadstools in vinegar, and Barclay and Percins (*sic*) brown stout.

Much mineral wealth lies, in all probability, concealed amongst the mountains, as lead, copper, and sulphur are continually found in this neighbourhood, though the veins are not worked as yet. A careful mineralogical survey would, no doubt, reveal the hidden capabilities of the country; and, unless a hopeless but fierce revolt of the inhabitants should break forth, will, it is to be hoped, soon be carried out. The dwellers in one village can frequently not understand the language spoken by those living in the neighbouring hamlet. The variety of languages is something bewildering; Baron Haxthausen is, perhaps, the best authority on a point about which we know nothing.

Next morning we started at 7, with a new escort of irregular cavalry, this time arrayed in black dresses with yellow capotes and black skin caps; most of them wear their cartridge-cases with beautiful Niello work to the tops of each. This is the peculiar work of Daghestan, from whence it has entered Russia. Their pistols were carried in richly embroidered holsters. Skirting the road for some time, we turned to the N. W. passing many herds of goats; most of these animals had long horns that twisted around themselves in a quaint fashion. We passed a small encampment, where a coal mine is indolently worked, and a shaft had been sunk for sulphur, which is procured in plenty —the coal is very indifferent. After halting for luncheon we rode through a chasm cleft by nature and a small stream, in the rock, which appeared to tower at least 1500 feet above us; the sides were so near together that sometimes we could not see the sky. Of course the echo was great, and our escort made the most of it during the 300 yards' passage. Coming upon a small river, we skirted it for some time, until we crossed it by a rough wooden bridge, with an arch ingeniously contrived to make every passenger get off his horse before crossing; thence we ascended a wild and peculiarly steep rock, and after reaching the summit, found ourselves on a plateau in a sort of valley extending to Khunsakh, our resting-place for the night. The rock was of a friable nature here, and the road, therefore, tolerably well made, except when consisting of loose round pebbles very trying to our horses' feet and our own balance.

We saw our destination long before we reached a mud wall, in front of which we dismounted, the whole population (not large) assembling to view the unaccustomed strangers. We then entered (by a large wooden gate) a court-yard surrounded by low mud buildings, the Russian official habitations, and were shown into a room at the farthest side of the court, where the only furniture consisted of a table, two chairs, and one bedstead in a rickety condition. The floor very damp. After some time, an old tin bread-basket was brought in (to serve as a bason,) and a camp-bedstead. Gounib towers away on the south-east, here not seeming so isolated as in reality, from our looking over the hills in front of it. To-day we passed some of the smallest cattle we have ever seen.

Riding out again next morning we followed a very level road, on a mountain ledge, for some time, till we came to an abrupt descent, where we had to dismount and have our horses led. Ascending again, we skirted a valley, ourselves high up, till we came to a hill of white marble, on whose flat and long apex we rode, being able to see into two valleys at once, one on each side. Coming to the end we descended by a path still steeper than before, and soon arrived at Tlock. We were conducted through twisting lanes between stone walls, to a rather grander house than the others, that, probably, of the principal, if not the oldest, inhabitant. This gave us an excellent opportunity of studying the interior economy of a Lesghian house; with which intention we immediately proceeded to poke our noses into all sorts of uncomfortable places. Through the outer door we had entered a court-yard about 20 feet by 30, around which were built the kitchen stables, and other warehousing rooms; a colonnade of wood in front; the walls themselves of the rough unhewn stones that lie about the mountains. On one side, above the kitchen, rose the second story, with an open-air colonnade in front; under this were our rooms. This second story is exceptional, as the majority of houses have only one, and all have flat roofs. Hay and peaches cut in halves, lay on this one to dry in the sun, when ready the hay is stored under the colonnade, or perhaps verandah, in front of our rooms. The court-yard is uncovered. We had not been installed ten minutes when we were informed that another place had been prepared for us, so out we marched bag and baggage, but no trumpets blowing as none were handy. We were led again through the village, out of it, and into a magnificent forest of walnut trees, looking old and majestic enough to have descended from nuts left by the flood, when retiring from Ararat and the neighbourhood! Indeed we found this a perfect oasis amongst the mountains. We next came to a splendid orchard of every kind of fruit tree; Indian corn growing amidst all. Presently we came to a low mud hut, without any window, where we found a carpet and bed spread for us, and a leg of mutton judiciously hung up in a corner. However, on objecting that we preferred our former halting-place, we were marched back again. We then found the inhabitants of the neighbouring houses congregated on their roofs to look at us, as we sat in the verandah eating excellent peaches.

The leg of mutton was cut into kabobs * for dinner, cooked in their own fat, and vinegar, exactly resembling the way of roasting pork in the south of Spain. Grazzini here informed us that had he known the voyage we were going to undertake he never would have come with us—would even

---
* Small pieces of meat, roasted as described.

rather have remained with his wife! We find him an excellent and ready servant, and honesty itself. The doors here are four feet high, and the windows in proportion. Our host is a rough-looking Lesghian, with a grizzly beard, which he has tinged a bright red colour, the custom of many of his countrymen,—and others!

Many of the tombs that we passed are square upright stones with a cavity at the bottom, in which is the inscription. Several have long poles stuck by their sides,—a succedaneum for the spear of the chief whose tomb it is.

CHAPTER III.

On the 9th of September we started and rode along a black-looking stream for the greater portion of our way. Swallow-tailed butterflies are the prevailing variety, and yellow ones with black tips to their wings. The end of our journey took us near some slight hills; the dark blue sky above us showed off the rugged rocks around us to great advantage. In the middle of the day we arrived at Botlick, the chosen home of fever, though *why*—it would be difficult to conjecture. It lies in an exactly similar situation to our morning's starting point, which is entirely exempt from this disease, between rocky hills at the bottom of a valley, and has as many or more walnut and other fruit trees growing around it. The vines are most beautiful, festooning tall apple trees up to their very tops.

We had started early intending to pass this place without stopping, but we were told that the time of fever was just over by a week, so finding agreeable quarters in the officer's house, we remained; the sun was certainly very hot in the middle of the day. Our Lesghian officer, who has accompanied us from Temichanshura as our guide and interpreter, (the natives understanding no Russian,) here quitted us, as we enter another circle of government. At a small village, on our way hither, the inhabitants turned out, offering us fruit, cold roast chickens, and strong water of some description. The time of fever here is June, July, and half August; it attacks, to a certainty, every person who remains three days here.

The fort is in a lovely spot, on a low hill in the centre of a valley, surrounded on every side by bold, lofty rocks. The Commandant, like almost all the others in Daghestan, is very wisely absent, having given himself leave. In the cool of the evening we wandered with our three military hosts into an orchard, where we eat peaches, grapes, and plums to our hearts' content. As none of the officers could talk anything but Russian, we passed the evening smoking cigarettes, and carrying on an animated conversation in detached words, occasionally summoning Grazzini, when a more knotty point than usual arose. Next morning we started early, having a long day before us; we immediately began to ascend a very steep hill, forming the boundary between two circles of goverment. This occupied us three and a half hours in the ascent. From its summit we saw the higher Caucasus, clad in eternal snows, to the south. Riding on over comparatively level ground, we came to a charming little lake with intensely blue transparent water. We judged it to be about five miles round. The treeless nature of its banks somewhat detracts from its beauty. Our horses went in some distance to drink. Unfortunately our noble steed took it into its head to lie down here, a proceeding which, though no doubt affording intense gratification to itself, was by no means so pleasant to its rider.

After some time we began to descend through a valley enclosed by lofty granite rocks, upon which the most luxuriant herbage was growing and being cut down in every practicable spot, our road became narrower and narrower, and altogether execrable, consisting chiefly in the precipitous bed of a mountain torrent, running down the gorge we were now in. Soon brushwood began to clothe the sides of the ravine; and small birch trees, together with huge ferns hung on the damp rocks. The vegetation became grander and grander, until at length we could fancy ourselves in an English park. Our path led us through so many windings that we could never see a hundred yards in front, and thus every change in the vegetation burst upon us by degrees. Having ridden over a treeless waste in the morning, we now, towards evening, were threading a forest glade. The torrent increased in volume as we proceeded, and we were continually fording it. Night set in at a quarter to eight, while we were yet on our march, and our very ragged escort, who did not know the way very well, got off their horses to perform evening prayer; mounting again, we rode on in such darkness that we could hardly see, the tails of the horses in front of us serving as a guide. However, at 9 P.M., we reached Videne, our destination and a Russian encampment, surrounded by a wooden palisade, of which the gates were shut at night, so we had to knock at one of them for a considerable time, and only got in with some difficulty, the guard evidently taking us for a party of Tchetchens come to a night attack.

On getting in we rode to the commandant, Colonel Golachekoff's (we apologize if it is misspelt,) house, where we met with the customary cordial reception, here doubly grateful to us after our long ride. Unfortunate Grazzini had to sleep out all night, as the escort of our luggage refused to proceed. On arriving next morning, he remarked that if ever he returned alive to Moscow "sara un miracolo!" Videne lies in an extensive plain, surrounded on all sides but one by well-wooded mountains.

After our night's rest we walked out in company with a Polish officer, who spoke French, and said that he had had no other opportunity of speaking it for five years, the time he had been quartered here. We walked along the plain until we came to the fossées dug by Schamyl to defend his aoul or village against the Russians, before his final retreat across the mountains to Gounib. After the third comes the spot on which stood his own house; here the Princess Chavchadazy and two other Russian ladies were imprisoned; but no traces are to be seen either of this or of the village around, the rank vegetation having completely covered them and their ruins. Buffalo were lazily cropping the grass, perhaps in Schamyl's dining-room; wild hops were growing about. Dinner at 2 P.M., and then the fashion is to rest for two hours. Our colonel's amiable weakness is "sweets;" at least a dozen boxes of bon-bons and dried fruits lie about his bedroom which he kindly turned out of to accommodate us.

It being the Emperor Alexander's name-day, a ball was given in the officers' clubhouse, to which we drove in a huge sort of brougham, with a strong flavour of the dust of ages about it. Arriving at 8 P.M. we found a moderate sized ballroom, decorated with fir branches and festoons of wild hops hanging from the tin chandeliers; a billiard and cardroom, and a library, are also here. The portrait of the reigning sovereign occupied the place of honour on the wall. Our Polish exile received and conducted us to the room, where we found some eighty officers already congregated, each with more or less decorations on their breasts. The ladies, mostly officers' wives, mustered some thirty strong. The force quartered here amounts to 4,000 men, and thus all their officers were present. The wife of the regimental doctor, a Georgian, was perhaps the only pretty person in the room—dark complexion. We made the acquaintance of an officer commanding natives, whose father was a Frenchman, and who informed us that he had not talked his paternal language for fourteen years! A waltz was played by the military band soon after we arrived. We were lucky enough to be introduced to a lady who did not dance what are in London called "round dances," and, then, to another just as the music ceased; neither of them spoke any language, so it was just as well that we could not dance with them. Quadrilles and Lancers were the other dances; in these chairs were brought out for the dancers to sit on when their turn was over, the ladies gracefully folding their arms, or munching peaches whilst standing up in the figure. The whist played here was of an astonishing nature; no trumps allowed; the dealer always threw his hand on the table, as in dummy whist, and the highest card of the suit led, invariably took the trick; more than fifty points could be made in one hand, their value six a penny. Supper was served in a large tent, open to the air, which now became rather chilly. The garden around decorated with coloured lamps. The Emperor's health was drunk much past midnight.

We set off in the morning in an old rattletrap with four horses, that the colonel kindly lent us. Passed many plantations of sunflowers, and elder shrubs six feet high and more, lining all the road. We soon emerged from the brushwood-covered low hills on to the plain; here our off-horse managed to tumble under the carriage which was stopped, and we got out, whereupon the other three horses bolted, running the heavy carriage over the stomach of their unfortunate comrade, who, however, rather seemed to like it, as he then got up and trotted after the others, which were luckily stopped in due course opposite a small fort. Here we halted for some time to rest the horses after their escapade. An additional fort of stone was in process of construction. We found the thistle now flourishing along our road, only occasionally relieved by a field of maize. The houses in the plain have thatched, slanting roofs. We crossed the Argoon on a long wooden bridge, and saw several battalions of soldiers exercising beyond.

At sunset we drove into Grosna, a large village, but with much unutilized space enclosed within the boundary ditch. After driving over a stream, the Sunjan, we drove back again to find the commandant's house; here a lady, who was standing on the doorstep, and purported to be that commander's wife, informed us there was no room, and advised a trial of the clubhouse. Following her advice, we drove thither, but finding preparations for a grand ball going on, we had to make a third effort for house-room, which we at last obtained by going to a shop opposite; we found that the proprietor had travelled down the Volga in the same steamer as ourselves, and Grazzini immediately claimed a cordial acquaintance with him, which so far affected his tender bosom, that he procured us two dirty rooms at the back for some exorbitant sum.

Having again got into "postal districts," we sent Grazzini off to engage a telega for us for next morning, when we again took to that jolting vehicle, this time in only one, with all our baggage in it; our trunks were our seats for the next thousand odd miles. Passing many bullock-carts along our flat road, we changed horses twice, and our carriage once, as one of the wheels came off, leaving itself and ourselves in the road before arriving at Slipsowsky, where we found a fair going on; so leaving our cart at the posthouse we walked thither, and found a thriving trade going on in leather and drink.

The Tchetchens have a pretty dress; the usual cartridge-cases on the breast, with red tips; then red shirts edged with silver, and displaying a white under-shirt; red morocco boots, and the tunic black or white, with a black or white Astrachan cap tipped with red to correspond. Getting in again, we drove over low hillocks to Nazrah, passing numerous round tumuli, and a cavalry encampment, at least 2,000 horses strong, with no shelter for the quadrupeds and wretched tents for the bipeds. The thick mud dashed plentifully into our faces as we spun along. At Nazrah we slept (more or less) in a private house, but the dismal howlings of many dogs sadly disturbed us. At first we could get nothing but eggs, and they were all bad, but after great struggles a fowl was discovered and cooked by Grazzini. Rough wooden look-out towers are attached to each village.

Next day, proceeding again through a rainstorm, we changed horses once at a fortified station containing the dirtiest room we ever saw. Then fording a small stream, we observed that villages on the plain present the appearance of a large collection of haystacks, as the thatched roofs looked like so many of them. We reached Vladikavkas in three hours. It is surrounded by a low stone wall, pierced for muskets, with martello towers at intervals. The post-house here is dignified by the name of hotel, where sheets and towels are extras to be charged for per diem. The town covers a vast extent of country, but principally in the shape of gardens within the walls. We are surrounded by hills, except on the East. Walking out, we came upon the bazaar here—a long straggling street of shops, with nothing remarkable for sale. The motto appears certainly to be "Nothing like Leather," if one may judge from the quantity of it exposed for sale. The Terek river flows through the town, a noisy stream. A small public garden descends from the main street to its bank. The trees are planted so thickly as to afford a delightful shade in hot weather. There is a wooden pavilion in the centre, where concerts are given. On the right of our hotel a badly-kept allée runs along the bank of the shallow river, which is crossed a little further on by an excellent iron and stone bridge. Standing upon this and looking down the stream, here rapidly flowing, the red tiled roofs of the houses intermingling with the many gardens and tall trees present a very pretty appearance. Some of the houses are very well built. Of the number is *not* our hotel. It is a great straggling building of brick stuccoed over, two storys high, with a wooden verandah running along the interior side towards the post stables. The eating, however, is very tolerable, and the wine good. The roads (streets) are shocking, and appear to be always the last things thought of throughout the Russian empire. Thick mists cover the surrounding hills, except when dispelled by a cursory burst of sunshine, which discloses a vista of snow-clad mountains rising above the lower ones near us. The Governor Boris Melikoff returned from a short absence to-day. We saw him in an open calèche galloping along, with a large escort of native cavalry, his baggage, to all appearance, consisting in half a portmanteau following in a telega! Some of the natives wear most astounding reddish felt hats conical in form, with broad turned-up brims. The noise of the stream is distinctly heard from our rooms here. We find the quails excellent, and generally dine upon some of them.

On the 15th we strolled out on a nasty Scotch-misty day, through inch deep mud, in a south-easterly direction. We passed a small Christian cemetery, badly kept, and Mohammedan tomb near it— a square stone enclosure surrounded by a ditch, with two short wooden columns surmounted by enormous turbans also carved in wood, and overshadowed by a poplar, a walnut tree, and a weeping willow. Then we came to a narrow country road which took us through a perfect jungle of nettles, dwarf elders, and thistles, to where brick kilns appeared to flourish. Some distance further we ascended the nearest hill to look panoramically at Vladikavkas, which we found very irregularly built, and with the usual diversity of opinion with regard to the best colour for a roof. We on returning engaged in serious deliberation as to the expediency of visiting Piatigorsk, the Baden-Baden of the Caucasus. We duly weighed the pros and cons; the former being; that we ought to see the fashionable mineral-water baths of South Russia, and that the highest mountain in Europe, Mount Elbrouz, is to be seen from it. The "cons" being; its distance out of our road, 130 miles, having to return the same way, the expense, and that the season was already over. On a division, the numbers were—for going, 2; against 0; so we accordingly set off in our usual vehicle, this time with very little baggage.

Before crossing the Ardon, at a village of the same name, we traversed several rapid streams, but always on bridges. This village, one of the largest and best built we had lately seen, seemed to be entirely inhabited by soldiers. Whilst we were waiting for fresh horses, a lumbering old (evidently European) travelling carriage with four horses abreast, came up, and out stepped a Circassian with a little boy; our astonishment was great when presently, hearing us talk English, the apparent Caucasian came up and addressed us fluently in our own language. He turned out to be a well-informed Russian who had travelled much, especially in America and England, and now was living in Circassia in Government employ. Amongst other things he told us that he was about visiting a curious temple high up in the mountains, that he had heard was raised ages ago by the natives, to the Spirits of the neighbouring range! We hoped he would not be disappointed, and then drove on, passing several tumuli; the road quite level, indeed sometimes we drove simply through the grass, getting grievously jolted. We observed the usual Caucasian Simon Stylites, on the top of his wooden watch-pillar in front of each village.

After five hours' drive we came to a gap in the low mountains, and, emerging again, were on another large plain. Here a singular tube-like building, used as a watch-tower, was standing, looking very like an ornamented English manufacturing-district chimney. The sides of the mountains forming the gap were perfectly covered as with a dense matting of wild hops and vines— a charming scene. As if to contrast with it, the half-eaten skeletons of some horses and oxen lay about along the road. On the north the Kiare river wound along, but not through our mountain passage. In a short time we arrived at the Melka, which forms the boundary between the Tchetchen and Circassian districts. Here our scanty allowance of baggage was examined carefully by a soldier, in search of tobacco. We halted at dusk at Proslainaia, and slept in the common room of the post, as a small house used as an hotel close by was crowded beyond the limits of even Russian endurance.

At the changing station, we had bought two pheasants for as many shillings; of course these stood us in good stead by way of dinner. From that station we drove upon one of the best roads we have seen in Russia, Macadamised and equal to a French Chaussée. As if to tantalise us, it only lasted for about an hour, and then our road was worse than usual. We have apparently entered the climate of pumpkins, as they are sold about in great quantities. We are following the line of telegraph from Odessa to Tiflis. It is, to all appearance, newly erected, as the date is carefully carved on each post. The wires serve as a grateful resting-place for countless birds, including small Hoopooids (?) and pretty jays with blue breasts and green feathers, besides quantities of the hawk tribe. We saw a pack of doves in most dangerous proximity to these their arch enemies. The road we had found good, is kept up by a toll, exacted on leaving

Vladi; the ticket we then received, on payment of something more than double the proper charge, was taken from us on crossing the bridge over the Melka, at a toll-gate just resembling a German one.

On continuing next day, we passed many white-painted landmarks, resembling exactly an enlarged edition of our pillar posts. These are evidently intended to point out the road in winter, when snow is on the ground. However, the telegraph posts, which conscientiously follow every winding of the road, must have entirely superseded them. At length, after jolting about in the most heart-rending manner, we reached Piatigorsk, "the Baden of the East," at 5 P.M. On approaching, we came suddenly to a valley sunk in the plain and formed by the action of some almost antediluvian river now reduced to a small stream. The town, which we could not see as yet, is situated on the north slope of this sunken valley. Before reaching it four or five isolated mountains appear, the last spurs of the Caucasus detached from the paternal range. From hence there is, we believe, almost a dead level all the way to the Baltic. The town is so situated that none of it is seen until within twenty yards of the first house, as it nestles on the southern flank of a mountain rising some 2,000 feet above it, and sheltering it from the North and East. On entering, we passed the usual amount of shabby wooden huts, and then came on the decent houses. We are in an hotel kept by an Italian Jew of the name of Carotto—Hebrew prices. It is a roughly-cemented stone house of two storys, with pretty good rooms and civilised appliances, but no sheets. Opposite this, on a little slope, stands a house built in modern-English-watering-place style—Bastard Tudor, answering to the "desirable villa residences" stuck up in a house-agent's shop. We discovered afterwards that it belonged to a Mr. Upton, the Sebastopol Englishman! More information we cannot give.

The best Caucasian wines are pressed at Kahetie, near Tiflis, where there are most extensive vineyards. The morning of the 18th turning out rainy, disappointed our hopes of seeing Elbrouz on that day. We however sallied out. The mud being something too awful, we went along the boulevard in front of our hotel. It is tolerably well kept, but the trees are young,—as in everything else, *that* is a fault that soon rectifies itself. Entering some jewellers' shops here, we inspected the lovely Caucasian belts, and niello silver work, only regretting that we had not the fortunes of several nabobs to buy up the whole of the shops with. Walking up the gully, we passed the library and reading-rooms, near which an iron plate with a ditto inscription commemorates the only ascent of Mount Elbrouz, some years ago; then into the garden leading up to the pump-room on the elevation. In this garden are some very curious old monuments: one like a semi-Egyptian human figure, with its hands folded over the breast, a sort of drinking-horn in the right, and below on the pedestal the sports of the chase rudely carved. The pump-room we found an oblong stuccoed building, with its open colonnade in front, and two rooms—one at each wing, the right-hand one containing the spring. We entered the deserted halls, and woke up a solitary soldier, who gave us some of the water to taste. We found it like Seltzer, with a decided dash of rotten egg, the basis being partly sulphuretted hydrogen; but we are not analytical chemists. Then walking out along the colonnade, which opens on to the slope down to the town, we sat down in the opposite room on leather divans, wooden benches in the centre. The springs are said to be very efficacious in curing rheumatism and affections of that description. The principal bathrooms are on one side. The situation is very charming; green trees and little bowers all around, and a good view. The inhabitants are Kabardians here. They are building a church very much on the model of St. Saviour's at Moscow, in white stone which is obtained in large quantities in the neighbourhood. The Russians appear to delight in magnificent superfluous churches, whilst utterly neglecting the roads. The cemetery lies on the south side of the town, a low stone wall around, and a small church in the midst of the tombs. A solitary mountain, rising some 4000 feet to the west, is very picturesque, forming a sharp cone, with two lesser satellites of the same shape half-way up it at each side.

The next morning being tolerably fine, we took advantage of the last trip of the omnibus to go to Kislovodsk, another bath some twenty-seven miles distant. We drove along a plain that rose gradually the whole way, till it finally merged into low mountains, between which we found our watering place situated. An allée of poplars, some quarter of a mile long, leads to the pump-room, the first, or last house in the town. A gentleman of the Hebrew persuasion, the only other passenger besides ourselves and a decayed subaltern, observed during our drive that there was nothing in the rest of the world to equal this. However, he had probably never been out of Piatigorsk before. The room in which the springs bubble up with great vigour at one end, is a long covered walk, wall at one side, colonnade on the other. A few well-dressed ladies and some officers were walking about here. These stared considerably at us being, probably, the only Englishmen who had ever drank the waters here. The ferruginous springs bubble up in a large well some twenty feet round. Procuring a glass tied to a string, we let it down, and found them to taste again like strong Seltzer, but of less decayed egg than at Piatigorsk. They are said to be very efficacious to debilitated constitutions. There is yet a third watering-place near, yclept Isslavodsk. To one of these three all Russian officers quartered in the Caucasus during the summer and off duty take their wives, if they have any, and themselves if not. Leaving the room, we got into a very nicely laid-out garden. Following the course of a clear mountain rill up a valley for about a mile, the shade delightful, we mounted an eminence whence the whole could be surveyed; and we found the native town situated on another slope of the hills, well separated from the swell part. Returning and sitting down, to await the return journey of our omnibus, we observed a Russian officer sit down on a bench opposite, then gradually drawing closer to us taking all the seats on his way, and at length locating himself on our bench. He was evidently intent on addressing us, so we looked unconscious, until he presently uttered the cabalistic words, "How are you?" Thinking that he had, perhaps, taken us for interesting patients undergoing a course of Kislovodsk water, and had kindly enquired after our healths, we answered, " Pretty well, thank you. How are you?" However, this did not seem to be the satisfactory answer, as presently came the other question "Whom are you?" Now this was a thorough "argumentum ad hominem," so we ventured the evasive response that we came from Vladicavkas, which contented our inquisitive friend for the time being. However, after we had got into our omnibus, in which he was also going, and which was now quite full, he once again inquired "What business is it?" We entirely satisfied him by saying "House breaking!" In the morning we had passed the freshly skinned carcase of a horse; at 5 P.M. we again passed its skeleton on the same spot, magpies and dogs having done the rest.

20th. At length, after the sky had been overclouded for five consecutive days, the sun shone out brilliantly at dawn, and we saw magnificent Elbrouz rising into a sharp snowclad cone from our point of view, far above the other, also snow-topped mountains. It is more than fifty miles off.

The clouds assembled again before we started on our return journey, our only adventures being, bolted with on two stages, and having drunken isvodskys (Russian, we believe, for drivers) twice, of course for the longest stages. We discovered this day to be a church festival, which caused this exuberance of spirits on the part of our drivers but not on ours. A third driver, more sober than the rest, insisted on standing up, waving his cap, and shouting at his horses to make them gallop. We passed a station called Soldatsky because it was the only one on the whole road where we did not see a single soldier near, and stopped the night at the station, Preschiskaya, where the pheasants were to be got. The only room was a large one, with a division, effected by a thin hanging; so we gave up one part to Grazzini, and took the other ourselves. The window was imperfect, indeed, only consisting of one shutter, the other having decayed long since. To remedy this, the oldest piece of felt we ever saw was brought in on a pole, (nobody daring to touch it,) and leant against the open window. After we had just fallen to sleep, a cat thought she would like to examine the strangers, or perhaps what they had had for dinner. Moving just then, we caused such a panic in the feline breast that she hurriedly bolted through the window, carrying this piece of felt along with her and smashing the other shutter; so the window was open for the rest of the night, to let in a vast amount of rain which fell most furiously. In the morning no better, so we put on our waterproofs, and in a short time our telega and ourselves resembled a huge mass of mud. We rather regretted that we could not make a sensation by driving thus round Hyde Park Corner. We passed a lot of soldiers smoking round a large fire kindled in the centre of some waggons containing cartridges! We are in a position to aver that the road between one of the principal towns and the principal watering-place of the Caucasus is, like most roads in Russia, a disgrace to a semi-barbarous nation. We except the the three miles after the Melka, which are a credit to the same. This was constructed by soldiers.

CHAPTER IV.

ON the 27th we got off at 10·30 after some trouble, and drove up the mountain gorge leading towards Tiflis, which gets gradually narrower and narrower. A dense bank of clouds hanging over the mountains. The post-houses are excellently built now. After the first station we passed a fortress commanding a bifurcation of our defile. We kept the north bend. The Astrachan caps are worn very low now—indeed, sometimes the head-gear only consists of a circular piece of skin with long hair hanging down all round the head, imparting the appearance of having very unkempt locks to the wearer; felt pork-pie hats also obtain. The natives all look very cold and frost-bitten. Some of the physiognomies are not so sharp-looking as in Daghestan. At the second station four horses were attached to our telega, which we now have to change at every one—a great nuisance, as the loading and tying the baggage always takes some time. Shortly after, we passed a fort built in mediæval style, with Saracenic buttresses, but quite modern. Here was a toll-gate, where we delivered our ticket taken at Vladi, and we now entered the province of Georgia.* The clouds now lifted occasionally, giving us glimpses of glorious snow mountains above us. However, much of the snow had evidently only just fallen. We now entered the defile of Dariel; the road good, and soldiers mending any ruined portions. We were following the Terek stream, here only a mountain torrent; one or two very small patches the only visible cultivation.

At 5 P.M. we reached Cazbek. Here we were surprised to find the best hotel since leaving Moscow. The Government has built this and some other stations for the accommodation of travellers, and the prices, extremely moderate, were according to tariff. The eating was good, and we enjoyed the luxuries of iron bedsteads and spring mattresses.

---

* Iberia of Romans, Gog of the Hebrews, and the Colchidis of Democritus and Eratosthenes.

The cold is sensibly felt, but not so much as to call for a fire, though there are iron stoves in each room. A very neat little red sandstone Armenian church graces this small village. In front is a Gothic monumental cross, two horse-shoe arches, supported on three pillars on each side; behind, a belfry in the same style. On the summit of a mountain just under the lee of Cazbek, which rises, covered with eternal snow, in front of our post-hotel, stands a small, probably Armenian, church with another belfry. The height of Casbek is given at about 17,380 feet, but there seems to be considerable doubt as to the relative heights of mountains in this part of the world.

Next morning the clouds had disappeared, enabling us to see the snow-clad summits on all sides of us—we could not, however, discover any glaciers. The incline up which we were driving is so gentle, up to the very last five miles after the first station, that one hardly realises the immense height of the pass, 7000 German feet. Small patches of snow lay about but not on our road. When the culminating point of the Pylæ Caucasia is reached, then, indeed, the descent on the other side into Asia is rapid. The hill on the left of the pass is called by some German geographers the Kreuzberg, as here was erected a small cross, marking the confines of Europe and Asia. The road down the steep incline is excellently well engineered. Some way down, the hills appear generally composed of bad slate. The telegraph, which is adapted even into some of the post-houses, lined the whole road we have come. The snowy peaks now disappeared gradually, none being visible near us after the first station down the South water shed. At one of the stations there were some wretched little shops, in which, curiously enough, the chief commodity on sale was " Frend's double stout," and German matches, made at Vienna for the English market, with the remarkable lines, " If you want a light, I'll shine so bright," printed on the etiquette. In the humblest post-houses we generally found English crockery-ware, the willow pattern largely predominating.

The scenery now lost in wild grandeur but gained in peaceful charm, cultivation assumed the upper hand, and elsewhere brushwood coppices began to encroach on forest trees. Turning off to the right we followed the vale of some river, all down hill to Ananoor, where we stop the night; the posthouse not so good or so large as that at Cazbek, but still a glimpse of Paradise to the stations on other routes. A gay-coloured (probably Armenian) church was in course of building at the station before this; the cross on the top golden, the cupola dark blue, the pedestal of this a cream colour, the under part light blue, and the octagonal roof with conical points also cream colour. The beasts of draught appear generally to be two Bulgarian bullocks (buffalo) in the shafts and two oxen in front. The horses we got were not by any means invariably excellent. Above our halting-place rises a picturesque old Armenian convent or monastery. The weather-beaten walls, as much intended to keep out the attacker as to keep in the monks or nuns, run slantingly down the side of the hill on which the convent is built, and the church rises at the highest point of the enclosure. A few ruined castles, scattered along the road at points easily defensible, give a look of romance to the scene which even enhances its natural beauty.

Shortly after Ananoor, we left the torrent we had skirted, and turned up a branch gorge rather westerly, then mounting a few miles until we came to a point whence we could see an endless succession of undulating valleys, their soil fertility itself; near the next station we passed, at some distance, a most flourishing village, all the land around being arable. Still descending gradually we crossed the broad stream of the Kur, the ancient Cyrus, at the last station before Tiflis, on a well-built stone bridge. Here there were two churches with the greatest pretension to simple architectural beauty that we have seen in Russia. They were of stone, half stuccoed over, as seems to be the invariable plan for spoiling fine buildings in this empire. The windows were of Norman character, and the double roof Gothic. This may sound incongruous to the contributors of the *Building News*, but the effect was charming in the extreme. Here also we observed, some miles away from us a deserted Armenian monastery, built on the summit of a tall broad hill. In one of the Gothic churches the tombs of almost all the Georgian kings are preserved. We had not time to see them, and indeed did not know of this till we reached Tiflis. For the last two stations the road was not artificially made, but left to chance and traffic. As we approached the capital of Georgia the increasing number of vehicles and travellers on foot clearly demonstrated our approach to a large town. At last, when some ten miles off, we reached a turn whence we surveyed Tiflis. We, however, reserve our impressions till we have entered it. Before the last stage we passed some Bactrian camels quietly browsing among the brushwood by the road side, their immense loads of cotton piled into a heap awaiting replacement. We now were on an inclined plain between mountains, at the apparent end of which lay our present destination. A large encampment of soldiers was situated on the opposite side of the Kur. The various styles of architecture in vogue at Tiflis rather puzzled us at first. We on entering came upon the common wooden thatch house, gradually merging into Swiss chalets sort of affairs. Then one-storied stuccoed buildings, then two-storied, and last a Boulevard, where we felt considerably ashamed of ourselves in our disreputable vehicle and dirty waterproofs (for it had rained slightly) exposed to the gaze of the "Row" of Tiflis. We "descended" (authority for the term, *Morning Post*) at the Hotel de l'Europe, kept by an Italian and a Frenchman in partnership, and really a miracle of cleanliness for this country: the eating good, though everything was preposterously dear.

At 7·30 o'clock we went to the opera—nay! start not!—a real Italian opera in Georgia—to see the company and the " Ballo in Maschera." The performance reflected infinite credit on the management and the actors. The baritone especially, who rejoiced in the music-breathing name of Kolliwo, would not have disgraced many an European stage. The same can be said of the tenor and the prima donna Mdlle. Dsenoni, as she chose to spell her name. She was evidently a great favourite with the audience, who, however, were not professed critics. The scenery and appointments were both well done, and the orchestra, of whom the greater proportion were Germans, was excellent. The little house was well illuminated with oil lamps, the decorations in white and gold in Moorish style; the stage boxes lined with blue silk, and the upper boxes decorated à l'Alhambra. The Georgian ladies in the boxes were hardly to be called even good looking; indeed it requires great beauty to carry off the effect of the head-dress worn by them—a sort of flat pork-pie hat looking object of coloured silk, yellow the fashionable colour, studded with silver stars, which presents a tinselly appearance. Sometimes it is prettily embroidered instead; a white lace veil is attached all around this, excepting on the forehead, and falls over the shoulders. The ladies then present all seemed to have black hair in ringlets of the "Follow me, lads." description, and plaited behind. The Imperial box was empty, as the Grand Duke Michael, the Governor of the Caucasus, was not then in Tiflis. The stalls, and indeed most of the house, were crowded with Russian and Georgian officers, every one with at least three decorations on his breast, including the inevitable one of two crossed swords, given in commemoration of the final submission of the Caucasus to any officer or soldier who happened to be near this Russian dependency at the time. Many of the native officers wore gold-tipped cartridge cases. Evening dress was adopted by those individuals who happened to have the misfortune—in Russia—of being civilians. Between the third and fourth acts an Italian dancer executed a solo very creditably, being encored by an enthusiastic public, which, during the other pauses had always left the theatre in a body to smoke cigarettes. In the upper boxes we observed two Englishwomen with their husbands, engineers engaged on the line of railway now in course of construction from Poti on the Black Sea to this place, and then on to the Caspian. There is a performance three times a week during the season.

This morning we had a long hunt after some one who would replenish our almost exhausted purse on the faith of an English letter of credit. The representative of the (Asiatically) wide-spread house of Ralli scornfully refused to have anything to do with it. At length a nice old German chymist said he would think about it. The town is built on both sides of the river, and slopes down to it according to the incline of the mountains on which it is built. We wandered down the intricate streets to the bazaar, where we found the lanes crowded with shops on both sides, and crammed with people of all nations—Italians and Germans are most numerous; indeed the latter have a regular colony on the left bank of the river.

The Persians and Armenians have their regular quarter apiece. The noise was deafening, the shops one mass of litter and confusion. To have anything made you have to enter four or five shops to buy its constituent parts. Nothing ready made excepting in the civilised "emporiums" out of the bazaar. Lace work, silk, tobacco, jewellery, wine, wine skin, linen, boot blacking, fruit, and omnium shops, each had their separate quarter in each separate national bazaar, excepting, perhaps, those for tobacco, which seemed impartially distributed, averaging every third shop; one street is covered over at a considerable height from the ground, resembling somewhat Lowther Arcade reduced to the dirtiest possible level; another street leads to the Tartar bazaar, with little intricate passages lined with shops, principally linen; before each of these wooden benches were placed, where the customers sat down in front of the shopman to make their little bargains, which always seemed to require some time before a mutual agreement was effected. The scene reminded one more of the Arabian Nights, plus the dirt and minus the romance, than of anything else. The bustle, the hurry, the jostling of Europeans and gorgeous or filthy Asiatics, presented a scene of confusion strangely at variance with preconceived notions of Oriental laziness, and utterly bewildering to the unaccustomed spectator. However, as we never have any preconceived notions, we were not so disturbed as we might have been. Getting up to the Boulevard, we found this lined with more civilized shops; out of it on the right hand side the public gardens slope down steeply to the river; they are not of any great extent, hardly one acre, but prettily laid out. At their foot, a bridge crosses the Kur, which here divides into two branches, leaving a small, stony, uninhabited—because probably inundated in spring—island between. This bridge

K

is almost a quarter of a mile in length, with shops on each side of it where it passes over this island; these are, however, bad and shabbily Oriental. The main stream, here already as large as most English rivers, flows rapidly underneath. On the left hand, leaving the bridge, five or six houses, some fifty feet above the level of the river, are built in the style, and from their position, evidently in imitation of some of the palaces on the Canal Grande at Venice. The very narrow roadway between them and the river is the only drawback to the illusion. The native women walk about with a long white linen sort of sheet over them. All letters from England, and even from Italy, pass through Moscow on their way hither, thus going some 4000 miles out of the road to their destination.

27th. Walking out in a south-westerly direction, we found that the houses are built up a steep rocky hill, so close to each other as hardly to leave room to pass through the lanes. They are here all low flat-roofed mudbrick houses of one story; Eastern dirt apparent everywhere. Above these, on the summit of the mountain, rises an old and ruined fortalice, whose outer walls are, we should say, certainly not less than three hundred yards in circumference. We entered through the original passage under one of the towers of the southern extremity, and found that though built with almost Roman solidity, the interior buildings had fallen to the ground, owing in a great measure to the bad quality of the cement, which crumbles at a touch. The ground plan of the fortress can, however, be traced with very tolerable distinctness, some underground cellular apartments evidently having formed dungeons in days long past. The only arch remaining, part of the roof of one of the chambers, was in the old style with an angular apex instead of the improved semicircular one. The north wall is built over a sheer precipice, which must have been very convenient for the Georgian kings to throw their superfluous wives down, when they got tired of them! Underneath are the new botanical gardens, which seem pretty; and on the other side of the ravine rises the high flat mountain which bounds the plain of Tiflis on the west. From the ruins the view over the town beneath is very interesting. Flat and angular roofs are used very impartially all about the town, excepting in the extreme west—the European quarter—where slant roofs obtain. Armenian churches, with extinguisher steeples painted black or green, according to the taste of the architect or founder, abound; we could only discover one mosque, with its minaret crowned by an egg-shaped apex of glazed green and yellow tiles; there are, however, some more in the town. The river winds like a serpent through Tiflis. Almost all the better houses have the open verandah before them on each story.

The banks of the Kur are rocky, and at the south portion rise abruptly from the stream. Some fortified barracks, with a church in the centre, stand at the south bend. A little higher up there is a low muddy island, given up principally to cattle and temporary wooden huts; here the river is spanned by a wooden bridge. Lower down the left bank is flat, then it rises again covered with houses, mostly flat roofed; at the extreme north are the public gardens, still surrounded by houses.

Then walking along the pathway under the walls of our fort, we find the houses on the slope almost perpendicularly below us. The portion of hill on which they are built now merges at an obtuse angle into the higher flat one, and our path leads downwards into the town, here built between the two projecting flanks of the west mountain. The first building reached on getting to the town is a small church with four or five pretty tombs near, in a small churchyard. We were particularly struck by one in white marble, erected, as the inscription in Russian tells, by a sorrowing husband to his dear wife; underneath in French, "Tout mon bonheur. Toute ma joie. Tout mon orgueil." The design, a square raised pediment, angels' heads at each corner, and above a cross covered by a winding-sheet, surmounted by a carved wreath of roses and convolvuli. This was an extremely windy day, but still warm. The principal portion of the town, and almost all the grand houses and government buildings — the palace of the Governor-General is on the Boulevard—are built on the right bank of the Kur.

Cigarettes are smoked as extensively as in other parts of Russia here. The bakers' shops are level with the pavement, and have a counter in front, behind which stands the officiating *German*, and again behind him the furnace is let into the wall, so that he has only to turn round to fetch the loaf out of it, and present it to the purchaser. The loaves are baked in a round shape, very brittle and brown, their appearance generally unsavoury. We found throughout the whole of Russia that fancy bread bakers almost always belonged to the " Vaterland." Many of the shops are situate in cellars as in Hambro' and other towns.

The Armenians wear a long flowing garment, generally black or dark violet, tight at the waist, with an opening in front, under which is a sort of waistcoat, with a coloured border, buttoned or hook-and-eyed up. Large full-grown ox-hides are used as the wineskins, and water is conveyed about the town on horses' backs in skins, apparently those of the thigh of the buffalo, the skin of the leg still attached as a pipe to empty them by. On a clear day, the high range of Caucasus we had passed can be seen clearly; Cazbek stands well out, above the lower mountains, resembling from here, rather, a doge's cap in shape. We went again to the Opera to see "Ernani" for the first time. We thought that almost a sublime and especially grand idea when the hero in the last act exclaims, " In the meanwhile, and to fill up time, I'll kill myself!" and suiting the action to the word, stabs himself for no other apparent reason. This part was taken by a Signor Biondini, who acquitted himself very creditably of it.

The 28th was a day devoted by us to shopping. Having seen a pretty pipe, for which the shopman asked three roubles, we managed, after a deal of bargaining, to get it down to two and a-half; thereupon we tendered a three rouble note in payment. The proprietor, with true Oriental laziness, preferred giving us one rouble back to sending out for change. In the jewellers' row the working is continually going on at the shops, which have no front, but a glass case with the small stock-in-trade exposed in the centre. Hardly anything is kept on hand, but all is made to order.

However, by careful inspection some fantastically-shaped plate may be picked up. The little cabinets in which instruments and odds and ends are kept are sometimes artistically inlaid in ivory, &c. The tobacco of Imeritia is very cheap, and smokeable when made into cigars. We discovered a tolerable restaurant, kept by a Frenchman, on the Boulevard. A countryman of his has established a brewery some miles from the town, where beer not unlike German Weissbier is made at fourpence a stone jug. At Tianelee, a village some thirty miles north of Tiflis, we are told the inhabitants, as yet uncontaminated by the rude hand of civilization, ply their ordinary every-day life avocations dressed in complete suits of armour, such as the Crusaders wore, the round low helmet ending in a point, and chain armour. Very romantic! An enthusiastic German traveller we met at our hotel wanted us to verify this, but we thought it would encroach too much upon our valuable (?) time. We have engaged a new servant, Joseph Seffer by name, *vice* Grazzini, as he would be of no use to us in Persia. We parted with regret from an honest, faithful, and ready, though perhaps somewhat grasping, servant.

30th. Walked out to the public gardens some two miles off to the north. On the way to them is a private garden called "Mon Plaisir," where a military band plays almost every night during warm weather. The walks in the gardens are laid out nicely, but they sadly needed gravel when we were there, and the carriage road was full of ruts. An enterprising Frenchman has established a restaurant in the gardens, with a music pavilion and a dancing platform, attached to another refreshment platform he has built regularly out over the bed of the Kur, on a level with the gardens, which are here some fifty feet above the stream. Excepting when the river is much swollen, the water does not reach this bank, but leaves a wide shingly margin between. Good-sized rafts are built above this, and floated down for firewood to Tiflis. The trees seemed young and lately planted, with the exception of some most venerable willows by the principal road. Some of the walks are charmingly arranged, with vines over them on trellises across. Hardly a grape is to be seen. This, however, cannot be wondered at, considering the publicity, and that the large soldiers' encampment we had seen coming from Ananoor is at the further extremity of these gardens. This was formed to accommodate the soldiers from other cantonments who were sent here to assist in quelling the riots that took place in this town last July, originating on a question of taxation. The Armenians were the chief instigators of this disturbance, which assumed rather formidable proportions; indeed, they regularly gutted the house of the mayor; (who was particularly obnoxious to them,) which stands in the centre of their portion of the town. The ruins were still unrepaired in September. The streets here are principally lighted by the moon—when it shines! The season is far enough advanced for every third day to be rainy. This, the 1st of October, is one of the third days! We clomb (?) up a portion of the pathless mountain to the west of the town. The streets leading up to it are simply the beds of torrents flowing between two rows of houses. On the hill hardly any vegetation, but a friable sandstone soil. A good view of the town from here, but much resembling that from the ruins. We saw two soldiers, heavily manacled round the ankles and wrists, escorted through the town by others with loaded muskets. They were probably deserters.

The fish caught lower down the river are excellent and of large size. Not having been able to procure horses easily, it was 5 P.M. before we started from Tiflis on the 2nd, and jolted right through the bazaar, on our way out of the town, which extends for a considerable distance in the direction we were taking; we were following the downward course of the river Kur on its right bank. Huge lightly made waterwheels supplied the irrigation of the plantations along the river in the most rude manner, the water adhering to the large paddles being brushed into a trough by loose brushwood, and then conducted down to the grounds through a wooden channel. We reached Suganloo at a quarter to seven, having driven some time by a brilliant moonlight, and passed several droves of sheep and camels.

Getting off tolerably early next morning, we drove along a bleak undulating plain, bordered by mountains on both sides, high at first on our left and low on the other hand, then high on both sides. During our second stage, the driver beguiled his time by telling Joseph stories, which he immediately translated for our benefit. One of them was of such a highly probable nature, that we think it worth recording; be it observed, that to all appearance the story-teller implicitly believed what he was stating, and expected us to do the same:—

"One night as our driver was passing some lonely Tartar tombs after dark in his Telega, he espied something white moving about amongst them; with considerable strength of mind, he got off and walked towards the object, which he presently discovered to be a very pretty little white dog. This immediately began jumping upon and caressing him, playing about in a dog-like fashion. Pleased with his find, he took it home in his cart to the posthouse, where it was much admired, fed, and petted, and at last put into a room for the night. Strange to relate (indeed exceedingly so!) on opening the door in the morning, the little white dog had disappeared, and a dead body lay in its place."

The same gentleman had once again wandered about these tombs at night (one would have thought he had had enough of them), and heard a voice crying out of one of them: "Help me! Protect! Save me!" Whether he rendered the required assistance, deponent sayeth not.

At the third station there was a large Tartar cemetery, perhaps the home of the white dog. Joseph looked about carefully for one. Upright stone slabs, rounded off at the top, some of large size. The habitations of the natives are hardly distinguishable from the surface of the plain, as they are excavated in it, and then the ground is heaped up on the roof, so as to present exactly the appearance of a low oblong tumulus. When some distance off, on the slope of a hill, they look like fit homes for Troglodytes, nothing but the open doors being apparent. We met several curious waggons covered with tenting, on two wheels, each wheel at least seven feet high, and much larger in proportion than the body of the cart itself. Reaching Salahlee in a storm of rain, we determined at 4 P.M. to halt here, more especially as we were told that there was no accommodation at the next station — though for that matter the accommodation here was what Irishmen call "no great shakes," as at first we could get no food, and candles were not to be found. An old candlestick and the samovar—the "hot water urn" (we carry our own tea and sugar) were procured with some difficulty, and bread and new laid eggs from the usual little shop near. Unfortunately perhaps, for our palates the black bread was musty. The stone floor of our room afforded, by its unevenness, a model on a small scale of the Swiss Alps! Near this place we saw a land tortoise of some size, its shell a foot in diameter lengthwise.

In the morning we drove along a road as broad as you like over the plain, the telegraph to Persia alongside. On a mountain to our right a ruined house, we were told, was once a robber's lair. We continually met long strings of camels, each laden with two bags of cotton as large as themselves. The soil evidently only wants irrigation to turn it into a land flowing with all sorts of good things, for wherever a stream ran through it there the vegetation was of a most luxuriant character; hops, walnut-trees, elms, vines, and apple-trees, vied with each other in beauty and fertility. We remarked an enormous spider, its body quite an inch long, creeping along the ground. We soon reached a low ridge of sandy-looking hills which we crossed, and then entered upon another plain for about twelve miles, when we got into the defile of Dillijan. The river of the same name flowing through it caused fertility around, and the mountains became well wooded. At 4 P.M. we reached Istibulleh. Here the postmaster refused to allow us to proceed (which by not giving us horses he could, effectually), alleging as his reason that there were some brigands on the mountains we had to cross. The band, he said, were fifteen strong, and had plundered some caravans lately, so that no travellers were allowed to proceed without an escort, which was not to be got that night. Having lately killed a colonel who objected to being robbed, a body of three hundred soldiers had been sent against them, so that the danger could not be very overwhelming. It will be observed that killing a colonel has the same effect on the Russian army as including a bishop in a railway accident is hypothetically estimated to produce on a railway company in England—causing the powers that be to show some energy.

The postmaster informed us that a "billet" was required in order to procure an escort, but that if we would stop one night he would give us one in the morning without this formality. We accordingly stayed with as good a grace as possible. We observed oxen used as beasts of burden on the road to-day, the load conveyed in immense saddle-bags. Up to this place in the pass, the carriage-way is quite unartificial, and the boulders cause awful jolting. The fat-tailed sheep look most ludicrous when their caudal appendages waddle about in their walk. The women wear the white sheet over their mouths and foreheads, only exposing the eyes. The process of covering up the nose, we thought, must have its great inconvenience when a severe cold is caught! They all ride astraddle, side-saddles not being known here. We are now in Armenia, and the first natives we saw had a decidedly cunning look about them, though not to such an extent as to justify the proverbial expression about them which is current in Turkey. This is, that it takes five Christians to get over a Turk, and five Turks to cheat a Greek, five of these latter are required to swindle a Jew, but it requires five Jews to "do" one Armenian! However, as our dealings with them have been limited, we are not entitled to speak from experience. W. is studying Shakespeare hard, and has lately come on a passage in "Richard II." he wishes embalmed herein:

> "Oh! who can hold a fire in his hand,
> By thinking on the frosty Caucasus!"

At 7.30 A.M. next morning we looked around for our escort, one miserable horseman with the usual rusty matchlock. He would certainly have bolted had he seen "the fifteen" descending from the mountains, as indeed should we under similar circumstances. However, there was not the slightest appearance of danger on our road, indeed we met several solitary pedestrians and horsemen, so, after the first stage we declined the services of another escort. We passed many caravans of camels kneeling in a circle round their loads of cotton by the roadside. The scenery is fine and wild, well wooded hills on each side, some of it where the mountains approach so close together as only to leave space for the road, and the Dillijan much resembles portions of Norwegian scenery just north of Christiana, but the general scenery is very different, lacking the magnificent firs, the " Norwegian pines" of Milton, and the waterfalls. At our second station, Dillijan, we were informed that we could not have horses, as *all* were out and the *rest* had to be kept in readiness for the post, which was expected to arrive immediately. Nothing for it but to wait till it turned up. The common black soldier's bread is along our route as dear as meat is cheap in Tiflis. A nasty drizzling day. After two hours' waiting, the post arrived in the bodily presence of one horseman, so we got off, taking the bag along with us. The road was up-hill almost all the way, and more fitted for a "gemsbok" than for a heavily laden cart like ours.

The influence of early autumn was just beginning to show itself on the foliage of the trees clothing the mountain sides, and imparted the most varied tints to the leaves. At times the groups of timber were so symmetrically arranged by nature that we could fancy ourselves in the well kept grounds of an English park. The west wind blew very cold, and as we neared the top of the pass, a dense mist surrounded us, luckily clearing away at the very summit, allowing us to see snow on some of the surrounding peaks. Here the road was comparatively level for about ten miles. The aspect of nature had completely changed from that at the northern side of the pass. On our way up we passed several carts on two wheels, these being made simply out of two slices of good-sized tree, the body flat, in fact as near as possible the plaustrum of the ancients in which Thespis is said to have transported his theatrical paraphernalia.*

---

* "Dicitur et plaustris vexisse poemata Thespis."—*Hor.*

The landscape being totally devoid of trees, we here saw the lake Gooitcha, of considerable extent, not unlike a Swiss one; we descended slightly to get to its edge, and came to a halt at 6.15 P.M., on the western bank at Shibookli, a very small station. Here eggs were the only eatables to be got. It froze hard during the night, and was bitterly cold even in-doors. We managed to get off at 8.15, and drove for about ten miles along the west bank of the lake, generally about two hundred feet above its level. The panorama of the hills on the further side was very fine. There is a small island at the northern extremity of the lake on which stand two old Armenian churches called Sievan Killeasea—the latter word meaning church (ecclesia) in that language (Armenian). The lake cannot be much less than forty miles long, and at least half as broad for the greater part of it. Many fish are caught in it, especially excellent trout, of these we saw some dried specimens at Jellanook, the next station still on the shore. Some small boats were returning from fishing with enormous nets; there are also plenty of wild duck. The land side is cultivated in cornfields, the soil when ploughed up looking as black as coal. Jellanook is a very squalid village, but the houses are above ground, owing, no doubt, to the proximity of the lake on whose level they are. We passed the Zengi river just where it leaves the lake to flow hereafter through the streets of Erivan. Then leaving the lake on our left hand we turned into a stony undulating road, round and over small mountains, until we suddenly saw the snow-capped peak of Ararat in front of us. On the left some recent snow covered the higher mountains, and on the other hand rose a four peaked mountain eternally snow capped, called Darahleglass. We now gradually descended until we were in full view of Ararat, which standing like a solitary giant looks down with proud contempt on the lesser pigmy mountains around it. W.'s waterproof unluckily fell out of the carriage somewhere here, so he and Joseph went back to look for it, but were not successful, and we managed to get to the nearest station, some eight miles off, before W. caught us up in the carriage. Here, having sent Joseph back to look for the coats, we stay for the night, arriving at 5 P.M. The climate here is again tolerably warm, unlike up in the pass.

Our servant is a Chaldean Catholic of that branch which acknowledges the sovereignty of the Pope, about whom he knows just as much as a non-elector does about the "man in the moon." However, we have again been lucky in getting a good, though extremely dirty servant at short notice, and he speaks French very well. We strolled out upon a small hill just opposite our post station, and got a capital view of the country, the only drawback to the perfect beauty of the scene being the total absence of all vegetation—nothing green to be seen excepting a little stunted brushwood on the distant mountains; even the corn was all cut, thus adding to the general desolation. Mighty Ararat appears a mountain of easy ascent compared to many Swiss peaks, at least from this point of view, as the west side ascends with a very gradual slope to the summit, looking very nice to climb up—from a distance! Perhaps actual inspection might tell a very different tale: at all events, we shall not make the attempt. The snow only covers the apex then, as aforesaid, a slope and then a flat surface of small extent, another slope, and a precipitous south and west side, a few thousand feet downwards. On our right, Darahleglass, looking very black where not very white owing to snow, and other lower mountains completed the panorama. The dusty road we had come wound up to the north in tremendous zigzags,—troops of camels grazing unrestrained on the broad surface of the plain. Only scanty herbage theirs here; though on the other side of Dillijan they would, or had, found plenty of young trees, the tops of which to devour. The ploughing is carried on laboriously in the parched soil. Two yoke of oxen harnessed to a pointed forked tree branch, the lower limb being cut off sharp and sharpened so as to form the ploughshare, and the other branch the handle. One man leans on this contrivance with all his might, whilst another sits on the bar connecting the heads of the two leading oxen to guide them! a peculiar position, which it must require considerable practice to keep for half a second. Joseph returned next day at noon without the coats, and we set off from Yogunarshie, or the "long stream," so called from a miserable rivulet that runs behind it and is carefully hoarded up for purposes of irrigation. In about two hours, down an incline all the way, and after passing a village on the road surrounded by willows, walnuts, and poplars (proving thus that it is only for want of planting that trees do not grow in other spots near which there is water), we reached Erivan. We found it lying in a valley, in which the trees were so numerous that the town looked like many houses buried in a forest. They (the houses, not the trees) are all of mud, and have flat roofs. We drove through most of the town, and stopped in front of a building calling itself the "Ararat Hotel," where two nasty little rooms without furniture were offered us in exchange for some exorbitant sum. So we drove on to the post-house, where we got a tolerable room at a cheaper rate,—nothing per diem! In the bazaar we found nothing very much calculated to tempt the European purchaser, though the fruit is magnificent. There is a large mosque in the midst of it, with the usual bakehouse dome and glazed tile minaret. Here we for the first time heard that six persons had died of cholera while we were at Tiflis. However, happily that disease did not extend its ravages. The bread is of a pancaky nature, baked in pieces about three feet long and half as broad. Not bad. Ararat is at thirty miles distance, though from its immense height it is utterly impossible to judge by the eye. It might be any distance off, from five to fifty miles.

CHAPTER V.

ON the 8th we procured horses and carriage to take us to Etchmiadzin, not without some trouble, as the name of this monastery was not written down in our padarojna, which only indicates the straight route towards Persia, and this is eleven miles to the west of Erivan. We passed the bazaar, and then the fort opposite our rooms built apparently of mud, but still (to the unmilitary eye) on most scientific principles. It has lately been renovated, as the original fort is coeval with this town, the capital of old Persian Armenia. Descending to cross the Zengi, the road again mounted on the opposite bank; the fort now opposite on the precipitous left bank, some huge poplars on our right. The road for the first four miles is rather stony, and then very good on the elevated plain.

After about a two hours' intensely dusty drive, we reached the first of the Ooch Killeasea or *three* churches, another name for Etchmiadzin, which is so called after the manner of nomenclature obtaining in England also, because there are here *four* churches within half a mile of each other. However one of them is more modern than the others. We met numerous pilgrims on the road, this being Sunday and St. George's day. Each church has its own grounds, surrounded by a high stone wall, those of the principal one being much the largest. Etchmiadzin is said to have been founded by "Gregory the illuminator," in the ninth century. When we visited the monastery, the seat of the patriarch of orthodox Armenians, who is also called the Catholicos, that post was vacant, the last occupant having died a month since; and the new one, who is elected in a peculiar manner by the votes of all male Armenians whether Turks, Persians, or Russians, was not yet chosen. We made the half circuit of the strong walls to get to the west door, where we found three priests and an Armenian, a native of Tiflis, who spoke French, ready to receive us, though we had given no notice of our arrival. The priests are dressed in a long flowing robe of dark blue cloth with a "moire antique," silk "capuchon" over the head, replaced indoors by the little red Turkish fez.

We now entered a court-yard surrounded on all sides by dwellings for pilgrims and visitors, and quite full of every variety of the human race, presenting a gay picture of Eastern life. In one corner we saw several women seated round their dinner, each of them holding up with one hand a large shawl over themselves to hide their features whilst eating. Most of the women have only half the face covered, but some wear the whole face under a thick veil, (punctured with holes to see and breathe through,) a precaution which, considering the extreme ugliness of all the women we have yet seen (the features of those who wear the open veil are easily discovered), it were only common charity to extend to all. Passing thence through a passage under one side of this court, we entered the large square in which stands the church. The portico, of old red sandstone, is evidently a later addition as the other walls are well weather-beaten. This is curiously carved in Armenian style, the design of it being Gothic. Two frightful daubs of saints, of most modern date, disfigure the inner pillars of the principal entrance. Just outside are the tombs of two patriarchs, one of whom built the immense tank, which is beyond the outer gate of the monastery and oblong in form, of solid stone. By the side of the patriarchs lies an Englishman in fraternal and tolerant juxtaposition. This is Sir J. Macdonald, and his neat tomb is of white marble, with an inscription setting forth in Greek, Arabic, and English, that it was raised by the East India Company to Sir J. Macdonald, K.C.B., who died at Tabreez in 1830, when proceeding as their envoy extraordinary to the court of Persia. The other tombs are alabaster. The service having already been performed, the church was closed, but we entered by a side door, and were received by a most venerable priest, with a long, majestically flowing white beard. The interior is very imposing, though the style in which the walls and cupolas are painted, more resembling the pattern on a Persian carpet than anything else, is perhaps a little gaudy. The tawdry gilding of a Greek church is, however, absent. In the centre of the church, on the spot where our Lord is said to have appeared to St. Gregory, rises an altar, on which is a picture of Madonna and Child, in Greek style, wearing a sort of breast-plate of carved silver. The light streaming through the windows on to the high altar shed a wonderful rose-colour over it. The railings are of alabaster, painted over, principally with figures of the twelve Apostles, in the style of the Vivarinis. The patriarch's chair was covered over with a cloth not to be removed till the late Catholicos' successor should be appointed. It was, however, raised to allow us to see the exquisite carvings of the back. It is of some Indian wood, and the species of pavilion overhead is of tortoise-shell, inlaid with mother of pearl.

We then walked round the exterior. The church is built in two intersecting oblongs in Byzantine style, with little Gothic towers on each of the eight corners.

We now went into the third court around which are the patriarchs and priests' rooms; we ascended a very narrow staircase to the library. It contains 2040 volumes, all in manuscript, principally relating to sacred subjects in Armenian. A copy of the Evangelists is kept in a wooden box, and shown as a chef-d'œuvre. Its binding in curiously Byzantine carving is certainly remarkable, and the writing is beautifully executed; the monks say that it is 800 years old. All the books required for the use of the monastery, or the various churches, are printed at a press on this spot. At the present moment the work being performed consisted in "setting up" theatrical playbills! and posters. Our French-speaking Armenian and two friends were going to open a native theatre in Erivan; the performances to commence in a week with an original drama and a translation. Ladies' parts, to be performed by one of the three men. From the library we went into the patriarch's rooms; they were plainly furnished, portraits of Armenian kings hanging on the walls. A few of the rooms were painted in the Persian carpet style aforesaid, interspersed with agreeable martyrdoms. A small "Madonna della Seggiola" in Gobelins, a bad Riberesque Crucifixion of small size, complete the patriarch's boudoir. We now again entered the first court, and went up through the wooden verandah that completely surrounds it, to the room of one of the priests, where we sat for some hours talking, drinking black coffee, and smoking cigarettes, the worthy priests joining vigorously in all these pursuits. Some dozen persons came and sat with us at intervals.

The modest furniture consisted of a bed, table, four broken-down chairs, a trunk, and a Persian carpet. The noises in the court below were of the most varied and continuous description. Now an enthusiastic pilgrim would fire off a pistol, then another would begin practising on a large drum, and now a quarrel arose, not without some fighting. Presently a musician with a sort of bagpipe would set up unmusical sounds, to quell strife by melody! Then an amateur indulged in a piccolo flute. The women all wore ornaments on their heads or necks, sometimes only glass beads, but more generally gold coins strung together. We were not accosted by a single beggar whilst walking in the monastery.

An Armenian from Constantinople, who spoke French, and rejoiced in the archangelic name of

Raphael, was very mysterious on the subject of his visit; and from his conversation we judged him to be an emissary of the Turkish Armenians, sent to enquire into the state of feeling among the Russian Armenians,—whether they were ripe for revolt or no. He was speculating on an insurrection in Turkey at no distant date. It appears there is a "King of Armenia," who habitually resides in Italy, the Turks having an unconquerable but natural objection to his domiciling himself amongst them. His name is Leo, a lineal descendant of the old kings of Cyprus, the Lusignan family. After our two hours' converse, we bethought us of sending for horses to take us back to Erivan, as our telega driver had refused to stop for us at the post. Meantime we went to see the westernmost church. It is not ornamented outside, and the interior is quite plain, even the whitewash having peeled off. Outside are some fine alabaster slabs covering the tombs of patriarchs and princes. The ordinary tombs are of red sandstone, and in shape exactly like a gigantic common round-topped envelope box on a pedestal, with the inscription on the top.

A few relics are preserved on the high altar, but we wondered much at not seeing a piece of the true Ark! We asked the priest in attendance whether no piece was preserved in the monastery, when my friend bursting out laughing spoilt the idea completely. A low arch in the west wall under the high altar leads into a passage only three feet high and ten feet long, which descending with a taper we were in a cellar, in a recess of which lies buried Gaiamee, a female missionary, who laboured amongst the first Armenian Christians. We returned to the monastery to find that there were no horses to be got at the post, so we determined upon walking back, though most hospitably pressed to stay, but we could not, as we had brought nothing with us.

On our way we took the easternmost church, about half a mile off. Its very weather-beaten walls of Saracenic order contain nothing remarkable excepting the tomb of Repsimah. We were told that this lady had been a beautiful Armenian, educated in Greece, where she imbibed the principles of Christianity and returned to attempt the conversion of an Armenian king. This gentleman not being anxious for conversion, but wanting a mistress, asked Repsimah to act in that capacity. Upon her refusal he began to persecute her in various ways; so she wisely fled to the spot where she now lies. Her death so affected our Armenian king that he became a Christian. The tomb is down another short dark passage, which we had to creep through to get to a small and dimly lighted cellar, where a woman who was howling vigorously was getting herself healed (!) of whatever disease she had by lying down at full length upon the grave!

After a slight shower we saw a rainbow in heaven, perhaps at the same spot where the first messenger of Divine clemency appeared unto Noah! Just as we were leaving to start off on our pedestrian excursion to Erivan, two men from the monastery came up and informed us that a Troika was being got ready, so we walked back, and were met by our priest and first Armenian friend on horseback, the priest in full canonicals! Of course when we got back no carriage was visible, so we entered the room we had before sat in, again and waited somewhat impatiently for more than an hour. It was getting late—already five—when we were told the Troika was ready; so after a glass of tea we again left the monastery, and had to wait outside for twenty minutes longer, when at length the horses belonging to the monks arrived. We bad adieu to our courteous hosts, and lying down on the hay in the telega, were soon jolting back on the same road we had traversed in the morning. Two armed horsemen escorted us the whole distance, being changed once on the road. In the evening a drunken man created a disturbance in our posthouse by beating a woman with a baby in her arms. However, we consoled ourselves by the reflection that if she did not deserve the blows *then*, she probably had, and would again. At last a very small soldier, looking frightened, came in and quelled the riot by seizing hold of the wrong man. We left Erivan on the ninth of October, and for the first station we drove, perfectly south, through numbers of poplar trees enclosed in mud walls, the rare intervals being filled up by castor oil and dwarf cotton plants. The greater and lesser Ararats were on our right hand during the whole of the day; the greater slopes down to the south to half its height, and then rises again into the lesser, which had a very little of this year's snow on its summit. As seen from the north it much resembles Vesuvius, and the greater, W. tells us, might, with the assistance of a little imagination, represent Etna. Thus the two seem like a baby by the side of its nurse! Our road was impossibly dusty. The second station was in a larger village than usual, with a small open bazaar of principally English cotton goods, of which the women and even the men are very fond. After this the cultivation was nil, and the road perfectly flat. We now met several darkly bronzed Kurds driving unloaded cattle along the road. Near the fourth station we passed a tomb raised to one of their chiefs; it was about thirty feet round and fifteen high, painted white, with a round dome, something like Dante's tomb at Ravenna. We reached Sadarack at 5.45, and stayed the night in the clean post-house.

Here a woman came in to dust the table—an unheard of thing. W. complained of midges at sunset, but they do not interfere with us. Next morning we found the first two stages unusually long, twenty-two and a quarter versts a-piece, or about fifteen miles. The plain partially cultivated. We now skirted the low mountains on its east, and saw in a drove a camel almost perfectly white. It appears that it is the arrangement of the pack-saddle which gives the camels we had yet seen the appearance of having two humps on the back; for in those animals that we saw without one hardly a single hump was visible. After the second station, where we were detained for two hours, whilst a runaway horse was being caught, we crossed the Arpahchi, whose stony bed is at least half a mile broad. At this season it divides into at least ten small streams, each of which we easily forded. Just as we neared the third station, a north-west wind began to rise, and without much warning it came on, rolling clouds upon clouds of dust before it—a perfect simoom—before which nothing could have stood. Fortunately we were going with it, but as it was, the road was utterly invisible, even the horses' tails not being discernible. We luckily stumbled upon the posthouse, and there waited for half an hour, when a heavy shower allayed the dust, and after an additional thunderstorm we were able to proceed. On our left hand Ilandagh, or the serpent's mountain, stood out well from the surrounding hills, in shape like a sugarloaf for all its height, with a cleft at the top. At about 6 we came in sight of Naxshivan, built on the slope of a hill—a very insignificant place now. There was only one room at the posthouse, and nothing but bare walls to that; so we drove on to what our Yamshick pleased to call an hotel, a mud hovel with glass windows, but not a soul near. Our servant Joseph had, however, heard of one kept by a German, so he and the coachman, who wished to patronise his absent friend, had a wrangle, only put a stop to by threats of personal chastisement if we were not driven to look for our German. At length we found the house, but "Vaterland" had left, not finding it a paying concern. Some very civil

Russians had succeeded to the goodwill of the house, and the remains of German civilisation were still hanging fondly about in the shape of one sheet apiece for our beds, and a clean tablecloth!

The wine of Erivan we had found not bad, and resembling Kahetie, but here it was atrocious with a bitter taste. The inhabitants are more or less afflicted with ophthalmia; those fortunate enough to escape this scourge of the East had fever. For the information of future travellers we would say that our hotel (?) here was called "Billar," from the fact of there being a billiard table in the house! In the front room some European trumpery was exposed for sale. In the morning we sallied out and made our usual *inspective* tour of the bazaar, which is extensive but with nothing worth buying, as everything was either brought from Tiflis where we had been, or Tabreez whither we were going. The streets are very narrow, bounded by mud walls.

This town, a flourishing one under the Persians, is now half utterly destroyed, most of its poorer inhabitants having migrated into Persia. We got upon the ruins of a quarter of the town, and thence enjoyed a magnificent view on to the mountains on either hand. We were forcibly reminded of the panorama to be seen from opposite Turin, when looking on the Piedmontese Alps in mid winter. On the east the greater portion of the mountains, though looking low, owing to our own elevation, were covered with snow, much of it of recent date. This range extended on either hand north and south, as far as we could see in an almost unbroken mass of snow. Ilandagh rose darkly against the snowy background. Ararat, on the north stood clearly out against the clear blue sky—a contrast to yesterday, when we could hardly see it for clouds. The lesser Ararat, though between us, could hardly be made out against the dark side of its mother. On the west the mountains were not yet all snowed up. We saw below us a large Eastern-looking building, and being told that it was a Tartar Khan's palace, we determined to pay him a visit if he would receive us. A much dilapidated octagonal tower stood outside the brick wall near; the sides of this were exquisitely ornamented in bricks arranged in all manner of Arabesque figures, each panel of the octagon having a different design, and light blue glazed tiles being let in to form the reliefs. The old brick archway was flanked by two round towers of some elevation, and on the arch were Arabic letters, also in the blue glazed tiles, most probably setting forth the usual welcome to the coming guest. We entered through this into a garden in the front courtyard, the bricks in the walls still arranged in exquisite figures, and the garden itself planted with flowers and fruit trees, though in no great order, as a tasteful arrangement of a garden is not a Persian accomplishment. More is left to nature than to art. We now sent in to ask permission to visit the interior, which the prince (the Russians had made him a prince to keep him true) graciously accorded.

We entered a low, whitewashed room where he was giving an audience, and found him attired in a gorgeous blue silk close-fitting coat with gold trimmings and collar. On a Persian carpet in front of him three Persians were seated on their crossed knees, one writing in what one would consider an uncomfortable way in England—that is, holding the paper on the flat of his left hand, taking the ink from his portable writing-case or kalamdaun, which every Persian of at all a literary turn of mind always wears about him! The pens are always reeds. Sometimes the paper is held on the knees. We were then conducted into another room, where the floor was being covered with common blue thick paper pasted on in squares. This was to be glazed, and then the carpet to be laid over all! Here the chimney-piece was some seven feet high, all painted in the Persian style, somewhat resembling lacquer work, rather tawdry. We then went out into the inner court, also a garden, and through this into another portion of the house which was undergoing complete repair.

In one of the upper chambers—properly devoted to the wife or wives, who were absent then—there was a lovely Persian carpet with trees and birds of many colours wrought into it; divans with embroidered cushions all round. Outside was a roofed wooden balcony, carved in Arabesque trellis work, little pieces of coloured glass being let in, forming the pattern. We sat down, and the Khan produced a pair of opera-glasses by Chevalier. In front of us, about ten miles out, flowed the Araxes, the opposite bank being in the dominions of the Shah. This was thus our first view of Persia. Some eight miles on the other bank rose the range of black mountains we had seen yesterday. The Russian side is cultivated; on the Persian side only the two miles next the river. In the winter the vines, of which there are large plantations near this place, have to be covered over deeply with earth to preserve them from the intense cold. We observed that the Russian princes' coronet on our host's property had the crescent instead of the cross on its top, and the initials K. X. underneath; rather an alarming name he must have had!

The common water jars here are very prettily shaped, as the ancient amphoræ. At a little after noon we started on our last telega journey. A portion of the last piece of road was rather bad, as it led us through the bed of a torrent amongst very rugged red sandstone boulders. We see Ararat for the last time, after being in full view of it for six days. The tints of the mountains around us now presented the most exquisite possible colouring, from light grey blue to deep red. On our arrival at Joolfa, the frontier station on the Araxes, the sun was setting, and all the hills in the East were covered with an intensely purple haze. As we gazed, the shadow projected from the Western mountains gradually rose as the sun went down, at length leaving the hills in their former cold colours. We found the post-station a very good one, and thought that this might be owing to a wish on the part of the Russians to present a more vivid contrast to those on the Persian side. Our first care was to order horses for our onward journey. This had to be effected by screaming across the river, which luckily is not much over fifty yards in width at this point. Our servant Joseph having wisely told the Custom-house man here that he (Joseph) had a quantity of silver money to carry over for a friend (!), the Customhouse man very naturally objected, as the exportation of coin is strictly forbidden by the Russian authorities—an evil practice, by the way, as it encourages white lies.

CHAPTER VI.

ENTERING a new country affords an opportunity for a new chapter, of which we avail ourselves. A judicious bribe secured an unquestioned exit for our baggage next morning, when we crossed in a rough wooden boat with two pointed ends. Bakshish demanded and tendered, we found horses brought down to the river for us; and getting our baggage tied on to the pack-saddles with ropes of horsehair and flax mixed, we rode to the post station, custom-house, and passport office all in one, some hundred yards off—a mud house. We went up-stairs and bowed to two Persian swells sitting cross-legged on a carpet in the verandah. Our Feringhee names were then neatly inscribed upon two Persian passports, which were handed to us by way of an excuse for getting money. They were roughly lithographed with a huge lion at the top, and a female face looking out of half a sun, just over the lion's back.

Kaleouns were brought in, but never having smoked one we declined, fearing to muddle the process, which at first is rather difficult, though extremely pleasant when acquired. The smoke is vigorously inhaled through a wooden stem, and inflates the lungs, whereupon it emerges through the nose. The wooden stem communicates with a bowl, nearly full of water, out of which proceeds another stem supporting the tobacco holder; they are sometimes gorgeously decorated. The tobacco is called Tumbak, and the best grows near Shiraz. We got off at 10 o'clock, with an escort of three men, who followed us for two or three hours, and then remarked that the danger (!) was over. We were making straight for a gap in the range of hills in front of us, then up and down hill with an upward tendency, through an arid country with considerable cultivation however, wherever flat. We passed a ruined caravanserai of great extent, the foundation walls being of old red sandstone blocks, and the rest brick; the gateway almost perfect and beautifully ornamented in coloured glazed tiles. In five hours we reached the first post station where we changed our baggage horses, and then proceeded onwards to Merand. We witnessed another glorious sunset, and had to march after for four hours by the sole light of the stars, our horses sometimes fancying that going down on their knees would be an improvement, "*Stumblings by 'Starlight,'*" indeed! We forded plenty of small streams near the stations, but the intermediate ground seemed very arid.

At length, at 10 P.M., we entered Merand, and marched up what appeared to us a stream skirted by trees and walls on both sides, constituting the high street of the place. After knocking for some time at the posthouse, the huge door was opened, and we rode in. The post houses are always of mud bricks, in square form, presenting a dead wall on all sides, with one large entrance in the centre of one wall, and one room built above this, which is the grand strangers' room. We entered this here, and found that it boasted of three windows, the outer one extending the whole size of that side, and none of them having, or being ever intended to have, glass in them. A broad lattice of woodwork is the only protection from the air outside, and this is generally wanting. Thus these rooms are more adapted for summer than for winter travellers. In winter we found one of the two rooms *under* the archway always the warmest. The square courtyard of these posthouses is formed by low stables on three sides. On the door side generally are the attendants' rooms. Cribs are let into the walls in which the horses feed whilst waiting to cool down. On going into our upper chamber we found its entire furniture (!) to consist of two carpets. Little niches in the walls had to serve as receptacles for our moveables. We found considerable difficulty at first in writing at full length on the floor. A huge lantern of wood and linen was presently brought in, and after tea we slept soundly on the floor.

At 3.30 P.M. next day we reached Soofianeh, first passing on the road a most venerable Persian dressed in a most magnificent blue silk flowing garment. We find now a piece of sentiment in our journal! "We passed the carcases of two camels, their toil over for ever!" The gardens around the various villages are the only objects breaking the dreary monotony of the parched scenery. Next morning we left after the usual squabble about money; the Persian appears to be not easily satisfied. We rode over a plain here ploughed up on all sides, streams of brackish water very plentiful, but "not a drop to drink." This we found rather a hardship as the sun shone burningly hot overhead. On our left the rocks were of a deep gory red, on our right we saw the mirage of an extensive lake. After about five miles we caught sight of Tabreez, lying at the end of our plain, surrounded by mountains on three sides. We rode on and on without seeming to get much nearer, until after five hours the mud walls of the first gardens became distinctly visible, when we halted to allow our baggage to come up, and then we began a march through high twelve feet mud walls, surrounding flourishing gardens with every sort of fruit tree. After a time the streets got narrower, and then we threaded our way through the most intricate windings. We presently halted in front of a large house, that of the English

Consul-General Mr. Abbott, upon whom we made a most sudden descent. Though totally unexpecting English visitors, he and his wife immediately, in the kindest manner, placed two rooms at our disposal. The house was entirely Persian in shape—of one story, with a charming garden in the front courtyard, and an open gallery supported on stuccoed pillars at one end. Under this were our rooms. This town stands at an elevation of 4200 feet above the level of the sea. It is liable to earthquakes, but there had been none for some time. A strong easterly wind blows almost constantly in summer, but by a merciful provision of nature ceases in winter, or the climate would be insupportable. All potable water is brought down from the mountains by a succession of wells dug at stated intervals, and having a subterraneous conduit connecting them. These are sometimes called Canauts. This is the most commercial town in Persia, and almost the most flourishing. It is said to contain 120,000 inhabitants, but the truth in that respect is very difficult to arrive at. Having a letter of introduction to a Mirza Abdul Nahib

Khan, a species of lord mayor with a seat in the Cabinet, we sent it him; whereupon he returned us a tray with four sugar loaves, two pounds of tea, and some sugar candy, as a complimentary present, no doubt very useful, but to travellers rather cumbersome. The servant who brings these presents expects a sum or sums of money, which constitute his pay! The sandgrouse are very good eating, and water-melons flourish, some of them charming baby ones as large as an orange. We walked on the top of the house, and had a good bird's-eye view of the town. The object which strikes the eye most, and which indeed we had seen as soon as we were at all able to discern Tabreez, is a mass of brickwork towering over the town, the wall of an ancient mosque. There are only two consulates, English and Russian, here; a French one was in course of institution. On riding through the town we observed that many of the doors of private houses were solid blocks of stone some six feet high, with pivots cut in them at the top and bottom to act as hinges. The wooden doors are studded with immensely large copper or iron-headed nails, much resembling those to be seen on some doors at Toledo, in Spain. The custom here is to take coffee early in the morning, then breakfast later, between 10 and 12, and to fast more or less till dinner, say 6 P.M. This being Sunday, the old flag of Great Britain floats over the entrance porch, where are stationed four Persian (so-called) artillerymen, as the guard to the consul; two of them are habited in something like cast-off English shell-jackets and trousers, the other two are got up anyhow, though always with the tall Astrachan cap with a dent at the top. This they never remove on entering a room : shoes off! hats on! The climate is said to be drier here than in the hottest parts of India, but not so high in temperature. Thus trunks that have stood Indian heat warp upon being brought hither.

16th. The bazaars are very extensive: miles of arched ways. The European caravanserai well built; a court-yard in the midst of the bazaar with a fountain in the centre; red brick buildings all round containing rooms in which the traveller can unroll his carpet and sleep, besides the regular offices of the merchants who trade with Europe; our banker's establishment we found in the centre of one of the sides of the court-yard where it forms a graceful curve, with the bazaar running underneath at the depth of each of the four curves. We got our first Persian money here. It is very roughly coined and consists of Tomauns in gold, about eight shillings, and Kerauns in silver, about tenpence.

It is said that the exports and imports of this place amount to something like three millions sterling per annum. This is no doubt a flattering estimate but still a very large trade is carried on, as it lies on the high road from all north and central Persia to Turkey and Europe.

On the top of the surrounding hills which look so black and poor, many flowers grow, including "gentinilla," "wild tulips," and "Pride of Peru."

A Dr. Cormick, whose father was physician to Abbas Mirza when governor of Shiraz, and who himself holds the corresponding office now, called here. He has passed the greater part of his life in Persia, and tells us, as indeed we imagined, that the stories about the deadly effects of the bite of the Meeanee bug are absurd fictions. It is a small red-coloured insect whose bite is supposed to take effect upon strangers sleeping in Meeanee (which we have to pass), by causing them to waste away and at length die, the natives not being susceptible of the bite, and a lighted candle keeping off its attacks. Now Dr. Cormick stayed there, and his cook was bitten by a red bug on the chest. Nothing but quiet was prescribed, and no evil effects ever followed; but owing to the low rice plantations about Meeanee the place is most feverish, so much so indeed, that out of a party of twenty-two Europeans who lately slept there, twenty were taken ill, and all declared they had been bitten by the insect, though they had slept in tents outside the town. This latter circumstance affords a clue to the mystery, as they all had low fever. The fable no doubt arose from some persons catching a malignant fever in the place and dying from exhaustion, this being attributed to the little insect which certainly infests Meeanee, but whose bite is little worse than that of the ordinary domestic " cimex."

This morning the Alvizoreh came to pay us a visit, attended by twenty-four ferashes to clear the way for him. He seemed a portly, good-natured, olive-complexioned man, talking no European language, so Mr. Abbott kindly undertook the office of interpreter, though our conversation was not marked by any particular brilliancy, beginning with the usual compliments and merging into the weather and the comparative antiquity of English and Persian families! Our friend stated that one family whose title of nobility extended back three thousand years, was just extinguished through failure of heirs! Something like our Welsh pedigrees: " About this time the Flood occurred !"

The wall of circumvallation is in ruins here as in most Persian towns. Mr. Abbott has attempted mending a few of the roads in the immediate vicinity of his house, but bad are the best. Being invited to dine with some Greek merchants, we walked out in the evening, preceded by men carrying huge linen lanterns. These are proportioned to the dignity of the individual before whom they are carried; no one is allowed out after dusk without them, and indeed it would be rather difficult to avoid perpetually tumbling about were it not for them. We find considerable difficulty in getting a muleteer to take us on, but hope to achieve one to-morrow, 19th. The quinine, jujube, and rose trees grow well here. We returned the Nahib Alvizoreh or lieutenant of the ministry's visit to-day. (It will be observed that we get more learned in the titles of this individual the longer we stay at Tabreez.) We went on horseback, as walking on such an occasion is "infra dig." and found the broken state of the roads to interfere considerably with our comfort whilst riding.

A large proportion of the regular (?) Persian army was loitering about the prefect's courtyard, as he, like most Orientals, keeps up a great and useless state with regard to his retinue. We sat on the civilized appliances called chairs and smoked Kaleouns, though as an exception our host did not indulge in them. Two tiny cups of coffee and two ditto of tea were handed round to each of us at intervals, and after half an hour's not lively twaddle we departed as we came. Mussulman cemeteries are all over the town. The tombs are generally the common flat oblong stones, with a low one at the head. The government of this town and district being the most important in Persia, is always given to the heir-apparent. At present (1865) he is a boy of fourteen.

On the 19th of October we parted from our kind hostess. Mr. Abbott rode out a considerable way with us, showing us the blue mosque on our way, a ruined place of worship still beautifully overlaid with the tiles from which it derives its name. We are now travelling " en caravane," that is without one! for the main body of heavily-laden horses and mules always travels by night, whilst we have hired five horses for ourselves and baggage to go by day. We were soon overtaken by a European, escorted by a Cossack, who turned out to be a Russian secretary to the consulate. The first question he put to us was what our names were. We made with him a detour through a nice poplar wood, in whose centre we found an octagonal pavilion of three storys in a bad state of repair, but still retaining traces of Alhambresque decorations.

This he informed us was called Khelaut Shah (?) as here the khelaut, or robe of honour, which the shah sends every year to his son and chief officers of government, is put on by them. This is a sign that the king's good graces are still continued to them, and they come out these nine miles to meet it. We passed through a well-cultivated country and over two fresh-water streams before reaching our first halting-place, Cay (?). An extremely dirty caravanserai received us about three farsacks or twelve miles out. Next morning we set off again, having been kept awake most of the night by the noises produced by our caravan, which started at midnight. Shortly after leaving we began to mount. Seeing one of the old massively-built caravanserais on the way, we entered it, and found strong arches of brick, the level being below surrounding ground. Thus the basement was dug out, and the whole interior very dark, in arched galleries. We passed a small piece of water, on which were a large number of ducks. We tried to get a shot at them, but failed to get within range, so fired our Colt's revolver, loaded with ball, at a lark flying. Oddly enough we missed. At Hadjala we put up in (and with!) a mud room, without going to a caravanserai. Another plain and ridge of hills to cross before getting to Danadgar, where there are only three houses. We put up at the posthouse, as our friend the Alvizoreh had given us a road order; though, for the matter of that, no doubt bakshish was the one thing needful. We passed several horses in caravans laden with huge clothes' basket affairs, having a semicircular hood over them. In these, one on each side of the horse, sit travellers who prefer this mode of conveyance to riding; it is the only alternative in Persia, excepting a thing like a double sedan chair carried by two mules in shafts—one before, one behind. In this one can lie at full length, but in the clothes' basket the only postures are sitting cramped or curled up, or with legs dangling over.

This day (21st) a succession of hills and vales, each valley getting higher up as we advanced; our village is in a low valley, and is called Chodjakias. Same sort of road next day and latterly following the broad bed of a stream for three miles to Meeanee, the chosen home of the cimex. Here, as usual, we were shown into a mud room by some inhabitant. In a few minutes a man, who turned out to be the proprietor, rushed into the courtyard, objecting to our installing ourselves. He was cuffed on the head and then quietly retired. The town lies in a low district by the stream we had followed, and beautifully green beds of unhealthy rice grow close around. Having to keep our candles lit for fear of *the* insect, we passed a good deal of our time in reading, and now follows a Persian story, in consequence:—

"Once upon a time, long, long ago, there flourished in some part of Persia an academy called that of Silence, whose tenets inculcated a vast amount of thought, a very little writing, and no talking at all. The number of academicians was strictly limited to one hundred; and as may well be supposed no ladies belonged to it. It so happened that in due course one of the members died; it also occurred that at that very time there was living at the other extremity of Persia a most learned man, Zeeb by name. He had written many treatises, as 'On the art of living for ever,' and others too numerous to mention. No sooner had he heard of the vacancy in the Academy of Silence, than seized with a laudable desire of filling it, he posted up, as fast as horses could carry him (the Indo-European telegraph was not in existence then, and would most likely not have worked had it been!). Meanwhile a court favourite, renowned for his talking propensities, had been installed in the vacant place. The consternation of the fellows may therefore be imagined, when the learned Zeeb sent in his name as craving admittance. The President determined to give him an audience in full council to show their regret. Zeeb, therefore, was ushered in, and the president taking a glass, filled it as full of water as it could possibly hold, so that another drop would cause it to overflow. Zeeb, like a wise man, understood the allegory, but seeing a roseleaf lying on the floor, he picked it up and placed it gently on the water, which did *not* run over! The fellows were so charmed at this, that clapping their hands, they instantly admitted him a member regardless of all rules to the contrary. The book was brought to him to sign his name in, which he did, adding the numerals 100, and then prefixing a nought, thus, 0100, showing that the number and worth of the academy were not increased by his admittance. However, the president charmed with so much modesty in so learned a man, scratched out the nought, and added a one in its place, 1100; thus implying that the academical worth was increased tenfold by his presence!"

Near the lake Ooroomeah, west of this place, on the borders of Turkey, there are chalybeate and sulphur springs of great medicinal effect. The lake is seventy miles in length, and on its west bank is the town of Ooroomeah, where some Presbyterian American missionaries have established a station and schools, which are said to do much good, especially amongst the Nestorean Christians. Our candles effectually kept off the insect, and most of our sleep.

Eggs are seven for one penny here, but the price of fowls fluctuates considerably in the different villages, from the moderate sum of two-pence to the enormous charge of fourpence ready cooked! In the morning we crossed the stream of yesterday by a long flat bridge, and began ascending a steep mountain. We passed a bush covered with rags, as every Mussulman passing by tears a strip off his already scanty raiment, to hang it upon this solitary bush, making a prayer at the same time, or a wish for something which is to be fulfilled as long as the rag remains fluttering upon the branch. Outside Meeanee and other villages we saw two or three families of lepers, living cast out in tumbledown mud huts. We found the upper portion of the road over this mountain to be paved spasmodically in bits about a quarter of a mile long, with rough intervals, but totally regardless of inclines, so that no human being riding on any animal would venture on the pavement, consisting of various sized stones hid in the ground with their flattest side uppermost, and this was generally a jagged point! Descending we crossed a river with a strong current, on a high bridge, and then ascending again, we came to a vast high table land, intersected by shallow ravines. Our road was very wild and solitary; in our seven hours' ride we hardly met as many people; no cultivation visible. We observed on the road some curious animals with the tails of lizards and the bodies of toads, also some rat-like animals with bushy tails, burrowing in the sand and called Sichan by the natives. The latter part of our road was a descent to a stream and the village of Sharshan.

On the 25th we marched for seven and a half hours along a level road, following the course of the stream all the way. Along the flat banks corn and rice were growing, and we saw several Kurdish or Eeliaut encampments, a congregation of tents made of dark felt, of goat's hair, woven by the inmates. Neekbash our halting place. One gets used to the smell of a stable at night. Here it was rather nearer to us than pleasant. The inhabitants seem gladly to put their mud room at European travellers' disposal, no doubt on account of the expected donation. We apparently halloaed before we were out of the wood, for at Sharshan, we were bitten by some insect, assuredly *the* bug, that left a round and perfectly deep crimson mark, about the size of a silver penny, with a black spot in the centre. On our servant's right arm these bites caused a very considerable swelling; grape treacle was recommended him as a cure, and was very efficacious.

On the 26th we followed the valley of a river we find spelt Naclowzum in our journal: it abounded in poplars and willows. In seven hours we reached Zengan, the largest town between Tabreez and Teheran; a blue glazed tile mosque with a round cupola, rising far above the other buildings, we saw a great distance off. We installed ourselves in a very dirty caravanserai, but luckily in an upper room. Of course in these places we always have to send our servant out to see whether there is anything to eat, and then to light a fire and cook whatever there may be. The first morning after our arrival here we departed from this plan, in so far as that our servant went out to buy eatables, and came back with some beastliness resembling a sausage with the skin off, tasting more of garlic than of anything else. We stopped here this day, as we had a serious disagreement with our muleteer, who wanted us to stop *two* days; we even got half our money returned to us, as this place is supposed to be half way between Tabreez and Teheran, though really nearer the latter, but as the sequel showeth, we were obliged to give in!

We went out alternately to-day, one of us staying to look after our things. *We* went out first in search of a new muleteer, but they were all engaged or going the wrong way. During our voyage of discovery we strolled through the bazaar, which is a solid new brick gallery, and shows considerable commercial enterprize to exist here. The nights are already rather chilly, though in the daytime the temperature is good. We find that, in American phraseology, we "caved in" on the 28th, and stop here to-day to proceed with our former muleteer to-morrow. However, he apologized, and as we could not find another we take him on again. Just outside our windows there is a large open space only partially occupied by underground baths, whose round mud roofs project a few feet from the surface. Here there are constantly playing a quantity of youths, age from seven to thirteen, whose garments are of the most elementary description, just consisting of sleeves and a portion of back. A large cemetery is just beyond and there are female mourners constantly passing to and fro. A dark blue sort of serge appears to be the fashionable mourning dress. The women not engaged in mourning we find to be generally dressed in a black and white chequed cloak. The coppersmiths, whose bazaar is close at hand, seem to drive a " roaring trade," as the noise of their hammering continues ceaselessly from early morn till dewy eve. The mutton is excellent, and the best quality is sold at three halfpence a pound; then they have had no cattle-plague!

Starting on the 29th we rode over a perfect flat, until we imagined ourselves at the end of the world. The plain on which we were riding was bordered by two chains of mountains which seemed to end about twenty miles further on and then— nothing. Our thoughts were however recalled from these reflections on attempting a gallop, when our horse fell on its nose and pitched us very neatly over its head. After about seven hours' riding we reached Sultanieh. About a mile outside this village stands the most picturesque edifice we had yet seen in Persia. On a small hill, made higher by art and rising abruptly from the plain, we saw the fortress palace of the Shah, to which he often comes during the summer heats to review his army, which encamps below him. It is a square on two platforms of brick rising one above the other, with arched glass windows. There are about fourteen sentinels' boxes excavated in the hill and looking like gigantic rabbit-holes. Mohammed Khodabundeh, the son of Ghazan, one of the successors of Zingis Khan, that "scourge of the Lord," founded Sultanieh as a great town; now it consists of a few wretched mud huts, though the traces of former grandeur are still distinctly recognisable, as we passed through ruins for some few hundred yards before entering the present village. These are however now almost level with the soil, and indeed sometimes ploughed over! We saw the remains of a mosque and two circular-roofed buildings on the west side. This city did not escape the ravages of Tamerlane, who spared it from utter destruction on payment of an enormous ransom, which perhaps contributed to its ruin, though no doubt, as in other parts of Persia, misrule is the principal cause of its decay.

We Christians were conducted into a very clean room with carpets belonging to a Mussulman priest, Tolerance! (perhaps pecuniary). The son of the priest was of a gossipping turn of mind, and fell to talking with Joseph. He informed him of the derivation of the founder's name! "When he (Khodabundeh) had founded this city, he took up his abode in it. Most probably feeling hungry one day, he sent to a neighbouring village to demand two fowls as a tax. The villagers did not send the animals, but instead a complaint of the exorbitant nature of the impost, which amounted to two shis (one penny, the common copper coin of the realm!) Now two shis, it appears, in the Tartar language are called Khodabundeh. From henceforth Mohammed was called nothing else! just as Dean Swift explains the derivation of Alexander the Great! He was buried here, surrounded by his own creations, and his tomb stands close to our room. We went to inspect it before starting in the morning. It is an octagonal building of fine brick, encrusted with blue tiles. At the top of the octagon a gallery runs round the building outside, with three horseshoe openings at each side. The roof of this gallery is fretted and apparently inlaid with red tiles, which of old time were evidently gilt. The entrance and portions of wall have tumbled down, so we entered through a breach, and found ourselves in a space quite as large as the body of the Pantheon at Rome and resembling it in shape, excepting that where the high altar stands in the Christo-Pagan temple here an open arch leads into a square high room. The height of the roof from the ground appeared to us to be almost double that of the Pantheon. It is a perfect concavity, exceedingly well built in brick; these being laid in circles, each circle getting gradually smaller till there is only the one at the apex. These bricks were then covered over with some sort of mud plaster into which the lacquered tiles were fixed. Those parts of the edifice which strike the eye most are very carefully worked, each tile being baked in the form required by the design. The prevailing colour is light turquoise blue. The roof has several large cracks, and is evidently hastening to decay. No trace of the actual tomb is to be discovered, nor did any inhabitant know of its existence; but how can we expect a people whose annals preserve no record of such monarchs as Xerxes and Darius to exhibit any interest in later kings? Khodabundeh was the first Persian ruler who embraced the Sheah heresy, now the dominant religion. Accounts of this are no doubt to be found in many encyclopædias. We rode eight hours over the plain, discerning the remains of many villages and watercourses, and stop at Koorumderah, a large and well planted village.

Leaving the plain next morning, we ascended the hills on the east, which we crossed, and in six and a half hours arrived at Meskeen: a cold north wind blowing. Next day, it took us just as long to arrive at Cazveen. Shortly after starting, we met a Persian bound for Stamboul, who talked French, and asked us where we were going to and why! His wives and other baggage came after him. A short distance amongst hills, and then into a plain, which to judge from the comparative multitude of towns and villages seemed very populous and flourishing. Six miles outside Cazveen we began marching through vineyards, which extended to the very walls in unbroken succession; grapes were also ludicrously cheap, as we bought a pennyworth, and received rather more than six pounds weight of them for that sum. Until within a mile of the town, we seemed to be approaching a forest of poplars, as no buildings were visible; then a finely decorated mosque and some blue minarets made their appearance, and we gradually got into the village. We put up at a caravanserai in the bazaar, which is long and dirty, with nothing remarkable for sale. The dwelling houses are all beneath the level of the street, which runs between the garden walls of each one. This is no doubt owing to the fact that the bricks of each house were dug up out of the mud on the spot, thus sinking the soil. The drinking water is conveyed through the town in a subterraneous brickwork channel, the access to which is gained by an inclined plane, or long sloping staircase, arched over. At the entrance to this stands a pretty porch-like open edifice, gaily decorated in tilework. Then a regular tube and cock communicates with the aqueduct below. This arrangement, however, sometimes as at this place, allows the drainage of the town to filter into the water, thereby not improving its taste. After a prolonged search after our muleteer, who deserted us here, but was brought back and slightly cuffed, we started next morning at $10\frac{1}{4}$ A.M., and reached Hassarkoobad in four and a half hours, when we got into a room whence the inmates bundled out leaving all their portable property about. Our road lay over the yesterday's plain. We observed that the ants of this country, contrary to the practice obtaining amongst their civilised congeners, burrow under ground instead of erecting ant hills! Next day we rode for seven hours, passing some Eeliaut tents and a large flock of cranes. We now see the snow-capped mountains of the Elburz range towering over the lower range on our right, stop at Aptarasseen, and next day at Sophiabad purporting to be thirty-two miles off, where we got the worst rooms we had yet been in, the place swarming with children, and all the inhabitants looking diseased.

CHAPTER VII.

On the 5th of November we started early for our last day's journey before reaching the capital of Persia, Teheran. We cross a good-sized stream on a good-sized bridge, we ride on for six hours without discovering any traces of a large town, though Demavend towers loftily above and before us. At last we see Teheran before us, in a sort of embrasure of hills (though in reality rather far from any, and on the plain). The impression conveyed by a first sight, as to the size, is that it is smaller than Tabreez, which is indeed the case. Nothing striking about it, as trees as usual conceal all the public buildings. We met hundreds of unloaded camels going out of the gates; then passing through some very crowded streets and dark crooked bazaars we reached a narrow well paved street where the pavement was frightfully slippery, and halted before the British legation. The first objects that struck us were fireworks placed in readiness for letting off before the door. This was appropriate—Guy Fawkes' day! Mr. Alison, our envoy, in the kindest manner offered us apartments at the embassy, and the same evening he gave a grand entertainment to the Turkish minister, where we saw all the Europeans then staying at Teheran. The Persian Minister for Foreign Affairs and the Shah's Aide-de-camp also dined, and the two Persian ambassadors respectively to London and Paris, who much prefer Teheran to going about their business!

The first news we heard was that of the death of poor Lord Palmerston. This had come by telegraph, which traverses this town, coming from Bagdad and also from Tiflis. We found here a billiard table, brought all the way from England with great difficulty. The Persians played at it with more or less (rather less than more) success. Two Persian bands played alternately in the large garden in front during and after dinner: one was led by a Frenchman, the other by an Italian: this latter much the best. The fireworks were creditable, but the art of colouring the fire did not seem to have been brought to any great perfection, and the smoke was much too great.

On the 7th we went into the bazaars, accompanied by Mirza Jan, the second moonshee or interpreter to the mission. These were positively interminable, and filled with every sort of commodity. Old arms are seemingly a great article of trade, and the jewellers, who are always Christians or Jews, are also very numerous. These enamel very beautifully on gold, though when the subjects chosen are human beings the drawing is anything but perfect, and the perspective always ludicrous. The bazaars are very solidly built of burnt bricks, and the various caravanserais are commodious. At one end we came out upon the Shah's palace. This is surrounded by a moat long since dried up. Then an arched gateway leads into a street well paved, and with little shops on both sides; these are the outer precincts. Then a large garden courtyard with a large tank brimful of water in the centre. This was added by the present monarch, Nusreddin Shah. In this (the courtyard, not the tank) quantities of soldiers were lounging about, and in one corner we saw about twenty rough-looking fellows with nothing distinguishing about their dress excepting dirt, who, we were told, were the executioners—as handy with the baston or the bowstring as with the sword. The whipping-post is only a stout pole with a loop of cord in the centre, into which the whippee's feet are placed, and thus held up to be bastinadoed. Taking off a man's toe nails neatly with the stick is one of the executioners' greatest accomplishments. On the right of this court stands the royal palace, flanked by two tall broad towers. Before getting in here we passed some corridors decorated with designs worked in white plaster. Here is the English telegraph office and a staff of English operators. Some of the walls of these corridors are painted in barbarous style, but withal picturesquely.

In the evening we dined with a solitary French attaché, who filled the post of chargé d'affaires, first, second and third secretary all in one at this moment, and for some time before. We went on horseback with attendants on foot bearing the lanterns, as the road is very treacherous, full of holes and desperately slippery. Returning on foot, we were vigorously attacked by the watch-dogs in the bazaars; they were however repulsed without much slaughter. A few dim oil-lamps were stuck up here and there in niches in the walls. The Russian mission having determined to build a house in grand style, they got the plans drawn out, and the building was commenced by laying the foundations and cellars in solid stone. Then no more money being forthcoming, the rest was built of mud. The Russian Government has now (1865) about 650 cases calling for redress of wrongs done to Russian subjects by Persians, for which they have received no satisfaction, and thus it is only waiting its opportunity or the withdrawal of British countenance to seize upon the provinces of Ghilan and the port (!) of Astrabad, in the Caspian, as a compensation for those cases.

On the 7th the races, a national institution, came off. As we were riding into the town we saw at a distance a building open in front, which looked something like a grand stand, and it turned

P

out to be so. The course is about two miles out, and purports to be two miles round. The foreign embassies are always invited, but it appears have never gone, owing to a point of etiquette, the minister for foreign affairs always allotting them a position not by any means suited to the dignity of representatives of European sovereigns, — a room on the ground instead of near the Shah. On this occasion a message was however sent round to the various envoys to say that this had been rectified and that the room generally appropriated to the queen mother had been allotted to them. We therefore set out with Mr. Alison in the morning, forming a cavalcade of nine Europeans, preceded by the Gholaums (the mounted attendants and foreign-office postmen to the envoy), and the Kaleoun, as that pipe is always carried about on state occasions. We had hardly got out of the town when a messenger rode up bringing word that the arrangement of rooms had again undergone alteration, and that the missions were to sit in a room below the Shah. This, of course, was an indignity not to be overlooked, so we turned our horses' heads away from the course, and prepared to return.

However, we thought that as we were mere travellers not diplomatically connected, we might have a look at the fun *incognito;* so we rode a little way up the course, which is enclosed by two low mud walls, and quite as uneven as the rest of the plain, and then turning, accompanied by two Gholaums, we got to the stand, where we dismounted and stood in the passage of one of the outer wings of this building.

Early in the morning, when the Shah prepared to go out of his palace, one gun was fired, then a salvo when he mounted his horse. This we heard when some distance off, so we cantered on through a multitude of people who lined the course for a great distance. The sight put one much in mind of a racecourse in any other country. The Shah's eldest son soon drove up in a carriage *on springs* most gorgeously got up. Then after an interval came a troop of camel artillery, each carrying a gun of the smallest calibre in front of its rider. Before these came a drum and fife band also on camels. These soldiers were dressed in perfectly respectable red coats. Then some mounted horsemen rode up clearing the way, and after these some fifty fellows got up in the most curious of helmets, apparently high cones of black cloth, flat at the sides and with bits of silver paper pasted on in bits; upon this a pasteboard erection, like a painted bunch of flowers, red coats and gold (or brass?) buttons. These were the Shah's "running footmen." Then the state coach, richly mounted in gold with a glass front; the harness of the eight horses also to all appearance of gold. After this, and preceded by all the dignitaries of the realm on foot, came the Shah himself riding alone, on a splendidly caparisoned steed and holding a red silk umbrella majestically open over his head. His complexion was olive, with dark moustaches, no beard or whiskers; his epaulettes one blaze of diamonds. After him came an immense and miscellaneous escort of horsemen wildly galloping about. Immediately on the king's entering the grand stand, which was in two storys and built of brick, the races began. Nine venerable-looking men got up in red robes like so many Venetian senators, took out bits of paper, and began writing, standing in the centre of the course, in front of the king; these were the king's scribes, " chiels taking notes." For the first race eight horses started, six times round the course—twelve miles! The jockeys were all boys, four of them dressed in red silk shirts and violet breeches, two in white and two others in green shirts. They each wore a handkerchief, of colour corresponding to the shirt, on their head. The start took place at an immense pace; no false starts here: should one jockey be behind the others, *tant pis pour lui*. Anybody is allowed to enter a horse, and should one not belonging to the king win, the jockey and owner are bastinadoed. Whilst the race was being run a band of drums and shrill clarionets struck up in front of the stand, the musicians sat cross-legged on the ground, and to this accompaniment the Shah's singing dervishes struck up a song in a quavering treble. Very luckily the sound hardly reached us, as the performers were on the other side of the course. All this time the sun was shining very hotly upon us all. The horses at each successive round seemed to be taking it easy, though, judging from the supposed length of the course, this could not be the case, as they finished the first two rounds in ten minutes (four miles), and the whole twelve miles in twenty-eight minutes! At the last round, the spectators who were on horseback rushed on the course and licked the respective horses they had any interest in with sticks to make them go faster. One of the red shirts won. There were five prizes; this is the number for each race we believe, irrespective of entries, so that if only five enter, each has a good chance of gaining one! The prizes, sums of ready money, were wrapped up in a sort of white linen handkerchief, and were laid on the ground in front of the king, before the start. Each winner receives one of these, which he puts on his head, and then walks in front of the king, to whom he makes an obeisance, as he did before the start. After this race we left, as all the others are the same, excepting that the distance for each gets shorter.

On the Indo-European telegraph being opened

in Persia the king went in person to the office and telegraphed to all the governors of the various provinces on the telegraphic line. The message sent was to this effect:—" What present have you brought the king on this auspicious occasion." Satisfactory answers were received, each governor giving a present according to his ability or the tax-paying powers of his province; and when the king retired, the respective governors at the various stations also left. They had, however, not proceeded far away when they were summoned back again, and received messages from the Prime Minister:—" How much have you brought for me?" The present minister of finance, a devout Moslem, who frequents the society of Mullahs and Dervishes more than any other Persian, lately acquired possession of a village in the neighbourhood, an Armenian colony, by name Van-eck. Upon hearing that his tenants were in want of a place of religious worship, he immediately gave orders that a church should be built for them; and not only that, but with his own hands presented them with a large crucifix to place in it; a rare instance of

Moslem toleration! A favourite present to make to a Christian here is that of a pig! which animal is supposed to be very useful in the stable. We had heard great things of the dangers of travel between Tabreez and Teheran, but at anyrate *we* found it perfectly safe. Our muleteer was constantly complaining about our liability to be attacked; but as we continually saw solitary horsemen on our road, it did not seem so very unsafe after all.

On the 8th we went out hawking towards Shah Abdulazeen, a village about three miles from town, where there is the tomb of a very holy Imaum of the same name. The cupola of the mosque in which he is interred is gilt all over, and shines accordingly. We soon found some partridges, but on very bad ground intersected by narrow and deep ravines; so they got away, and we turned to the right, away from the ruins of Rhè, the supposed site of ancient Rhagæ. These are to all appearance of mud. A few bricks lie strewn about, and rude sculptures have been found by careful explorations. The city (then called Rei) was destroyed by the Tartars in the 12th century. After a long search the dogs (of a thin greyhound breed), found a hare, which not having sufficient start, was run down by them before the hawk got a chance at it. Finding another, after ineffectually beating a castor oil plantation, we got a short run over a corn country, when it was soon pulled down by the hawk. Then we had tea and a kaleoun under a chinar or Oriental plane-tree, and returned over a bad country full of small ravines. The corn is already growing, about six inches high. It is covered with snow in the winter, and then shoots up to its proper height in the spring! We saw the top of Demavend peering out of the clouds. It is variously estimated to be from 19,000 to 22,000 feet high!

We on the 10th came suddenly upon a lion, led by a string in the bazaar, and nearly fell into its mouth. It rained heavily, falling as snow on the surrounding mountains. On the 12th, Sunday, we went to the Teheran Zoological Gardens, thus keeping to the fashion even here. We got to the animals, which were the king's private property, through a large garden, also belonging to the Shah. This has a summer palace at one end, and the walks are well planted and laid out. Thence we entered a smaller garden where the beasts are kept in small brick huts; some six tigers, two panthers, and one lioness, completed the collection of *wild* animals. The keeper walked amongst them very unconcernedly. They are much better treated than in many public "Zoos" in Europe, petted, never beaten, and always well fed. The birdhouse is a large building with wire for windows, where every sort of bird runs about indiscriminately. In a large yard were some gazelles and wild asses; one of the latter was very tame, and came up to us to be patted. We dined with the Russian minister.

On the 18th we visited Goolaheck, the residence of the English mission during the summer heats; we went on horseback in front of a sort of four-horsed landau, in which came Mr. Alison and one of his secretaries. We passed one of the Shah's palaces on the way—a lofty square stuccoed building, with a platform and trees on the top, and a nice garden in front. Some distance from this there rose a Persian cotton-spinning factory built in European style, and bringing reminiscences of the neighbourhood of Manchester into one's mind. It does not succeed as a speculation. The road is remarkably good, perfectly level for five miles with a trench on either side. At about seven miles from Teheran we turned off on to a less perfect side road, to Goolaheck, which stands on rising ground. The house has nothing remarkable about it, but a good garden and many trees in front. These latter throw a grateful shade on it during the summer, but hinder all view, excepting from the roof. A tent is raised in front where the mission eat their meals whilst residing here. The supply of water here is on rather odd terms. A stream runs right through the grounds, but the water may be only stopped for purposes of irrigation for twenty-four hours every week; on other days only enough for ablutions may be taken from it. These rules obtain for all the grounds through which the stream runs, though according to the various leases the time you may stop the water is shortened, or the same, but never longer than the twenty-four hours.

The passage walls of the house are Persianly ingenious, a sort of open lattice work of blue glazed tiles, which admits all air whilst excluding most heat!

CHAPTER VIII.

WE now determined to visit the Shah's town palace, so having obtained permission, we were escorted into it by one of the servants. We entered the court which has a long narrow sheet of water in the centre, with trees planted on both sides of it, and saw at its head a large room open in front, but now covered in by a huge sort of bamboo or reed mat. There the king sits in state during great public festivals, such as the Norooz, or New Year's Day. Then the Shah takes up his position on a richly gilded alabaster throne; this is simply a raised moveable platform, on which is spread a carpet, and a step at the further end of the platform is the post of honour, where he sits cross-legged on another carpet, until he varies his posture by sitting on a chair most brilliantly inlaid with precious stones, to be gazed at by his faithful subjects. The lower portion of the walls of the room in which stands the throne is coated with alabaster with raised gilt or painted mouldings; the upper is of the small mirror pattern with plaster ornamentations in Moorish taste. The actual roof is flat, and covered by pieces of looking-glass, two feet square laid side by side, and of European manufacture; the portion nearest the opening towards the court is supported by two pillars said to have come from Persepolis; they are of some white hard marble, with circular decorated flutings. We then entered the actual precincts of the palace by a side gate. The first court is inhabited by servants or officials and is proportionally dirty and ill paved. Passing a sentry, we entered a large garden, with ponds and trees and running streams; on our left was the Harem, in another court which we did not approach. The first room entered was on our right in this first court, the front again open to the garden; in it a throne of enamelled gold set with precious stones; by its side, leaning against it, a tawdry French daub not even hung up. In point of fact, magnificence and disorder, riches and squalor elbowed each other throughout what portion of the palace we saw. Here the chandeliers were of rich, perhaps too rich, Bohemian glass, decorations of room all in the looking-glass style. We entered then another room across the garden. This portion of the palace being built by Futteh Ali Shah, his portrait and name were stuck all about. Here there was a throne of more European conformation and one perfect blaze of jewels, as was also a chair of state in the same room. Then into a room hung all round with bad French chromolithographs in gilt frames, and English engravings out of the *Illustrated London News.* In the corners some newly arrived *French* carpets lay still rolled up.

Passing under this room we entered another garden court, surrounded by buildings still in course of construction, a tank of very clear water filled with fish occupied its upper end. Here, another room was inspected with the usual throne, now of carved wood; the interior walls very artistically painted. The new palace was built in two storys and flanked by two broad towers of the same elevation, with peaked roofs and rooms open in front supported by pillars on each story, thus presenting an utterly novel and singular appearance. The rooms in this palace were being tastefully decorated in foliage and arabesque patterns on looking-glass ground. We we were now conducted, as a finale, into an orange and citron-tree house in this court. A stream flowed right through it, and the channel being paved in light blue tiles gave a most cheerful aspect to the water as it ran rapidly along. After a cup of tea (and bakshish!) we departed. The Shah had gone into the country for a day, or we could not have gained admittance to his palace on the point of etiquette, unless to be presented to him. We did not see the crown jewels on this occasion, as their late guardian had been disgraced, and the office being in abeyance the Shah had sealed them up himself.

After a great deal of squabbling, the diplomatic difficulty about seats at the races has been amicably arranged. The king wrote an autograph letter to Mr. Alison, as the "doyen" of the ministers, to say that he regretted what had past, that it should not occur again; and hoping that the matter might rest here—as it does. The king's aide-de-camp who brought back a favourable answer from the ministers to the Shah, was presented by him with a diamond-hilted dagger, worth some hundreds of pounds, as a token of his majesty's gratification. The other day H. M. tried his 'prentice hand at telegraphing. The sole answer he could get was "repeat, repeat!" until he gave it up. The governor of Shiraz, to whom he sent some message, telegraphed back that one hundred Tomauns, say £40, would be his present for the honour done him (the Governor).

The 16th was a cloudy day. We can see the snow getting lower down the mountain's sides. Owing to the quantity of fruit, &c., diarrhœa is very prevalent here. We had some enormous shrimps caught in the Persian Gulf and *dried in the sun*, exceedingly beastly. On the 19th we, for almost the first time since last May, saw the rain coming down in a continuous pour. Last night we dined with the Sepah Salar, or commander-in-chief, who is also Prime Minister,* having attained that office in

---
* Removed 1866, we believe.

'64 owing to some victories he achieved over rebellious Turcomans east of Mazunderan. Our invitation was worded as follows; be it remembered that he had never set eyes on us!—The heading "O high in place companion of greatness and dignity, kind and bountiful friend."—"With reference to the pleasure we experience by meeting with kind friends, I beg that on the evening preceding Sunday, the 29th of Jemidee, one hour after sunset, you will take the trouble of making your friend happy by meeting with him and partaking of dinner. There is no further trouble. Wednesday, 25th of Jemidee." We rode out through the ark, as the king's palace is called, to the Sepah Salar's house out of town, and dismounting, walked through several garden courtyards to the reception-room, where we found our host seated on a sofa at the top of the room, and the various diplomatic or official magnates in order around him. Kaleouns were brought in and carried out twice before dinner was announced, each servant presenting the pipe to his own master.

Frequently there are great contests about precedence outside as to the order they are to march in. We observed that all the Persians present had adopted the civilised custom of wearing shoes; excepting a major and lieutenant-colonel who had to stand in the doorway, and behind the Sepah Salar at dinner, who were in their stockings! The dinner was a perfect medley of European and Persian dishes, and the wines tolerable. We received what we were told was sherry at first, but upon swallowing the wineglassful, discovered it to be brandy neat. Bordeaux was also handed round, and then the half-emptied glass re-filled with Malaga. We dined with our hats on. Ours was a wide-awake, not a graceful full-dress portion of costume! The adjutant-general and confidential adviser of the Sepah Salar is an Armenian Christian. At the conclusion, a plate containing clay in which jessamine and geranium blossoms were fixed was placed before each guest, standing thus in lieu of the old English rose water, as we were supposed to take the flowers away to smell at! We now passed through courts crowded with servants jostling each other and ourselves to two smaller rooms, open in front, with a colonnade extending into a large garden, where we witnessed a display of fireworks and the sending up of two fire balloons. The grand finale consisted of a man running about and twisting round, covered all over with squibs and crackers of every description, a sort of Persian fire king. On returning, a soldier of the regular army had to accompany our large cavalcade in order to procure us admittance into the ark. This was only obtained on pronouncing the password for the night; and during our progress through the palace we were continually challenged by sentinels.

20th. We have now got a Persian servant called Awa Baba, which name, slightly modified, recalls unpleasant recollections of the forty thieves! His son also accompanies us. Awa at present talks about twenty words of English (which is our only means of communication with him) indistinctly; however we found him to improve as we got on. By very special permission we were allowed to see the crown jewels to-day. We started at noon, and waded through a sea of mud, only partially alleviated by the covered way in the bazaar, slipping in our goloshes at every step. Of five Europeans we were the only one who possessed the luxury of an umbrella, and as it rained hard it came in usefully. We went through the first court of the palace, and were ushered up a very narrow and extremely steep staircase, into a small room, where we found the king's aide-de-camp awaiting us. The designs on the walls here were very well drawn, and the decoration more tasteful than of ordinary. The chairs were of pure chased gold, as also was a sort of huge dumbwaiter that stood in one corner. Of the chairs the Shah possesses forty, of the dumbwaiters nine! (Of course underneath the gold there are wooden supports, unseen.)

After some tea, the jewels were brought in for our inspection in detail. It would be endless and impossible to attempt to describe a tithe of them or even the impression they produced on our eyes. Their value, putting a moderate estimate on them, could not, in our own judgment and that of the four gentlemen who saw them with us, by any possibility be under forty or fifty millions of money! that is if they were to be sold singly. Of course, in the aggregate no fortune would suffice to pay for them, and therefore their value would be depreciated. We must attempt to describe a few in the order they were shown to us. An evidently French jewel case was brought in first and placed on a table, round which we eagerly gathered awaiting its opening. In this there were some forty gold rings, each with a single diamond, of which the largest (diamond, not ring) was some one and a half inch round, and the smallest a quarter of an inch. One with a large yellow diamond. Two diamonds were placed as pendants at the end of a necklace of pearls, and most gracefully, looking like two drops of dew. Two pearl necklaces, each pearl perfectly round and white and about the size of a large pea. In two little drawers two or three more necklaces, the pearls this time much larger; and in the bottom drawer another, of the largest pearls we had yet seen, arranged— an oblong one and a perfectly round one alternately, each, without the smallest exaggeration, being the size of a sour cherry.

This casket always follows the Shah wherever he goes; next came a collection of a dozen belts, each surpassing the other in costliness and taste. One of these had the fastening buckle, about eight inches long and three broad, studded with perfect rubies, each about half an inch round, set in gold. Another diamonds only; a third, the whole band set in emeralds and diamonds and so on. We then were shown four sabres; all had the flat side of the scabbard richly enamelled on gold; one was one blaze of diamonds on the hilt and scabbard; another was studded with pearls like large peas; a third was set with diamonds and other stones to represent flowers. Two other necklaces we were shown were about two and a half feet long each, and formed of large emeralds, each about an inch and a quarter long, alternating with bunches of pearls. An aigrette presented by some emperor of Austria was exquisitely worked as a bouquet of flowers, in diamonds, with one large amethyst set *a jour*. The last tray of jewels was the " bonne bouche." On this we saw a belt of pliant gold work, the buckle consisting of the celebrated "Deriehnoor," or "sea of light;" a diamond perfectly flat except at the edges, and almost two inches long by one and a quarter in breadth (?); it was set round with other smaller diamonds; with this there were some bracelets of uncut rubies and emeralds, quite as large as pigeons' eggs for the most part. The largest turquoise we saw was perfectly flat and about one inch by a half. Two beautiful amethysts in silver settings. We saw one of the royal crowns; the other is kept in the inner treasury in the Harem, which is only opened once a year; on the top of this is the famous ruby that belonged at one time to Aurungzebe, a good deal larger than a pigeon's egg and uncut. The aigrette in front, something in the style of the Prince of Wales' Feathers, is of diamonds (the largest is set as a pendant, alone); between this and the red velvet cap of the crown there is a plume of spun glass such as may be bought for the sum of one penny at the Polytechnic. A black velvet robe with diamond buttons and frogs looked lugubrious but priceless; others, with the collar and sleeves completely covered with large pearls, were amongst some of the various things we saw. We returned delighted.

After very prolonged negociations, the telegraphic convention between England and Persia is at last concluded. The existing English staff to have entire control over one wire for five years, when, should the Persians have acquired the art of telegraphy, the whole to revert to them—always reserving the right of transmitting any messages through it. At present the value of a message from London to Kurrachee (the first Indian station), is exactly £5. On the morning of our departure Mr. Alison received a letter from an anonymous Persian lady, stating that she wished to marry a Frank; she had no objection to change her religion, and was young and handsome, but somewhat expensive in her tastes. Mr. Alison told us it was not the first application of the kind he had received. As we were just departing, here was a chance for one of us gone!

23rd. For the last three days we were detained in Teheran by the rainy weather; we hardly went out of the house, excepting to Major Smith's, next door—he is the superintendent of telegraphs in Persia, a very agreeable and well-informed person —or to take a tour in the garden. It is the drawback (amongst many others) of a Persian town that when the bazaars and any other sights there may be to see are exhausted, you cannot go out for a walk with any pleasure; for just outside the walls there is a bleak sandy desert, and even to reach this you have to walk through endless uncomfortable and narrow streets, unless you have a horse or a carriage, and these latter are so few in number that they hardly come into consideration. After bidding farewell to our hospitable entertainer and the other members of the mission, we started at 12.30, as this was to be a short stage. Now we are travelling in great luxury, having bought wooden bedsteads, and we have also positively two sheets, besides an embryo " batterie de cuisine." The mountains that looked black and bare when we entered Teheran, seventeen days ago, now form a magnificent snow-capped range. We passed the gilded shrine of old Abdulazeen on our left, and steered (!) due south; road bad from mud. We passed the deserted shrine of one Ibrahim, and some of the immense irregularly circular tumuli which seem peculiar to the plain of Teheran. None have been opened within the memory of man we are told, as permission is never given to what is here considered an act of desecration. We saw also many small ruined villages; if we may form a theory as to the cause of their desolation, we should say that the vicinity of the seat of power and government rendered extortion too easy here!

Having sent on our baggage, and taken only Awa Baba with us, we managed to lose our way, as he had not the smallest notion in which direction our destination lay, although the village was only twelve miles out of Teheran, where he lived, and he had twice done this journey before! However, after wandering over some ploughed fields we were shown our village, at least the one where we had intended to stop; but we found our baggage had proceeded another farsakh (or four miles) to Housseinabad. The road between these two points was so covered with salt, brought to the surface probably by the heavy rain, that we seemed to be traversing ground after a most heavy hoar frost.

We found our baggage domiciled in a large caravanserai, and our beds set up in two very small rooms. Next to ours, in another room, partitioned off by loose bricks in the doorway, was a quantity of cocks and hens. We distinctly overheard one of them snoring during the course of the night, and at 4 A.M. the male portion of the community set up a simultaneous and long-continued crow. Starting in the morning, we rode up a hill and down again on through the Malek el Most or "valley of the angel of death," a succession of very barren ravines and small plains; the road very good. A caravanserai is in course of construction at the further end of the ravines, presumably to take the sting from the angel aforesaid, but the name is an exaggeration. Before entering the vale we passed an ice-house just like a gigantic beehive, built of the customary mud, in a cone in successive circular steps; also a fresh-water crab; and, whilst in the valley, Demavend at sunset glowed some time after all else was shrouded in darkness. Night fell just as we were getting out of the valley, which certainly is then very lonely, and after riding eleven hours altogether we reached Houz-i-Sultaun, an immense caravanserai, or manzil, as any place of customary halt is called, where we stopped the night. Riding on over the outskirts of the great salt desert, Deria Caveer, we stayed at the posthouse of Poole Dullak, or the "barber's bridge," a barber of Teheran having repaired the bridge here at his own expense. The small stream that flows beneath it is brackish and bitter to the taste, like the salt that lies about and of course impregnates the water. Nevertheless, fish of the dace kind are found in it. We passed a low range of hills before arriving. Our room here is twelve feet square and has three doors and as many windows to it; none of the latter shut, and the former let in all winds that blow.

A Persian officer whom we met here on his way to Teheran was most urbane, and gave us some cups of tea on our arrival, sending us a bottle of Hamadan wine later. We returned the compliment by sending him some brandy, of which he took a very little, and with rare courtesy said he would not deprive us of it, as he was going where there was plenty of it to be got, whereas we were not.

We rode on in the morning, a sharp wind blowing, across black undulating gravel hills, to Koom. We saw the great gilt dome of the sepulchre of Fatima "the immaculate" long before we arrived. This mosque contains also the sepulchre of Futteh Ali Shah, the "father of his people," at any rate of five hundred of them, thus rivalling Mr. Carlyle's favourite Augustus the Strong of Poland! We walked into the bazaar, where we observed nothing particular excepting that more than half the people we met proclaimed themselves Mullahs (priests) or Saids (descendants of the prophet), by the colour of their turbans. Koom ranks as one of the three holy cities of Persia, having deserved the appellation of the "Abode of the pious." We regret that the Persian of this is so badly written in our diary as to preclude deciphering. Those who have read Mr. Morier's amusing "Hadji Baba" will recollect that it is here the self-styled

Hadji fled from Teheran to take "Bust," or sanctuary! We visited the exterior of the mosque, which is of the usual shape; the tiles on the dome are not well joined together, but highly gilt. No fire was to be lit in our room on account of the smoke, which all obstinately persisted in mistaking the way out by the chimney; but we had to remain here all next day, as it poured drearily. Whilst in Teheran we applied for an order to see the tombs here, several Europeans having told us that they had seen that of Futteh Ali; but we were told that no order could be given, as it would only cause a collision between civil and ecclesiastical authorities. Perhaps, however, we might get permission on the spot, by making interest with the guardian. This however we were unable to do, and we strongly doubt the desecration of the mosque, by the profane tread of a Christian foot, ever to have been allowed!

We got off on the 28th, riding first right through the town, which is rather dilapidated, even to three little mosques with extinguisher tops. On one of these were perched at least seven generations of storks' nests. There are great quantities of these birds about. We arrived at Pasangoor by a flat road, it having taken us six hours to do sixteen miles, owing to the mud. Next morning we rode up an inclined plane, with Demavend behind us all the while, and passed one oasis in the surrounding barrenness, where one man was ploughing. Here there were the remains of a gigantic castle, whose mud walls were yet standing some thirty feet high. The oasis in front enclosed by earthen walls. The watch-tower at the gate still preserved slight traces of its former shape—tobacco growing here. We then rode downwards to Sein Sein, our halting-place. Next morning we left our baggage to come on after us, and rode on to Cashan, having a picturesque jagged range of low mountains on our right, and behind these a snowy range; road good. On arrival we immediately rushed into the bazaar, which we found very long and with little in it. The copper ware is famous here, cheap and well executed. The neighbourhood of this large village is well cultivated, and there are many smaller villages near the mountains. They are built in this situation owing to the old fear of the Turcomans, who used to make raids across the salt desert: the mountains presented a refuge for the inhabitants on these occasions. Some of the streets are quite as well paved as any in the capital—no very high meed of praise! Some six miles west of this place, on the slope of the hills, and surrounded by trees, stands Theem, one of the many royal palaces scattered over Persia.

On the 1st of December we started, buying some things on our route through the bazaar, and rode gradually up a stony plain, following a little stream up into the mountains, where it became a torrent, which we crossed and recrossed several times, getting higher and higher until snow began to lie under our horses' feet, and it became bitterly cold. We came upon a huge dam of masonry work, some twenty-five feet broad and fifty to sixty high, across the ravine we were threading, built up to bar the water of the torrent from devastating its banks below during the spring. Thus only a small portion of water was allowed to descend at a time, the rest being kept in by the dam. At this time there was little there, but we could distinctly see the water-mark on the rocks, where the pent-up stream occasionally forms a formidable and deep lake. At sunset, the rosy rays struggling for a time on the snow with the brilliant beams of a full moon were very pretty, until the latter gained the upper hand, and crowned the snowy tops with a silvery light. Up and up, till we came to a valley richly cultivated in terraces, and then rode through stone walls like those in Daghestan, enclosing fruit trees of every description; through a rich orchard country, past a small isolated mosque, finding our lonely path by the light of the moon, as we had dismounted to keep our blood in circulation. At length past a large cemetery on the side of a hill, we gladly entered Kohrood, and found the first house to be the post, where we ensconce ourselves in a lower room, making as large a fire as possible: fortunately wood is not scarce. This village has all the characteristics of a Caucasian one, the houses, solidly built of mud and stones, stand one above the other on the slope of the hill.

Starting again next morning, we rode up a gradual incline through the mountains, all snow, until our path appeared barred by a diagonal mountain across the ravine. On approaching, we saw a steep path which we went up and then "topped" the pass, for after this we rode down a valley which sometimes widened, sometimes narrowed. Here the difference between a north and south aspect was very distinctly visible, all the snow having melted off the southerly mountains whilst it remained on their northern slopes. We went a short distance up hill again, and then came on to a table-land, presenting on a small scale all the features of that larger table-land Persia—a small gravelly desert, then intersecting ravines and higher hills on each side. At 4 we reached a village, Zoog, where there is no post station, so proceeded onwards by a by-path to Beedush, of which the valley is cultivated. We find here a diatribe against P**l's waterproof boots. Certainly ours were heavy, clumsy, and badly fitting, though made to order; unbearably hot in sunshine, and deadly cold on a cold day. However, no doubt we were unfortunate.

On the 3rd we rode for four hours down a shelving plain, nothing but camelthorn and some other small plant growing on the wild waste around. We then espied five horsemen galloping towards us, who on approaching turned out to be Mr. Walton, the then superintendent of telegraphs at Ispahan, and Doctor Baker, the medical travelling adviser to the telegraphic staff, with three servants, each carrying an English fowling-piece. They insisted on making us mount two of their horses, after which we continued our course to Moorchacoor, but on the plain off the road in hopes of putting up a hare; with the assistance of two greyhounds and a retriever we accomplished this, and had a short run, after which we entered the village in triumph. Here we feasted on some ducks Mr. Walton had shot in the morning.

4th. There is a considerable improvement in the temperature here: it is almost mild, and poor Mr. Walton is accordingly seized with recurring fever, preventing his riding to the next station with us.

He had kindly come some thirty miles out of Ispahan to meet us. We started with the Doctor, and rode to a ruined caravanserai, deserted on account of robbers, where we breakfasted. Across a plain, where cultivation had evidently been attempted some years before, as the furrows testified, we started a fox, which after giving us a run, got away through a very dilapidated building. Still on the plain, we got a run at full speed for at least five miles over excellent ground, after some antelopes. They however easily outran our horses, as it is quite impossible to run them down in the open. They made for some small hills on which wild sheep are said to exist. We then rode twenty miles to Gezd, where an English engineer corporal on the telegraph staff came in to visit us; he was engaged in surveying the line and happened to be halting in the same caravanserai as ourselves. Watercourses and ruined manzils abound by the roadside. The south wind was cold here. Next morning our companions of yesterday came up, and we rode on towards Ispahan. The high pigeon-houses, like elevated Martello towers with a smaller one erected on the flat roof, are the principal objects that strike the eye besides ruins. We soon beheld the outskirts of the ancient capital of Persia, and some very tall slender pillars, in reality minarets. We got into a lane between mud walls along a canal or watercourse, here and there riding through a small bit of bazaar; this lasted for an hour's walk; then through an archway supporting rooms above, which had once been gaily decorated in coloured tiles now mostly fallen off. We entered the famous Char Bagh or "four gardens," probably so called because it consists of *one* magnificent alley of chinar trees. There are, however, four gardens on the other side of the wall on each side. We rode along this for more than a mile. The alley is composed of a narrow, ill-paved stone road in the centre, then plots of ground sown with grass, and scantily planted, about twenty yards across; then the superb oriental planes and another paved road on each side, bounded by a wall. There are occasional reservoirs and a canal flowing across almost flush with the pavement. At the alley's end we came to a fine massive brick bridge, whose surface certainly afforded the best bit of road we had seen in Persia; perfectly level, consisting of stones with gravel laid upon them. The bridge is about twenty yards broad; on each side a covered way allows foot passengers to walk under it; horseshoe openings at every two yards afford light to them. The river itself had sunk into a very small channel when we crossed it, and on the banks the trades of dyeing and bleaching were being actively prosecuted.

After crossing we were in Joolfa, a colony of Armenian Christians, whose ancestors were transported to this place from the village of the same name on the borders of the Araxes. Here we are installed in a house rented by the Indian government for the use of one of the telegraph officials who is now in Teheran, luckily for us. There are many churches here, all of mud bricks, with a semicircular dome ending in a point upon which a small iron cross is fixed.

After resting one night, we rode out in the morning over the long bridge. On each side of the Char Bagh there are at intervals houses, originally inhabited by officials of the court, in the time of Ispahan's greatest splendour. The Medressa, or college, is situated about halfway down the avenue. To-day we turned out of this, just below the college, and rode through gardens that must be perfectly lovely in the spring and summer, though of course in December there was no foliage visible; indeed, in the daytime, we see frost lying on the ground in shady spots, whilst in the sun it is quite warm. Each of these gardens was attached to some palace, of which more anon. We rode into a large square, where we dismounted, and walked on to see the bazaar. The first short arcade was devoted to the workers in copper, and out of this we emerged into an immense oblong space, the Maidan, that we should guess at about six hundred yards by two hundred. It has, however, been measured. One side is taken up by low buildings, soldiers' quarters. At the upper extremity rises the great mosque, an imposing structure covered with the light blue glazed tiles. The life and bustle at the sides of this space were greater and more varied than anywhere else in Persia that we had visited, and all sorts of trumpery were exposed for sale under small tents. We then turned into the great bazaar. Mr. Agenor, the British agent, an Armenian gentleman educated in Bombay and speaking English fluently, had procured us a guide from the governor, without whose assistance we should infallibly have lost our way. We marched about for some hours, purchasing amongst other things a tiger-skin for five shillings. The jewellers exhibit considerable taste. The old armour of Ispahan is famous, but much is now made in imitation of it. The Persian painting on wood is chiefly carried on in this town. The drawing of figures is always out of all perspective and proportion, but flowers and fruit are rendered remarkably well. The calamdauns, or inkstands, show the greatest variety in this respect; they are oblong narrow boxes, with a slide drawer, in which is fixed a small inkstand, and into which the reed pens, knife, &c., are placed.

On the 7th we walked out with "Hakim" Baker to visit the cathedral in this part of Joolfa. We entered a court in front of the church, where stands the belfry, a structure on four pillars in two storys, like those at Etchmiadzeen. Under this an Englishman lies buried, a Mr. Rich, who died at Shiraz, whilst visiting Persepolis, being at the time "Resident" at Bagdad. A priest monk, dressed in a black apron as at Etchmiadzeen, showed us into the cathedral. We were greatly astonished at finding so much splendour at such a distance from any other Christian community. The whole of the walls are covered with oil paintings, representing, some the life of our Saviour, some scenes from the Old Testament, and others martyrdoms. The largest of all is a Day of Judgment of somewhat grotesque character. The style of art is not high, as they were probably painted by local Armenian artists 310 years ago, but some of the pictures are evidently intended to imitate the North Italian styles at their best periods. The floor is carpeted, and the priest took off his slippers before entering; most exquisite tilework extends for the height of five feet along the wall, then there is a row of small paintings, about two-and-a-half feet high and, above, the same height of gold ground, painted with arabesque flowers and angels very tolerably executed. The circular dome is coloured blue and white, the high altar is painted with miniatures of saints and cherubims; above it is a large picture of our Saviour, one of the best in the church; only two missals on the altar, the treasury being here naturally poor. The church is not large, but no doubt sufficient for its congregation, more especially as there are ten others in Joolfa. The Doctor knew the monk—who seemed a lively fellow—well, and he conducted us to see a new refectory, building on one side of the monastery. There are rooms with open arched passages on each side for the summer air to pass through, and on the roof there are two rooms, open on every side, to serve as residences in the hot weather; we got on to the top of one of these, by means of a ladder, and had a tolerable view of Joolfa, though Ispahan could not be distinguished owing to the immense quantity of trees in it, and the excessive flatness of the ground. We paid the (arch?) bishop, who is appointed by the Catholicos, a visit, and found him sitting on a kind of sofa in a small, well carpeted room. A most venerable and affable somewhat portly old man, with a magnificent beard, who welcomed us to Joolfa. The conversation, however, between him and ourselves languished considerably, as he only talked Armenian. One of the monks translated his remarks into Persian for the Doctor, who then made English of it, and *vice versa.* The worthy father gave us kaleouns and cigarettes, and the entertainment wound up with fruit, sweetmeats, and English ale!

We were besieged in our rooms this morning by curiosity dealers, all unmistakably of the Hebrew persuasion. There really is considerable difficulty in selecting from the quantity of pretty things they bring. There is now a temporary governor of Ispahan, as the king's eldest son (but not heir apparent) is in Teheran. About a week ago a baker in the bazaar insulted one of the telegraph clerks, and then took " Bust " in the house of the chief Mullah; another man, however, who had insulted Doctor Baker, having been given up by the Mullah himself, the baker got frightened, and leaving while the police were not on the look out, positively sought sanctuary in Mr. Walton's stables here! The stables are considered inviolable in Persia. However the "Feringhee" do not admit this, and the servants told the baker so; thus he escaped again, Mr. Walton being too ill in bed to go out and chastise him. The "Ferashes" are again after him, and he will, no doubt, be caught and soundly bastinadoed in the bazaar, *pour encourager les autres.* We are now seven Englishmen who sit down to dinner together, a greater number than Joolfa has ever, perhaps, before contained within its walls. Lieutenant St. John, the superintendent of telegraphs at Shiraz, has arrived here on his way to Teheran, to take temporary charge of the whole line; whilst Colonel Goldsmith and Major Smith have reached this place *from* Teheran. These two gentlemen are bound on a journey to Yezd (the great fire-worshippers' city, to the east of this) and Kerman (the carpet emporium, to its south), there separating to discover a practicable route for a new overland telegraph to India. We might have joined them, but, alas! *non omnia possumus omnes,* we should not see Persepolis, if we went that way, and so preferred our intended route. The expedition was completely successful, and an additional line of telegraph is most probably now in course of construction.

We had *roast* porcupine for dinner one day, the idea is unpleasant, but the flesh is like that of very tasteless pork. Hulver, a sweetmeat, looking like very thick, dirty, yellow putty, consisting principally of sugar, honey, and treacle, is not bad, and "gez" is delicious, made of what is called manna, with almonds and cream, and eaten when hard in round bits.

CHAPTER VIII.

On the 10th we paid a visit to the telegraph office which is exactly opposite the bridge over the Sengarood, and a commodious well adapted building. Having gazed with astonishment at the working of the apparatus we walked across the bridge, through the Char Bagh to the first palace, about half way down. This was in a considerable state of *disrepair*, but a portrait of " the beautiful Strachey," as one of the Englishmen attached to Sir J. Malcolm's mission is still called in Persia, is well preserved on the wall facing the side entrance; and portraits of Futteh Ali Shah at diverse pursuits, such as hunting, feasting, standing up, sitting in state, and sitting in ordinary, are plentiful. We previously entered the Medressa, or college—a square surrounded by buildings once appertaining to the students studying there, but now untenanted excepting by stray cats with bushy tails. On the right rises an enormous circular roofed building, superbly decorated in coloured tile work. Having once been a mosque one may only enter it on taking off one's shoes. We proceeded on to the Chehel Sittoon palace, or that of the forty pillars. It has a portico supported on twenty pillars in front of it; the other twenty are to be imagined reflected in the water of the tank before it. The only objection to this is that there is *no* water in the tank. However, no doubt there was, in the palmy days of Ispahan. In this instance the appellation of *forty* is thus far correct, but that number, as is well known, is used to denote an indefinite number in the East!

The Shah allows 50,000 tomauns yearly (about £20,000 in round numbers) towards keeping up the royal buildings in this town, and not one penny of it finds its way to them, being all absorbed by the officials connected therewith. Thus these noble structures are gradually decaying. This one has stood some 250 years, with hardly any attention paid to it. Each of the pillars that support the portico, is coated with the usual small mirrors, and the roof is gaily painted—it seems to be at least a hundred feet from the ground. The whole has still a marvellous effect, and when new must have been positively dazzling. The bases of the pillars are of some coarse marble like fine granite sculptured roughly into the forms of four lions looking each way, and painted over. The walls of the palace slant inwards, forming a room opening out to the portico, and raised on two steps. This is decorated with frescoes and mirrors. Then, entering by one of the two low doors at the further end of the room, we stand in the great hall, whose walls are entirely covered with various large paintings, representing scenes in the reign of Shah Abbas, who is engaged in the same sort of pursuits as Futteh Ali Shah in the other palace. The drawing is of the most grotesque nature. One of the pictures has been partly painted over with a portrait of the present Shah in a rudimentary style of art. We went up to the roof, and saw the solid construction of the palace; some of the rafters were whole chinar trees quite seven feet round and unhewn. From thence we proceeded to the actual palace, where the king used to live when this was a royal city. Here we saw a room entirely paved and pannelled with marble, with an enormous sash window of coloured glass admitting very little light, a bath in the middle and in the centre of this a marble throne, forming a cool retiring-place in the heats of summer; the roof was supported by columns, whose pedestals of marble were carved in four female draped forms, each holding a hideous tragic mask in the left hand. Fountains used once to play out of their mouths. Behind the bath we entered a room with beautiful windows—a sort of filigree of plaster of Paris, with designs and Persian characters executed in small pieces of coloured glass. Thence into a large court, on one side of which we entered a large room, open in front, whose walls were decorated by scenes out of Persian history. Hence up a very high square tower, built over an archway leading into the Maidan. From its summit we had an excellent view of the town and surrounding country. Ispahan appeared to extend for at least two miles around us, the only very conspicuous building was the grand mosque, which was undergoing repairs, (and had been for the last thirty-five years!) and the citadel right in front of us, not greatly elevated above the town, mud walls as usual; below us lay the great square, with the execution pole in the centre. The criminal condemned to death used to be hauled up to the top of this by means of ropes, and then let fall suddenly on the hard pavement,—it appeared to be about 80 feet high. When an individual is bastinadoed in Persia the punishment is called "giving him the sticks," and the number of strokes is not counted, but the number of sticks broken on the *beatee's* feet by the violence. Thus, 50 sticks being a mild punishment, the number of strokes may amount to some 700 in that case. When the sticks used are of pomegranate wood 500 of them are sometimes broken over the criminal, but when they are of palm-tree the punishment is so much severer that the number of sticks is considerably reduced. The panorama of mountains girding the whole plain, and encircling it as it were with a barrier only passable at certain points, is very beautiful. One mountain, called by Franks "Hadji

Baba's," has a regular top-knot on its summit, looking like the cupola of a mosque. Descending, we strolled through the Maidan; five pieces of ordnance stood here in front of a guardhouse on the right. One of these was presented to Persia by Sir J. Malcolm, and has the East India Company's mark upon it; the others were either taken from the Turks or cast at Tabreez. We walked back through a ruined portion of the town, emerging on the Char Bagh through a deserted bazaar leading at right angles into it. Here, some fifty years ago, an insurrection, headed by the Imaum Juma (the chief spiritual authority), was quelled, as the governor of the town got some Armenian artillerymen to plant cannon at the entrance of this straight bazaar, and fired down it on the dense mass, killing all who were there. Ever since this is "the deserted bazaar." N.B. The object of the insurrection, to get the governor turned out, was accomplished! We dined with the British agent in the evening; the (Arch?) bishop was there and afterwards played at the English game of "horse-racing." Some Ispahan wine tasted as sweet as Malaga, but was strongly brandied.

On the 12th, we all rode out to see the "Shaking Minarets," probably distant relations of the "Minarets" that "waved o'er the plains of Stamboul," of Bon Gaultier. We crossed the river by a bridge about a mile higher up than the long one, and wound along mud walls and a canal sunk some 15 feet deep, into a small village, where stands the mosque over which these phenomena are built. We entered a court, where are a few tombs, and on one side, the mosque. On each side of a recess, some 15 feet deep, rise the minarets on solid brick foundations; they have lately been put into repair. There is a stone tomb about 7 feet high in the recess, and various offerings, like old clothes and spinning shuttles, hang above it. From the ground to the top of the minarets the elevation may be about 130 feet, but the minarets proper only rise some 30 feet above the main building, on each side facing the court. They are, perhaps, ten feet round and the ascent is by a very steep spiral staircase, then four windows. A man went up and putting one foot on a window-sill as a fulcrum, then clasping one of the brickwork window-frames, began to rock himself to and fro. They (the minarets) really sway about in a wonderful manner, so that a tremulous motion is observable even at the base of the whole building down in the court. We went up one of them and felt exceedingly uncomfortable while rocking ourselves about. In front of us rose the "Artesh Goor," or fire-mountain, a rocky isolated conical hill, of no great elevation, with a ruined building on the top, said to have been a great fire-worshipping temple in days gone by. We are informed that Ispahan lies some 3500 feet above sea level, and Shiraz 1000 feet higher. We are endeavouring to get our old muleteers to take us to Shiraz, as they themselves offered some time ago, giving them a little more than the merchants would; still we had great difficulty in getting them to come, till Mr. Agenor got the deputy governor to send a policeman after them and make them go, *nolens volens*, for a fair remuneration of course, part of which, no doubt, the "Ferash" pocketed. Thus affairs are carried on in this favoured land!

Yesterday a foot messenger was despatched to Teheran with letters. He is expected to do the two hundred and eighty miles in, at most, seven days. We once more started on our travels on the 14th, bidding farewell to the large company assembled and especially to Colonel Goldsmith, a man uniting rare kindliness of manner to benevolence of heart. Having sent on our baggage, as we had to do thirty-six miles, we rode out of Joolfa, finding the outskirts in ruins, and walked steadily up a sloping hill, thus obtaining a perfect view of the town, which lay stretched out before us as far as we could see east and west, a confused mass of mud buildings relieved by tall leafless trees and an occasional lacquered tiled mosque. The Char Bagh, we found, extended for another mile on the right bank of the Sengarood, and the " Hasht Behesht," or eight paradises, the gardens on either side of the wall of the Char Bagh, also extend to this side. On our right rose some rocky hills; a little way up one of these there was a picturesque summer-house with a rock parapet. We soon came to an almost perpendicular path, steps being occasionally hewn out of the rough shiny slate-coloured rock. This lasted for about sixty yards, and so precipitous was the ascent, that our saddle quietly slipped off our horse with ourselves upon it and deposited us on the ground! The rocks around appeared of primitive formation, and well battered and water-worn. On the barren plain before us, we saw large herds of antelopes, and far to the east very many towers, probably for pigeons. Just out of Ispahan we passed an immense graveyard on the slope of a hill, the stones dark and massive. As it was getting dusk we reached Mayar, and taking the wrong side of the wall, we wandered along it to find an entrance through ruins, one being that of a post-house, but we could not stay *there*, so we rode on to a khan of most magnificent appearance; two lofty galleries with rooms leading to the entrance of the khan proper—an immense quadrangle, with a broken reservoir in the centre. This being also deserted, excepting by two or three mule drivers, we, after enquiries retraced our steps, and at last found our Chappar Khanee at the other side of the wall.

Next morning, on continuing our ride along the level Valley, we saw that a steep rock rose just above the village. A house in front of us, that appeared quite close at hand at our start, turned out fully twelve miles distant, so clear was the air hereabouts. After passing this we left on our left-hand a village principally tenanted by pigeons, at least to judge by the quantity of towers therein, and rode on through a narrow valley to Komishah, which we reached at four P.M., immediately rushing out to wander through the small bazaar, where nought but heavy white slippers and sweetmeats of a dirty description, attracted our notice. A mile outside we passed a mosque, with magnificent brickwork outbuildings and a large caravanserai attached to it. Quantities of little pointed stones at the head of each grave here marked the situation of an extensive cemetery; many almond trees and liquorice shrubs grew about.

Next morning we rode through luxuriant rice plantations and richly cultivated fields for some sixteen miles. Many streams of drinkable water intersected the soil and produced this unwonted fertility, little villages dotted the valley in all directions. After this, however, we got on a wild and barren flat plain, over which we rode for twenty-two miles to the caravanserai of Ameenabad. Here we only found two individuals crouching round a brushwood fire in one of the rooms. The interior court was octagonal; we selected the cleanest room on the west side, this was full of dung, which we had to clear out before installing ourselves.

Early on the 17th we started again to ride over some barren plains at the end of which we perceived what appeared to be a rise in the ground. On approaching, however, we found a broad ravine between it and ourselves, which we had to cross; then ascending to a dreary higher plain, very cold, until we reached the post-house at Shoolgestaun; we had thus come 120 miles in four days, very fast caravan journeying.

Next day we rode for five and a half hours over the same dead level and halted at Abada. We found the gates shut in our faces, but being foreigners were admitted after much knocking and precautionary measures. A curious state of things reigned here. The English engineer attached to the intermediate telegraph station at this small village told us that the governor of Shiraz had lately appointed a new governor of Abada, whilst the old one was still in office, he having rendered himself in some way obnoxious. Strange to say, the inhabitants took the part of the old governor and determined to resist the new man, so that the gates were closed and the inhabitants on the alert day and night. The telegraph station only afforded one room fourteen feet by six in which the superintendent slept; so we had to proceed to a caravanserai just outside the gates. Now, the " Kat Koder " of this village may have been a very estimable gentleman, and no doubt was, as the inhabitants backed him up; but this caravanserai was the worst we had yet seen; a decrepit mud building with a dead wall on one side, and stables on the others; one of the stables was cleaned out for us, and as there was no fire-place, we lighted a fire in the centre of the room. This smoked so abominably that we had to give even that up, and there we were in a little dirty room with a huge opening as a door, no fire, and freezing hard outside. We observed some little boys gambling for halfpence with "nux" at the door of a mosque. The wooden spoons of Abada are celebrated for the delicacy of their carving.

Numerous villages, we observed next morning, studded the plain. About twelve miles out we came upon some two hundred men (most of them armed with matchlocks, or sticks with iron knobs), in detached groups surrounding a walled village; we were told that these were Abadians, who had come out thus far to arrest the new obnoxious governor, who was ensconced therein, and held an involuntary prisoner. The matter was referred to the telegraph, as the new man swore that the Shah gave him the appointment in consideration of a douceur of 12,000 Tomauns (just £5000). No doubt the sum was exaggerated, but there might be truth at the bottom of the statement. We, early, reached Soormuck, and for some time searched in vain for a hole to lay our heads in, as all the caravanserais were crammed. At last we got a small room in the post-house, where we warmed ourselves as best we could with burning charcoal. Just outside we passed a most massive mud-brick building (the corners so jagged by the hand of time that we doubted whether it was sexagonal or square), apparently an old Persian fort. On the 20th we rode up a gradual incline, the valley getting narrower. It snowed during the night, and as we progressed upwards, we came upon a patch or two of snow, then it began to lie an inch thick, and around Khana Khora, our post-house, it lay at least two inches in depth. A bitter north wind blowing all the time. Next morning we soon got into a foot's depth of snow, then into deeper drifts; we followed the tracks of an immense caravan and overtook it, passing with some difficulty. Then only two horsemen had gone on before us, so we followed their tracks, and at last, after a deal of floundering about, we reached Dehbeed. The road rose most of the way.

At this place the caravan road from Yezd to Shiraz joins ours, so that the traffic is increased, and we found next morning that the snow had been tolerably trodden down on the path.

We followed a slightly ascending, but tolerably flat path for five hours, until we reached a lonely caravanserai, where our muleteers had wished us to stop. We thought, however, that this was too close to our starting point, and determined to push on, so we ascended a steep mountain, coming at its summit to a flat of small extent, and then up another steep. The sun was just setting, and the path became so slippery that our horse fell down with us at intervals. At last we reached a level winding road which we followed for some hours (hills on each side of us), where we were far from any human habitation. We were walking by ourselves to keep the blood in circulation, and rather in front of W. and Awa Baba, when we suddenly heard the voices as of many men and women laughing, and the barking of dogs, breaking in upon the stilly night. The owners could not have been within miles of us, but the snow acted as a conductor of sound. We had been told that Moorgaub was only twelve miles from the lonely caravanserai, so after marching for six hours longer, we began to think that it ought to be in sight, but no signs; the brushwood on the hills gradually increased from little stumps to the size of tolerable trees looking like whitethorn.

At length, at nine P.M., we reached some houses, and here we learned, to our disgust, that we had passed Moorgaub six miles back, although we had not observed any habitation before. We got off our horses and crouched for a short time before a fire kindled by some muleteers, reflecting whether it were better to stay here or go back. At last, rather reluctantly, we went back, obtaining a guide to show us the way. At eleven P.M. we reached the post-house, off the high road, and there found no traces of our baggage. We lighted a fire and waited, but the night passed without anything to eat being obtainable, and a Persian coat was our sole bed. In the morning, till 3 P.M., we amused ourselves by squatting in front of the fire; then our baggage arrived. Our servant and the muleteers had slept out on the mountains all night, as they said that the mules were unable to proceed.

Early in the morning of Christmas Eve we heard some shepherds, who "were watching their flocks by night," playing on their rough curved cowhorns very melodiously, much more so than any Persian musicians we had heard before, their melodies being generally very unmelodious; these shepherds, however, performed tunes rather like the " Ranz des Vaches."

We left at 9 with scant regret, and rode for an hour before coming on the broad path again. We soon reached the village we had already visited two nights before, and in half an hour came upon the first ruins really deserving that name that we had seen in Persia. These were two blocks of stone at least nine feet square, hollow inside, and placed as if to support an arch. There being a mound close behind them we thought this might have been the entrance to some large temple, though the mound is only composed of shapeless stones. On one of these pedestals (?) lay a smaller stone, and by the side of the other a large block cut into steps, as if to allow of reaching the summit of the pedestal. It now began to snow to add to the forlornness of the scene. Some five hundred yards beyond, to the left, we observed some columns, so rode up to them, and discovered four pillars partially standing, square and hollowed out; between these stood another, some forty-five feet high, perfectly round and smooth, composed of three pieces, each piece standing on the other by its own weight and all of them supported on a round dark-coloured stone only a foot in thickness and about half a foot broader than the column. This evidently marked the site of a forum, or other public space in a flourishing city. The plain is supposed to contain the ruins of Pasagarda, and it is evident that a large town was once located here. We saw flocks of wild pigeons, ducks, storks, starlings, and crows about.

Riding on we came to the miserable village of Madre-e-Suleiman, where stands the reputed tomb of Cyrus. Some of the huts are built on older foundations, and in their midst is a square space surrounded by upright cut stones. A mud wall built between the intervals of smooth stone columns, which yet stand some eighteen feet high, surrounds the tomb, which is raised on six square layers of stones, each layer being smaller than the other, so as to form high stairs to the little stone parallelogram on the summit. Snow was lying on these, making the ascent rather difficult as each

T

step was four feet high and very slippery. We managed to crawl up, and entered a little smoke-coloured room, of which the walls appeared to be each in one piece, though outside there are divisions, perhaps only chiselled. However, the place has been described frequently. The interior walls have partially crumbled in; round the lower portion an inscription runs forming a frieze; nothing inside, excepting some of the shuttle-like tin offerings. At the right-hand of the door is an inscription in Arabic (?) Some modern grave-stones are scattered about outside.

Mounting again, we soon rode into a wild and picturesque defile. The romance of the scene, however, was sadly weakened by the snow which fell faster than we ever remember seeing it fall before. We followed a rushing stream which had watered the plain of Pasagarda. At one place the path was chiselled out of the solid rock, when the defile got too narrow to allow of a path by the stream. This we thought very probably coeval with the remains we had left behind us, as modern Persians would never have been at so much trouble, but would have waded through the torrent. We rode on and on till night fell, then our beasts all had a tumble in succession, our carpet bags fell into some water, and we lost our way. After some wandering about, we luckily descried the walls surrounding the gardens near Kumeenabad, and soon after those of the village. We found the gate closed, but by dint of knocking we obtained admittance. It had taken us ten hours to perform twenty-four miles, but we kept our baggage safely in view all day, mindful of our last day's experience. On entering the village we found that, whilst on horseback, we could see over the roofs of all the houses in it, so low were they. After much search, a room was found above the gateway. One part of the wall was broken down, and the door would not close, but it was better than nothing, so we lighted a fire in the middle of the room, and killed a kid, of which we eat a portion within half an hour of its slaughter. We bought a duck yesterday and are carefully preserving it for Christmas day. W., to-day, by a stroke of genius invented a plan for keeping ourselves warm in our beds which had got rather wet during our travel—we put lighted charcoal under them!

Christmas Day.—W. caught rather a severe cold yesterday (no wonder), so we determine to rest here to-day. Perhaps a description of the room in which we passed this day of rejoicing, 1865, may not be inappropriate. At any rate it affords us some useful occupation, of which there is no over abundance. Well,—our room is twenty feet long by eight broad: the door in the centre of one of the long walls, and our beds in opposite corners, with their heads to the short walls. Above W. there is a small cross-shaped opening and above that two square ones about a foot large, the only windows in the place. Our system is that on alternate days we choose which corner we prefer; this was *our* choice, and therefore farthest from the windows. The walls are brick plastered over with mud, and with recesses about a foot deep and four square along them. The wall opposite the door has bulged in, and part has fallen into the room, the floor of which is composed of broken bricks and mud. The roof is supported by rafters, upon which coarse matting is laid, and above that again, mud. The walls, however, do not reach the roof at all points, but have crumbled away. Cobwebs abound. There is no fire-place, so we light our fire in the centre of the room opposite the door; somehow it does not smoke much. We are sitting on a small box against the wall by the door and the fire, sometimes reading Murray's Handbook for Syria and Palestine (a useful book here!) carefully through. Outside there is another and larger room, but with only three walls; however it seems to keep out the wind more or less; outside this again is a mud platform, and a rotten staircase descending into one of the streets of the village. Our left wall is also that of the town. It is thawing to-day, so to add to our comfort the melting snow begins to drip through the roof in most eccentric style, now sensibly falling on the floor where it can do no harm, now inundating our carpet bags, then seeking to find a watery bed in our own, and anon attempting to extinguish our fire! The landscape without is essentially wintry; the village half snowed up, and all the hills close around as white as a winding-sheet. Kumeenabad is only some hundred yards square and wretchedly poor; the inhabitants are said to have been much oppressed by the Governor of Shiraz. Some of the bread baked here is very good, very white and crisp, as thin as a wafer and baked in round pieces about two feet in diameter. We set some nooses, out of our horses' tails, for sparrows, but most ineffectually! We determined to get up a plum pudding at any cost, so with the help of nine eggs, a little mutton fat, flour and raisins, and a dirty silk pocket-handkerchief, we turned out something that, with a little lighted brandy, gave us the idea of one. We wished ourselves a merry Christmas and a happy New Year, the former rather half-heartedly, the latter in hope of realisation.

Next morning we rode on again, and in about an hour entered a most romantic gorge. The aspect of the sky was very lowering, until at a turn in the defile the sun shone out. Five hours' riding through this, and down a shelving plain, brought us to a good-sized village, when we struck off at right angles, turning from east to south down a valley. The road wound about much in order to avoid a little stream. On coming to an abrupt turn to our left, we were upon Tacht i Taous, or "the peacock's throne," and saw some large hewn stones, just off the road, which apparently constituted the remains of some small temple; then to the right behind a little hillock some more hewn stones, with a small fluted column in two pieces with a shapeless capital, standing amongst them. Riding on to another abrupt left-hand turn, we suddenly emerged on an immense circular plain, that of Merdusht, and the ruins of Persepolis burst upon our view. They were now some three half miles off on our left, and the high rock exactly behind took off somewhat from their grandeur, so that we are bound to confess to a feeling of disappointment at first sight. Two miles farther we came to Kinara, our halting-place. We again waited in vain for our baggage, and passed an uncomfortable night on the floor, huddling over the fire. Rather unrefreshed, we got on horseback again in the morning, and accompanied by a guide—some inhabitant who boasted of a " yaboo " or pony—we set off to visit Tacht i Rustam and Tacht i Jumsheed, or the "thrones" of the individuals named; the latter the modern Persian for Persepolis. We discovered that we had passed Rustam's throne yesterday, leaving it some five miles on our right; but we had hardly observed it as it was so far off. Now we cut across a country abundantly supplied with running streams. We crossed the stream we followed yesterday, wading it at a ford, and soon came to a village where our guide procured men with ropes for the scaling of the Tacht. The streams swarmed with snipe and plover, and had we had a gun, we might have bagged them at the rate of six dozen an hour. A mile from the village we alighted from our horses, in front of the four memorials of departed greatness. A curious square stone building stands in front of them; three of the memorials are on one surface of a rock, and one on a projecting side of the same. Each of them is hewn deeply into the rock at a considerable elevation from the ground, so as to present a flat surface, which is all sculptured into figures and cuneiform inscriptions. There is a door in the centre of each lower compartment,—but luckily they have been very often described, especially by Sir R. K. Porter, who also describes Persepolis at great length.

Now one man contrived to climb up the perpendicular wall, probably "hanging on by his eyelids," till he got to a projecting shelf below the centre Tacht. Then he pulled another man up, and both of them dragged us up by a horsehair rope fastened round our waist. We were told to take off our boots previously, so as to be able to stick our toes into crevices in the rock, but this was of little use, as we were dragged up bodily! There was a very long cuneiform inscription on the outside surface, and on entering by the low door we found ourselves in a large room, all excavated in the solid rock; four deep compartments were cut further into the interior wall; in each of these, three excavations like baths with slabs to cover them—these were all broken. They are supposed to be the tombs of kings.

We then rode across to Persepolis. The hill

before which stand the ruins forms a fine natural quarry of itself; the formation (in blocks) being like that near Torquay in the bay. One block that the builders had cut out and left on their way to the buildings is still to be seen where it was originally quarried. On approaching, the grandeur of the ruins developed itself. There is a huge platform formed entirely of hewn stones; a magnificent double flight of steps up to this, each step not more than four inches high. On this artificial platform are the remains, to which it would be impossible to do justice under ten pages. The cuneiform inscriptions are numerous, and we also observed more in the snow, these latter the impress of pigeons' feet! Fronting the staircase stand two immense winged bulls about twenty-four feet apart, forming the entrance to the area behind. Below these, on their pedestals, are cut the names of most of the travellers who have visited these ruins—the vast majority were English. C. Niebuhr, 1765, and Franklin, 1787, close together; a Mr. Becher, 1704, was the oldest in date, and the most prominent a M. Emile Bernay *de Paris* —

as if Mr. Snooks were to add *of London* to his aristocratic cognomen!

In the rock above are excavated two more such monuments as at Tacht i Rustam. The sculptures remaining are all in excellent drawing, and some of them exquisitely finished. Eleven columns of the great hall are still standing, and two others front the staircase behind the winged bulls, thus thirteen in all, the same number that were standing forty years ago. The actual *living* rooms of the palace were apparently to the right; the side of the double flighted staircase leading up to these is exquisitely carved in basreliefs representing a long procession. The chief incident sculptured in all directions appeared to be that of a man catching hold of a lion by a forelock and sticking a sword into his (the lion's) stomach; with another representing a king with a well-trimmed flowing beard, having an umbrella held over him by a satrap, another attendant in front. The stone out of which these figures are carved admits of a very high degree of polish: probably the whole was formerly polished; now it is only so in a few places, and these are darker than the rest.

As we stood here upon the spot,—in the very dwellings of the proudest monarchs of ancient times,—whence orders had issued planning the greatest expeditions ever known, our thoughts turned involuntarily upon the degeneracy, the decay of modern Persia. Alas, how fallen! The stream we crossed going to Tacht i Rustam is called the Kour Ab, or water of Cyrus, thus perpetuating the memory of the founder of Persian greatness—the only memorial, by the way. This falls into the poet's stream, the *prince's river*, Bund Ameer, which we crossed on a bridge whose ascent was as nearly as possible at right angles to the road and the top flat. The stream though lacking (at least here) the well-known "Bower of roses," was far the largest we had yet seen in Persia. At this point its banks were desolate; it rushes rapidly through the three arches of the bridge, just where we left the plain of Persepolis, or Merdusht. A ridge of rock on the right. The mountains surrounding the plain are most picturesque. The best view is perhaps that from the platform of Persepolis. Three hills on the right were most curiously shaped, rising into rocky tablelands with perpendicular cliffs, snow on all of them. We soon reached Zirgoon, where we halted that night; just above the village, on the left were some high steep rocks, along which goats were climbing seeking their very scanty pasturage.

Leaving again next morning at nine, we began to ascend after an hour's ride. In three hours more we reached an isolated caravanserai, Barjgar, and soon after came to a winding descent, which became rather abrupt, till at a turn we saw a large heap of stones in the centre of the path a little above us, and on reaching this our gaze fell suddenly on Shiraz. The heap had been raised by wayfarers like ourselves, who coming here in sight of their wished-for goal, had cast a stone upon it as a memorial. Indeed the sight was lovely: we were looking down a gully on to the plain, where the town lay stretched out before us. At the foot of the hill we were standing on, rose two groves of tall, dark, full-foliated cypress trees surrounded by walls, between which ran the broad and perfectly straight road, ending in the town, the colossal blue dome of the chief mosque the most striking object. The plain was dotted all over with buildings, surrounded by picturesque though gloomy cypresses. The hills on the opposite side of the plain stood out fine and massive, all covered with deep snow. We passed a clean new house, with open rooms approached by a broad flight of steps, on our left, and on descending found orange trees growing plentifully in the gardens. A large grove of cypresses on the left formed four straight intersecting alleys; another grove a little further on. In the morning we had sent our servant Jaffer on with a letter to Mr. Babington, the temporary superintendent of telegraphs here, and one to the Persian " mirza " attached to the same institution; so a horseman met us some way out of the town and conducted us to Mr. St. John's house. On entering the town over a bridge, we found the houses in a most ruinous condition, Shiraz being very subject to earthquakes—having been almost totally destroyed several times; the streets were filthy.

We rode through a portion of the bazaar, and turning out of it came to the house, orange trees growing in the court, their fruit hanging golden upon them. However, the oranges are very sour as a general rule, and the wonder is how the trees manage to survive the winters. There is no actual snow on the ground here, but the mountains surrounding the plain on all sides are covered with it, and the temperature is very low. Mr. Babington's house was close by, and he entertained us most kindly during our stay.

CHAPTER IX.

WE entered the town on the 30th of December, and next morning of course paid our first visit to the bazaar. The principal one is a high well-built straight arcade, the bazaar "al Vakeel," but the stock is not very varied, hardly anything being kept on hand. The wine of Shiraz is famed throughout Persia ; it has much body. We were told that about three weeks ago there had taken place some serious bread riots, owing to the high price of the staff of life—the large proprietors, to whom belonged all the corn-growing country around, having the bad Bishop Hatto-like habit of keeping back the crop, and only selling at an exorbitant rate. Some arrangement was, however, come to, and the riot quelled. The "mirza" Hassan Ali Khan "Nawab" informed the prince governor of our arrival, and he sent us a present of sweetmeats in the morning—a rather disagreeable offering, as it entails a fee to the servant bringing it of about double the value. One hour before sunset, the Mirza insisted on taking us to see the Governor. We entered the old garden of the old palace, in whose outer wall is situated the telegraph office, and were shown into a small decorated room, with three chairs in it. We monopolised two of these, keeping our boots on and hats off in Feringhee style. Presently the prince, an elderly man with rather an European look about him, came in and seated himself gravely upon the chair at the other extremity of the room, upon which the conversation began,—after our bows,—as usual spasmodically. In the course of it we made out that the recalcitrant governor of Abada had fled. We had met, occasionally, on our road small detachments of troops going to rout him out, but the trouble, it seems, was spared them. The prince desired to know the number of the inhabitants of China—a rather difficult question to answer, but putting a bold face on it, we said 300,000,000, not having the remotest idea on the subject.

The population of this town is said to be 40,000.

The telegraphic line, which had been broken between this and Ispahan, was restored to-day, keeping our host at work till long past midnight; we had ungraciously to dine without him. On New Year's Eve we rode out accompanied by the Mirza to see Saadi's tomb. We soon got out of town and rode for three half miles over cultivated land—the chief produce, lettuce—to a garden, Del Cason—with orange trees in rows and a ruinous house in the centre—which we entered, to see what an orange garden in this part of the world was like. Behind this we came to a small village—on the left hand a high wall, with a small door in it. We entered through this, and were in a dirty garden court with five cypresses, at the farther end a dilapidated building, with three arched rooms. In the one on the right—a small hole about twenty feet square—lay the tomb of the second poet of Persia, a slab of common hard stone, some seven and a half feet by two, with the surface chiselled out in letters forming stanzas written by him who lay underneath; the whitewashed walls had more poetry painted on them in fading letters of gold.

Riding out next along the hills, we came to the large cypress grove in four alleys; this belongs to the king, nearer the town stood a walled cemetery, and in the centre the lowly tomb of Hafiz, some two feet longer and two inches broader than that of Saadi. Whether this be to show their comparative merits we know not. An alabaster slab about an inch thick lay on the top, very delicately carved into poetry; and almost all the graves, strewn thickly around, bore some poetical inscription upon them, probably owing to the presiding "*genius loci.*" Then crossing the road we entered the Bagh-i-no, or new garden, by a very small door in the wall. This also belongs to the king, and is planted with orange-tree rows—an open roomed house in the centre full of portraits of Futteh Ali Shah. Leaving this, we rode west for about half a mile to the Bagh i Tacht, or garden of the throne, once a royal summer residence, and still inhabited by the Governor of Shiraz in the hot weather. It is built on the summit of an isolated rock some thirty feet high, itself standing on elevated ground, and a series of terraces descend gradually to the garden, where there is an immense tank. The view from the dwelling-rooms at the summit is delightful. We have the tank, certainly not less than one hundred yards square, just below us, with four stone lions spouting water in the centre; then the garden spreading out before us, and a straight avenue of cypresses, leading down some half mile towards the town, of which we obtain a glorious bird's-eye view, on all sides gracefully shaped mountains surround the plain. We then descended by steps down the terraces; on the third from the bottom there were a quantity of concealed fountains, so contrived as to spring up suddenly and drench the unwary traveller—a right royal joke. Down the centre of the terraces a cascade is contrived but it is only supplied with water once a week. On looking up we saw the sun shining full on the terraces, which were partially tiled in blue. These and all the buildings were reflected in the mirror of the (somewhat dirty) tank, presenting a really fine sight. W. called it the Versailles of Persia, and we fully concurred. The sun now began to set, and the temperature became very cold, so we galloped home. Here, as at Teheran, a band of musicians with long horns and drums performs a hideous charivari above the principal gate of the palace at sunset.

1st January, 1866.—We wandered about the bazaars, which are very straggling in this town. We entered a court resembling that of the Medressa at Ispahan, but the tiling was not of so fine a quality as it is there. The telegraphic wire has been broken for a fortnight now, so that messages for which £5 have been paid in London, may perhaps reach Kurrachee a few days after a letter written at the same time! Many of the telegrams are most amusingly unintelligible, couched in language of which the key is only known to the correspondents, though, we apprehend, not difficult to decipher with a little care. As, for instance, "cotton, Paris; rapeseed, Avignon;" and so on. There is a Swede, a Dr. Fagergrim here, as doctor to the troops; we did not see him, however; but on the 3rd, a "père Clément," who had travelled from Ispahan to Busheer with two Frenchmen, and now returned, called upon us. As far as we could make out he was an Armenian Catholic educated at the Metacharisten Kloster at Vienna. He was an ardent numismatist, having, indeed, as he told us, studied that *science* for twenty years. Coins are continually brought to us, but most of them are counterfeits. It is rather strange, that the art of fabricating antique coins appears to be one of the few brought to any perfection in Persia. The padre showed us his collection of coins, bought on his last trip; a few, he said, were not known in Europe, and of course of great value, though picked up at small cost. He told us that once he had travelled in Asia Minor for six months on six pounds sterling, and had yet contrived to buy enough antiques to realise £40 afterwards! He also informed us that the pictures in the church at Ispahan were really by Venetian hands! There are only three Armenian families, with one priest and a small chapel, at Shiraz. The coins are exceedingly well made, and an inexperienced eye like ours cannot in the least distinguish between the true and false money.

We were told, and the fact was vouched for, that the cure for the bite of a scorpion (as for that of a mad dog!) is found in the animal itself. Immediately on being bitten catch your scorpion, cut his head off and rub the neck on the wound; then a drop of something that exists there will soothe all pain, and prevent any evil consequences! So much cotton was being sent down on mule and camel-back to Busheer for Bombay that we had great difficulty in finding any beasts to carry us; and for our shortest stage we found the hire to amount to more than for our longest (from Tabreez to Teheran), though still very cheap.

On the 4th we bade farewell to Mr. Babington and the padre (who accompanied us some distance on horseback), and left Shiraz for ever by a ruined gate—that of Kauzaroon. We left the Bagh i Tacht on our right hand, and rode straight west through rich gardens to the end of the plain of Shiraz, the sun shining warmly down upon us, until we reached the well-built stone and stucco caravanserai of Chenarada, where we found the usual opendoored stone-paved room, in which we passed the night. Next morning we started over a bridge just in front of the Khan, and began mounting small hills one after the other. After a rather steeper bit than usual we descended again to a pellucid stream with tall brushwood jungle and willows on its bank. Following this we reached Khauna Zenyoon. The first caravan-serai is bad, but two hundred yards further on there is a good new one, built by a lieutenant-governor of Shiraz. Outside this there was an arrangement as if for a fives court, we could not make out what it really was. There are no post-houses or horses beyond Shiraz, so all posts go by foot messenger.

Starting early, we rode along an uneven plain with hills at intervals, till we came to a regular climb, up which we scrambled, and then rode along this spur of a lower range of mountains, the snow coming down fast upon us. Descending into a plain we reached a most miserable tumbledown-looking village, and determined to proceed in a drizzling rain which wetted all our things and did not make itself generally agreeable. The rocks on our right had a perfectly wonderful echo. In about two hours we began to mount again, first gradually then by abrupt windings up a rocky well-wooded mountainside. Our horses' hind legs here gave way, and allowed us to slide gracefully off, and on to the snow, so we walked up with difficulty by a sort of natural staircase, made by the constant wear and tear of the mules' hoofs; without this we should have slipped at every step. At last we reached the summit, and then began the descent, showing not every "descensus" to be "facilis." This one was muddily slippery, loosely rocky, rainily sleety, and darkness set in about half an hour before we reached Mian Cothul, where we were very glad to find any room at all. The name of this caravanserai answers to our "half-way house," meaning "half the mountain." It is one of the best built "travellers' rests" in Persia, as we discovered in the morning, and the scenery around is wonderfully beautiful. There were many swallows' nests under the eaves, but the birds had sought warmer climes. The building stands on a flat piece of ground just above the road. The high grey mountain, down half of which we had come, almost overhangs it on the north, wild ridges of rock to the east, and a boundless vista of rocks to the south, about two miles below a narrow plain, then a tall range of mountains. Then another plain much lower down, and on the further side of it another chain of mountains. Thus we appeared to be looking down some gigantic ladder (as indeed we were), which led up by steps that the seven-league boots could hardly stride, to the tablelands of Persia.

Though it had rained torrents all night, in the morning on proceeding, we found that the sun, in about an hour, had dried the road. No snow now, as we were descending to a warmer clime; some of the trees around looked like gigantic broom some twenty-five feet in height. On reaching the bottom we rode along a plain through thickly-planted trees, which almost formed a forest. They appeared to us to be a kind of beech. We had been told numerous stories of terrific lions haunting them; but as we saw cattle quietly grazing amongst the trees, we thought there could be no imminent danger of an attack. On coming to the end of the valley-plain, the mountains on our right (south), which had gradually decreased in height, afforded a gap, through which our road passed almost level. We, however, soon came to the next descent; then the road became difficult; another turn, and we were descending the most celebrated path in Persia, the Cothul i Dochter; that which we had descended before was called the Cothul Pierazan, we were informed that the latter means the old woman's hill, and the former the daughter's ditto. Of course this suggested an old Eton quotation: "Oh matre pulchrâ filia pulchrior," though we were much inclined, regardless of metre, to read "horridâ" and "horridior" instead. Certainly the first was a tolerably stiff descent, but nothing when compared to this—a road composed of stones laid together unevenly and without order, some ten feet broad, a slight rampart of mud two feet high towards the precipice, the incline of about seventy-five degrees, with sharp turns. However, this is since the road has been, what in Persia is called, made. Formerly, mules and men had to scramble down as best they could. Half way down two men with guns demanded a backshish, which they did not get. We were then walking down by ourselves, and we pointed blandly up the hill as if the backshish was following behind. However, that was enough, as the natives are very chary of interfering with Feringhees; luckily so too, for we often thought when walking about unarmed, what a chance robbers would have if they only knew! The descent cannot be less than two thousand feet, and when we looked up, after fairly descending, it appeared to us an inaccessible precipice, the only wonder being how it was ever scaled at first.

Three villanous-looking men armed with pistols and guns were lying in wait for any solitary native, at the foot of the Cothul. Perhaps, however, we are wronging them, for they certainly did not interfere with us, but stories of robberies are rife about here. We met several caravans toiling up the steep, principally laden with English copper.

The temperature was now quite different and much warmer than that up above. For some time after the chief scramble the road was bad and still on an incline; a little lake lay to the south. At a turn to the right we came upon Tacht i Timour, a sort of attempt at an imitation of the Tacht i Rustam, executed by a living artist (?). A tablet cut in the rock represents Timour seated on a throne-chair, under which is the irrepressible Kaleoun. A waiting-woman presents a goblet to him; on the left a hawk sits on its perch; a vizier is standing behind the chair; the excavated sides bear also the figure of a man sculptured on each of them; a little broken down stone building encloses the tablet. We observed some Eeliauts encamped under a projecting ledge close by, and rode on over a rough causeway built upon a piece of marshy ground, with fine cane brakes all round and a running stream in the centre. The various kinds of thorn trees had their leaves still on them and the grass was fresh and green as if it were already spring; the plain was richly cultivated, and sometimes we saw hedges of cut branches.

Some miles off to the left we saw a village surrounded by palm trees, and in three hours from Tacht i Timour we reached Kauzaroon. We had to wait outside as Awa Baba had not yet come up with us, and there were so many roads intersecting each other that we were at a loss which to take. The wind blew cold at sunset. The town seemed in a very ruinous condition but prettily situated between palm and orange trees. Eventually we found a refuge in the Bagh Nazaar, outside the town, the telegraph station. There was no European clerk there at that time, as he had gone to Shiraz for his Christmas holidays! The garden in front of the house was perhaps three hundred yards long by fifty, and just in front rose a grove of some fifty magnificent palms planted regularly in rows; the rest of the garden was planted with orange trees; so high were these that we could ride under their branches without much difficulty; a little stone fountain in the centre.

On the 8th we started late (half-past 11 o'clock) for Shapoor, off the high-track to the north. A dense Scoto-Persian mist covered the landscape, but luckily lifted at midday. In about an hour we passed a grove of palm trees; in another hour we got into a stone-built village. Here we asked the way, and were told to follow two men. In half an hour more a horseman informed us that we were going wrong, and compelled one of the men to take us to a village called Sadowa (not in Bohemia !). The ground was covered with little bulbous plants like snowdrops, the flowers not yet out. We found Sadowa, where we halted, a ruined fort; the walls looked in good repair, but when we got inside we discovered utter desolation, only one round tower still standing. In this we ensconced ourselves. It was built on a slight eminence, and nomads' tents clustered around it. We determined to start immediately for the ruins of Shapoor, so we procured a guide, who set off at a pretty good pace on foot in an easterly direction across the valley, along a sedgy path where quantities of reeds had been cut to make the tents around the fort. We passed some large box-trees, and a little pond swarming with wild duck. In about an hour we rode amongst what appeared to be heaps of rough stones; presently signs of human handiwork became apparent, and we saw that we were in a ruined city. The massive foundations of walls could be distinctly traced, and close to a thick clump of box we noticed some cut stones, portions of an edifice of some kind; here we started a jackall, which ran into an old well; we rode amongst these heaps of stones for about a quarter of an hour and arrived at the foot of a low mountain (rather detached from the neighbouring chain), which had also been built over in olden times, portions of walls of unhewn stones cemented together still standing, and occasional arches not tumbled in. On the other side the hill appeared to have been once converted into a fort and escarped. Turning the corner of this hill, we entered a defile some 500 yards across (eye measurement); in the centre flowed a tolerable sized stream that we had already seen on our way. About 100 yards from the entrance to the defile, we came upon the first sculptured tablet. This represented a Roman figure kneeling before a monarch on horseback, another horseman stands behind the kneeling figure. This is supposed to represent the great Julian before Sapor (Shapoor); it is much defaced. Many oleanders grew about. Further on we came to the largest hewn tablet, in good preservation; it is divided into seven compartments. The centre one is the largest, and represents Shapoor with a round, high cap or crown on his head; a man offers him something that we did not make out. The other compartments are formed by a low framework of rock, and represent various standing figures; the whole cannot be less than thirty feet long by twelve high. We now crossed the stream, about twenty feet wide, not very deep, and rode up to the first of the four tablets cut into the rock on the other side of our defile. This one is not flat, but forms an angle as the rock turns, and is sculptured in two sets of small figures—some procession or other; the second, going up the defile, is more than half hid by a raised path of stones, so that only the heads of life-sized figures are to be seen. The third represents two persons on horseback with the round emblem of royalty on their heads; and the fourth another procession of small figures. These tablets are called Tacht i Feraoun in the district, though the country people point it out also as Naksh i Rustam, everything out of the common being attributed by the vulgar to their popular hero Rustam.

We now asked for the Tacht i Shahi, or king's throne, a cave in which there is supposed to be a statue of Shapoor cut out of the rock. We were shown a hole high up in the rock, some distance down the defile, and determined to ride there, although it was four o'clock. We skirted the north side of the valley finding the path nothing to boast of, and passed the traces of nomads who had only just shifted their abode, as the hedge of prickly branches, laid in order all round the encampment, was still there.

We put up a fox, and after riding some five miles, came to where it was necessary to get off our horses; high up in the rock above us we saw three caverns, situated like the eyes and mouth of some gigantic "jin." Our guide told us to enter the cavern representing the mouth—the lower and centre one. We began, therefore, to ascend, and we never had a steeper climb. To use a familiar illustration, Vesuvius was a front staircase to it. Sometimes we had to scramble over rocks forming as it were steps four feet high and more; at other times to climb up a mass of loose crumbling small stones, when each step seemed only to let us down further instead of taking us up. After a twenty minutes' burst, which appeared to us much longer, we were within ten yards of the cave. Here the rocks became almost perpendicular, necessitating some caution to get up. We found the cave very shallow, and of course the abode of various birds. Lighting a candle, we looked about us; at the further end there was a narrow passage into the rock, but nought there; and on one side a hole leading up to the cave forming the right eye. We managed somehow or other to scramble up to it, although we do not understand how we did it, for the rocks over which we had to make the short ascent almost overhung each other, and afforded scarcely a foot-hold. On emerging we stood on a ledge of rock —the platform of the upper cave; this also was of no extent, and nought there. Descending again to the lower cave we tried hard, for our own credit as "intelligent travellers," to make out a semblance of a human figure in the rocks strewn about beneath our feet, but in vain; we were obliged to confess to ourselves that here was only nature's handiwork, so we recommend further travellers not to toil up to this cave at any rate. We saw two others some distance off to the east, at about the same height, in one of which the statue may be, perhaps; but we were certainly told that it was in the one we had explored. It had become dark by this time, so our descent was characterised by more slips and tumbles than would, perhaps, otherwise have been the case. Our horses were awaiting us and we commenced our short ride home, following close upon our guide, who found his way on the little country path with hardly a mistake. Reaching our round tower at 9.30 P.M., we found therein just room for our beds and two feet to spare; it was an octagon without a fire-place or door. The fort, which was about one hundred yards square, appeared to have been deserted years ago, and was now being used as a stabling ground by the villagers. A centre square tower was still partially standing. Our antiquarian researches kept us up till the utterly dissipated hour of 11.30 P.M., some four hours later than usual!

On the 9th we reached a little defile in about

an hour, whence emerging we rode across a short plain, and into another pass where we had to ascend over slippery rocks for a short time. There was a ruined caravanserai here, and we passed a little village, Gamarej, leaving it on our right. Suddenly we came to the top of another descent to which even the Cothul i Dochter was a perfect farce. This was called the Cothul i Gamarej; precipitous rocks down which wound a path worn into them by the many feet of many animals, and this frequently blocked by fallen donkeys, which were going down laden with bales of cotton larger than themselves. The rocks on the opposite side of the defile which we were descending were upheaved as if by some tremendous convulsion of nature. The usually horizontal strata were perfectly perpendicular and the tops jagged. The worst parts came after crossing a little rivulet half way down. Here, by looking over at any point, we could see the whole path almost vertically below us. Where the precipice was very abrupt indeed, a low ledge of stones cemented together was built up, but otherwise the road was left entirely to nature and the traffic. We were detained for half an hour by an unfortunate camel which had slipped down whilst ascending. Its groans were very tiresome; at last it managed, unloaded, to scramble up to where we could pass it, and we reached the bottom safely. Here we came upon swarms of locusts in a dying state. On between lias rocks, which teemed with ordinary fossils, till we came to a rapid river whose banks we followed without crossing for about half an hour, when we turned off and ascended slightly, till again descending we came to the valley of Konar Tachta, whose caravanserai we reached in nine and a half hours from Sadowa, though the distance purports to be only twenty-two miles.

It rained so heavily all next day that we stopped in our mildewy room, whose roof was about to collapse at no distant date. The court of the caravanserai was turned into a swamp consisting of every kind of abomination; in the centre there stood a ruinous heap of stones, probably a cistern once upon a time. Our room faced the west; the eastern portion had tumbled down; every available hole was crammed. Bales of cotton lay in the wet on the ground. The amusement of the muleteers, besides swearing at each other—which was a "constant quantity"—was, firing at the sparrows which swarmed here. The village, principally a colony of nomads, looked picturesque, sheltered by palm trees. The dates are dried and made into a sort of half paste, half solid, some stones are extracted, others left in. The cultivation in the valley seemed to prosper, and grass grew well around. The aspect of the country was dreary enough when we saw it, but on a fine day it must be lovely. We were surrounded on all sides, at about five miles' distance, by lofty mountains, the range on the south being that which we had to pass before finally emerging on the plain extending to the Persian Gulf.

CHAPTER X.

LEAVING on the 11th, we soon got into the mountains and the descent began abruptly. The soil around was alluvial, with strata of hard conglomerate and limestone in sloping shelves, over which our track lay. The pass was called the Cothul i Mulloo, answering somewhat in name to the Via Mala, though there is no comparison between a "Diligence" road and one down which a single mule can only get with difficulty. The path was most slippery and treacherous owing to the mud. "Thus we remember in our youthful days, when the time was winter, to have attempted many a venturous slide, not without a tumble!" Even at the bottom the road was almost impassable owing to the accumulated mud. After riding on for some time, we saw a river far beneath us down to which the road gradually led. A herd of some dozen gazelles passed us within easy pistol range, but, of course, we had not got our revolver with us. We followed the river for an hour, passing a broken bridge, and arrived at the ford. Here we found that the rains of the last few days had so swollen the waters, that the caravans which had reached either side before us, were encamped there, waiting for the flood to subside. An island here divided the river into two streams. After waiting some time, W. determined to ford them. He got across the first branch easily enough, but at the second was very nearly swept away, proving it to be out of the question to attempt to lead a heavily laden mule over. Some men, who were on our side of the river, agreed at length, after a great deal of squabbling, to take us over a little higher up; so we retraced our steps for about a mile. Then six men stripped and led our mules over three at a time—the water came above our knees. The river was about thirty yards across, and the force of the current carried us at least fifty yards further down on the opposite side. Then we had to find a path up the hills on that side, for there was no road between them and the river. We scrambled up, although the leading horse fell down frequently, and had to be unloaded each time. We thus reached a level path (which had not been used for a long while) at the top of the hills; this probably was deserted when the bridge we had passed broke down. Soon we again descended to where the road abutted on the ford; then we skirted the river, sometimes ascending a little, and after riding some time, we turned up into the mountains. Darkness now came on, as we rode down a sloping shelf of rock, but not before we had seen that a flat surface lay extended before us; at last the road sloped very gradually down along the mountain to the plain, when we reached Dalachy, having taken the moderate time of ten hours to do sixteen miles. We find that the keep of a horse or a mule costs more than that of a man, for the food of the four-footed beast comes to about 1*s.* 1*d.* a day, whereas we lodge and board ourselves luxuriously (?) for about 10*d.*

12th. Like the little ratcatcher's daughter, who, it may be remembered, did not quite live in Westminster, *because* her dwelling was on the opposite side of the Thames, we find that we are not quite on the plain, *because* we are still in the mountains. Our course was a gradual descent with a few ups and downs. About half an hour after starting, we passed a large hot sulphurous spring, and further on, two more. We rode through a swarm of locusts, which flew high in the air, as numerous as the flakes of a heavy snowstorm. They were also on the ground eating up everything, which fact had occasioned the scarcity of fodder and its consequent high price. On our right stood an immense forest of palms, looking not unlike the pine forest of Ravenna; a spur of the high mountains extended into the plain on our left. We reached Barasgoon in five hours and a quarter. There was no caravanserai, but we found a long narrow room in a deserted house to sleep in. In the morning we rode through a grove of palm trees, and then got upon alternate sand and mud. We were indeed on the plain; nothing relieved the monotony of the dead flat except the occasional palm-groves and villages. A great deal of corn seemed to be grown here. We stopped at Achmedi, in the only mud hovel in the village, all other habitations being tents of matting. The only clean (?) place we could find was in a passage between the outer door and the court; large folding doors, with plenty of crevices, shut out the outer world, and the other entrance (not opposite the doors) had none. We laid our beds on a raised shelf of dry mud. The roof was of palm-stems cut in two, and matting laid over.

The 14th day of January saw our last caravan ride in Persia. We started early and rode over a muddy path, till we came to a place where water stood about two inches deep; through this and deep mud underneath we floundered for an hour and a half. At a distance we descried the masts of two ships at anchor in the Persian Gulf, which we could not yet see. We had to make a circuit of some miles in order to get upon the promontory on which stands Busheer, as the sea runs up and forms an extremely shallow bay here. At last we got to the neck of the promontory, and then were on rather better ground, so we galloped on into Busheer through a gate in the mud wall, which appeared to be here in rather better preservation than in other Persian towns. Guided by a small British ensign floating from a tall mast-head, we rode up to the Residency, where we found a few sepoys on guard.

The political resident was away, but the vice-resident, uncovenanted civil service servant Mr. James Edwards, received us in the office. In Colonel Pelly's absence, Mr. Edwards showed us the strangers' rooms where we installed ourselves.

The mail steamer had arrived the day before from Bombay and was just starting for Bassora, so we were in good time for its return. The bazaar we found bad and narrower than usual, though there were many European goods exposed for sale, owing to the facility of importation; indeed some ships trade direct from England to Busheer. The building we were in was an immense rambling construction, some thirty yards from the sea, and about ten above its level. Beach there was hardly any.

On the 18th a violent wind blew and heavy rain came down all day. The roofs of our rooms were leaky—everything was damp; the very soap in one's room dissolved as if in water. The sea, we were told, is gradually encroaching on the conglomerate rocks on which the town stands.

The 19th was a fine day but windy. The mail steamer returned from Bassora: the harbour is so bad that she had to lie some five miles out at sea.

On the 20th, our companion, W., started for Bombay at 3 P.M. We could not bring ourselves to face the seven days' sea; thus we were alone at some distance from England. We walked down to the place of embarkation on the land side of the promontory, where W. got into a little rough boat, rowed, or rather propelled, by six men. Even this little boat could not get within five yards of the rough quay, so W. was conveyed into it on the shoulders of two men. It was calm but raining when the boat started; soon afterwards the wind arose, thus diminishing any small regret we might have felt at not going to India. We were now fixed here for certainly four weeks.

The alternations of climate were perfectly marvellous in their regularity—one day warm and sunshiny, the next windy, cold, and rainy. In the summer punkahs are used here. About twenty-five miles out to sea there are two small islands; the larger of these, Karg, vulgarly called Karrick, was the station of the fleet during our desultory war with Persia. Here are some old reservoirs built by the Portuguese, and other ruins are said to be still visible. Near the island of Bahren, in the "Sea of Oman," off the Arabian coast and about two days' steaming down the gulf, the best sort of pearls are found. The fishermen who dive for them are so poor that they hardly can keep body and soul together; whilst the merchants who farm the fisheries and their services amass immense fortunes thereby. These merchants are all "Banians," or Indians, and this month many of them have sought refuge here, on account of some disturbances on the islands. There are many Indian merchants here, all of them British subjects; and all persons living in Busheer, not Persian subjects, are under English protection. The "Banians" wear a red turban twisted into a point. One of our chief amusements here was to go over to the gulf cable office and talk with the superintendent. The inland Persian telegraph and the cable office, are a mile apart, so that messages are always delayed here, a rather unwise proceeding, we should have thought, when combining the offices would both save time and expense. The charge for a message from Busheer to Kurrachee is £2 14*s*., and to England £2 10*s*. Such is the difference in costliness between sea and land telegraphy!

On the 28th a party of Englishmen, ourselves included, rode out to visit Reesheer. We rode along the coast about a mile from the sea, through partially cultivated country, by a very narrow and stony path; hardly any trees except a solitary palm here and there. About eighteen miles out we arrived at the Resident's country house, whither he retires in the summer, when his heavy duties do not compel his attendance in Busheer, or elsewhere. It was a small mud-built villa, with an open court on one side and verandahs all round. We breakfasted here. During summer the roof forms the sleeping apartment, and dinner is eaten in the open air after sunset, under a punkah. We then walked to a little mound about a mile off, and found the whole country strewn with immense quantities of large and small cornelians. We picked up some fragments of bricks with cuneiform inscriptions, on the mound, thus proving it to be formed out of some very ancient ruins. Permission to excavate it has been repeatedly asked and always refused, for the Persian government will neither excavate themselves nor let others do it for them, as they are under the impression, it is said, that inside *might* be found documents handing Busheer over to the English! After partaking of "tiffin," as English people *will* call luncheon in India and parts around, we walked down to the shore to inspect the fort of Reesheer; large slightly-cut stones lay all about, marking the ruins of some larger settlement. The fort is memorable for its gallant defence against the English in the late war. The commander of the small force to whom its defence was at that time entrusted, seems to have been a braver man than most Persians, if his remark be authentic:—" I will go: I know I cannot withstand the English, but as I am ordered to do so, I will sell my life as dearly as possible." He kept his word and was slain after inflicting much loss on our troops. The fort was only attacked in order to make an example of its defenders, and induce the capitulation of Busheer. The plan succeeded; for after the British landed to the east of Reesheer, and stormed the fort, the garrison of the larger town ran away, a few Persian soldiers only being killed by shells thrown from the fleet. The fort looked very insignificant from a distance—a square mound of earth—but on approaching we found that a trench some twenty yards across, surrounded it, and the earthworks rose some fifty feet on the other side, apparently raised on a natural elevation of rock. We entered through a breach, and found it to be about a quarter of a mile square. Nothing in the way of shelter for troops inside, but scattered stones on the ground testified to former buildings. The side towards the sea had broken down, but was still about one hundred feet in elevation and very steep; an old reservoir in the centre, near which an underground passage led to the shore, affording a means of escape to the garrison if attacked (and overcome) from the land side.

We got down to the beach; it was a beautiful day, and the waters of the gulf lay like a large lake tranquilly before us. We trode the sands in search of shells, but found none. A native doctor rode out with us on a magnificent donkey, the size of an ordinary pony. He (the doctor) had adopted European costume. We returned before the gates were closed, as they are at sunset, our ride being enlivened by the freaks of the servant of one of our party, who had got frightfully drunk, and rolled off his saddle every five minutes, getting on again regularly as if nothing had happened. At last his horse ran away from him into the town, and he walked home. Even at midsummer the days are only fourteen hours long.

No foreigners are allowed to possess house property in Persia, and the government generally waits till the house has been purchased, to put the money into its subjects' pockets, then it steps in and pulls the house down, granting no redress. In Teheran it is exceptionally permitted. The background of mountains to the plain was very picturesque, though we were glad we had crossed them.

The inhabitants of the town are hardly true Persians; we scarcely ever saw the conical hat—this is supplanted by the Arab Kefyeh—a blue and red cloth wound round the skull cap being the fashionable head-dress.

1st February.—The rain fell so heavily, accompanied by a gale of wind, that our room was perfectly wet through, from the drippings of the ceiling, entailing wet feet and a sore throat without our stirring out—" Fever made easy." When a shopkeeper in the bazaar leaves his stock in trade to go to dinner, or for any other purpose, he just throws a broad-meshed netting over the front of his stall. Thus anything might be stolen from it, were it not for the neighbouring tradespeople. One day we made an excursion along the narrow strip of beach extending outside the broken down sea-wall around the town. We observed several flamingoes lazily floating on the waves. Coming to the head of the promontory, we saw some decayed ships, one a largish pirate, captured by Colonel Pelly's ship the " Berenice,"* in the Sea of

---

*. Burnt 1866.

Oman; the style of build between a Chinese junk and mediæval galley. Then we soon came to the entrance to the bazaar, and went into a Jew antiquarian's shop, where we sat looking at various coins, most probably imitations, till after dusk. This necessitated our marching home, preceded by the Jew, carrying a tallow candle fixed in a bottle! Another day we walked out to the east, and found a good sandy beach, after passing half a mile of rocks. This extended for about a mile—only common shells on it, and a few sharks' heads; then on to rocks level with the sea and much worn by the perpetual action of the waves. We came to a village, in front of which a few boats lay on the beach, and, seeing that the sun would soon set, returned. One of the Persian servants of a lady here lost one of her earrings lately. On discovering the loss, instead of trying to find the jewel, she began to beat her bosom, tear her hair, and get generally into a most excited state, including hysterics; at length sitting down in the court and throwing sand upon herself, until a fellow-servant, hearing of it, came to her and showed her the earring, which she had picked up. All Persians, more or less, go into similar paroxysms of grief on the most trifling occasions.

On the 9th some of us English went down to the beach and shot at glass bottles with pistols but not unvarying success, as out of 50 shots we made 0 hits between us. Most of the population of Busheer gathered around us in about ten minutes. Next day we played quoits. The Vice-resident told us that Mr. Palgrave came here on his return, after travelling through Arabia as a Mohammedan physician, and left in his disguise. Colonel Pelly has been to the Wahabee country in the disguise of a British officer.

The steamer "Euphrates" arrived here from Bombay on St. Valentine's Day, two days late. N.W. winds are those prevalent in this portion of the gulf, especially blowing into the roadstead, and rendering the anchorage, except far out at sea, exceedingly precarious.

CHAPTER XI.

EXACTLY a month after arriving at Busheer, on the 15th of February, we set out again for Bassora. We played quoits till the last moment, 6 P.M., and walked down to the "Bund," or port, with a young Armenian of the name of Melcombe, then bidding good-bye to all English friends, we got off at half past 6 P.M. There were four oars to our boat, each about fifteen feet long, by six inches round in the thickest part, the blade oblong, two feet long by three-quarters broad. The rowers sat on the sides of the boat, and rowed pulling the oars towards the sides. We grounded when about half a mile out, so shallow was the water, and it took half an hour to raise the mast and hoist a felucca-like sail; then, with the assistance of a little rowing, we reached the steamer in three hours, having to make a circuit to avoid shallows. It was too late to start, so we were at anchor till 3 P.M. next day; luckily the sea was perfectly calm. The only passenger on board was an old Egyptianized Italian, who was proceeding to Bagdad to buy horses for the Viceroy of Egypt. Precisely at the appointed hour the ship's screw began to revolve. The tonnage of the "Euphrates" was 750; she was very long and narrow; we had the ladies' cabin. At 6 P.M. we sighted Karrick, a small round, elevated island.

On the morning of the 18th we were told that we were in the river Shat el Arab, although land was nowhere visible, until looking hard we observed some dim mountains on the north. The water was much discoloured already. The crew of the ship were all Hindoos, the officers and steward English. In the daytime we took a book out of the select library on board, and ascended to the upper deck, where we sat in an Indian blackwood smoking-chair, with our heels on a level with our head; the arms of these chairs extend to allow of the feet being placed upon them. At 10 A.M. we were fairly in the Shat el Arab. The banks were very low and covered with palm trees, here and there a canal emptied itself into the river. We passed a creek, up which lay Mohammud, the scene of some fighting during the Persian war; as the left bank is Persian ground and the right Turkish. At Fao we saw the crescent flag floating on its own territory for the first time. Fao is the terminal (!) station of the gulf cable, and two houses of palm-wood are respectively the English and Turkish telegraph stations. On the land line there are now two wires, and between Bassora and Bagdad the poles are chiefly of iron (as they are near Busheer), on account of the swamp. The English workmen and telegraphers have all been dismissed by the Turkish government, who have taken the whole management into their own hands. The employés are of all nations (rarely English) and their uniform is very neat. The forms are printed in French. Here a quarantine officer came on board, but no other formalities were observed. We now passed between very low banks, covered with palm trees, which belong partly to the government, partly to the Montifick Arabs, and partly to private individuals who rent the land on which the trees stand. They are planted from shoots, not datestones, as these latter rarely come to anything.

At 4 P.M. we sighted Bassora, the famed El Basreh of the Arabian Nights; a few ships in the river, and some mud walls amongst the palms, were all the signs of human handiwork we could see. A Turkish war-ship, resembling the landing-pier of penny boats on the Thames, had all its flags trimmed, and fired a loud salute—not, however, in our honour, but on account of the close of the fast of Ramadan, which takes place as the new moon rises. It had been seen the day before at Bagdad, and the day before that at Constantinople, much to the disgust of the impatient Mohammedans of Bassora! Another quarantine officer came on board and allowed none of us to leave the ship until a clean bill of health had been reported to the proper authorities. Captain Carter of the " City of London "—the steamer that was to take us up to Bagdad—came on board, and after a short time we got our luggage stowed on board one of the numerous boats that crowded around our steamer. We went straight off to the river steamer which lay close at hand, not without some demur on the part of the Customs' officer, who wanted us to go first to the custom-house; a little bakshish, however, smoothed over all difficulties.

At 10 P.M. we weighed anchor and steamed up half an hour to Margil, where is situated the British Consulate. The captain of the " Comet," the British Resident at Bagdad's ship, was acting as consul during the proper official's absence, and we found a brother of the (late) sultan of Muscat with him; he had visited Bagdad and was going back to Bombay on his way to Zanzibar,—a young and rough fellow, who, though an Arab, had an unconquerable aversion to a skittish horse. Our steamer lay about twenty yards out in the Tigris, and we went on shore in a small boat. The landing place was of palm trees arranged in steps, and uncommonly slippery. The English Consulate was close to the bank. We entered under an arch, into a large court-yard with walls all round; on the right-hand a door led through another smaller court to a colonnade and the living-rooms. These were lofty and well furnished, with a real English fire-place and chimney piece, blackwood furniture in the drawing-room. There was a nice garden attached, with all sorts of flower-trees in it.

After breakfast, on the 10th, the acting Consul lent us a horse to ride into Bassora. We went through a forest of palms, interspersed with the palm huts of stationary Arabs, and got on a sandy and marshy plain, where our horse ran away with us, doing about two miles in five minutes. We pulled him up close to Bassora, and rode in, to the steamer's office. The mud walls round the town appeared easier to get over even than in Persia, but the gate was still guarded by Irregulars. At first we rode through palm gardens, surrounded by mud walls, and much below the level of the road, which was elevated by the earth thrown out of these very excavated gardens. This was done to get the gardens on a level with the Tigris for irrigation. Outside the walls we passed some heaps like old ruins. When we got amongst the houses, we found them very ruinous. The court of the consular office is covered in, and the rooms are in two galleries around. We tried the bazaar, but found that, on account of the great holiday, all the shops were shut; and as it was Saturday, even those of the Jews. It seemed well built, but short. The glory has departed from El Basreh. The first object seen on approaching the town is the French flag floating from a tall masthead. This is under the keeping of a merchant, who is called the "gardien du Pavilion." The relations of France with Bassora are—that once a year a ship belonging to some Swiss merchants, calls here under the French flag! We went to the telegraph office; the operator, a Turk, spoke French. In Turkey the women do not seem to care so much about hiding their faces as in Persia. We must do them the justice to say that there is nothing to see. At midnight, after dining on shore, we went on board the "City of London," and started in an hour. We passed the "Garden of Eden," a few palms and Arab huts, in the early morning, and soon after sighted the tomb of Ezra, a square mud-brick enclosure with high walls, the windows at least 70 feet from the ground. A cupola of glazed tiles rises above the sanctuary, where lies the tomb held in high honour by all neighbouring Jews, who make annual pilgrimages to the shrine. We were told that one of the Barons Rothschild had given a large sum towards the establishment of schools here. The low banks were hardly four feet above the river; many Arab encampments on them; no trees; numerous flocks. The villagers generally turned out to see us pass, children in the costume once fashionable a little lower down the river, in the Garden of Eden, women with their faces unveiled. Occasional heaps testified to the ruins of ancient times. Numerous pillars of smoke arose at intervals about the plain, each seeming some "jin" released from a casket that had been sealed with Solomon's seal, but in reality the less romantic consequence of reeds burning near some nomad encampment. The river winds in the most eccentric fashion, so that the tomb of Ezra seemed to be now on our right, then on our left; now before us, now behind. We reached a sharp turn, nicknamed the Devil's Elbow, about noon. Permission to cut a straight course for the river through this, has been repeatedly refused by the Turks to the company whose steamer we were in. Indeed, the navigation from Bassora to Bagdad might easily be shortened by about one-half, simply by cutting through corners, but the Turkish Government, of course, does nothing, and will not allow others to do more. There are three English and two Turkish steamers on the river. The navigation is very treacherous when the river is low, and not without hazard even at this time of the year, when it is pretty full. Our ship drew four feet of water, and the deck was only three feet above the water. The cabins were built upon this deck, and the steerage passengers slept above them. The saloon contained about thirty square feet, and to get from one side of the table to the other at dinner, the servants had to go out at one door and in at the other. Some Arabs were continually racing the steamer on shore, bronzed fellows, very lightly dressed, with florid kefyehs. The breadth of the river varies considerably, and is generally deepest near one of its banks. We were now on the Tigris, the river below the junction of the Euphrates, and this being called the Shat el Arab. At 7 o'clock we reached Ordy, a large Turkish camp. A Turkish steamer which started thirty hours before us from Bassora, was now only eighteen hours ahead, so we were gaining rapidly on her. A large fire burnt luridly on the horizou; the glare was great and the light far spread.

At 7 A.M. on the 19th we passed the celebrated bridge of Alexander. The remains of one buttress are still visible on the (proper) right bank. It is of bricks, firmly cemented together. Higher up a few trees. The road to the bridge may still be traced on either side, in the shape of two parallel mounds. At 5 P.M. we passed the little Turkish steamer. The river was very discoloured. The bridge is called Fley Fley by the Arabs, from a sort of Hero and Leander story. A lady of that romantic name (Fley Fley) was enamoured of a young gentleman whose fame has not sufficed to preserve his name, but who, at all events, used to swim the river every night to get to his "ladye love." She, therefore, out of kind consideration for his health, and that he might not catch cold, built him this bridge!

At 7 P.M., we reached Kutellamara, about half way. At 3 P.M. on the 20th, we met the Dijillah, the other English steamer, belonging to Messrs. Lynch. She was much larger than the "City," and named after the Arab for this river, meaning "The Arrow," probably so called because it is one of the most crooked rivers going—or rather flowing.

At 8 A.M. on the 21st we drew up opposite the Tark Kesra, or Arch of Chosroes. Here the river makes an immense sweep, so that we could walk across the bend in half an hour, whereas it took the steamer two hours and a half to go round. Here Captain Carter and ourselves landed, and walked across to the Tark. On our right we saw the remains of a gigantic wall of brick. We crossed a broad canal. Here the city of Ctesiphon was situated in ancient times. The Tark is a most magnificent arch, standing out in bold relief against the sky; it must be some two hundred feet high by eighty broad. Part of the arched roof has fallen in, but the solidity of the remainder is imposing. It is built of large burnt bricks, cemented most solidly together. On either side of the arch are two wings of masonry as high as itself, with columnar decorations, the outer walls of a palace, of which the other sides have fallen in. On the west side of the arch there is a practicable way up owing to the decay of the bricks, which leaves a sort of narrow staircase going up, sideways. The greatest difficulty is to get up the first ten feet, as there the upper bricks project, and there is no foothold. After this we easily ascended to the arched portion, where the interstices between the bricks afford an easy climb to the summit. The plain near is covered with *heaps* of ruins, which look like ordinary hillocks. Getting down again we made for the river, through brushwood where we put up a few partridges. The banks were here very muddy. The water for irrigation is drawn up over a cross-bar by means of a large bucket let down into the river by a rope, to the other end of which a horse is harnessed, and then driven down an excavated hole, so as to afford leverage for the purpose. The ruins extend to the other side of the river.

At length about 2 P.M. we reached the first palm gardens around Bagdad, and in about three-quarters of an hour more we steamed into the city of the Caliphs. At a bend in the river we now saw the masthead on which ought to have floated the British ensign, but it was not hoisted till we fairly arrived. A bastion of the wall of circumvallation, which is of well preserved burnt brick, jutted out into the river. The gates are shut at sunset. Colonel Kemball, the resident and consul-general, received us most graciously. We found a real bed in our room, a thing we had not seen since Tabreez. Next morning we made our customary inspection of the bazaar, which is the best stocked one we had yet seen in the East; the arcades are wide and the building solid.

On the 24th we rode over the bridge of boats to Cosmein, the great Persian sanctuary, with two gilt cupolas and four good minarets in excellent preservation. The town on the right bank of the Tigris has very narrow streets which are continually thronged. On the Residency side, (the fashionable quarter,) latticed windows overhang the streets. The right bank outside the town is planted with palms, then an open plain, and Cosmein lies amongst more palms.

On the 26th we started on an excursion to Hilleh, the ruins of ancient Babylon. We hired three horses, and crossing the river by the bridge we turned south, after paying a small toll. After threading the streets for some time, we emerged out of the town to the west. On our right now rose the tomb of the celebrated wife of Haroun al Raschid, Zobeide; a burnt brick edifice in the shape of a sugar-loaf on an octagonal base, rising in steps. We soon came to a narrow canal that spread out further to the north, and found ourselves on the banks of the Tigris. We now rode through a succession of mounds and dry canals, past two khans, as the caravanserais are here called, and the bifurcation of the road to Kerbelah, a place of pilgrimage for Persians, whither immense cargoes of corpses are conveyed for burial in the holy ground around the shrine where lies interred the body of Houssein. We slept at Khan al Hassan, (thirty-two miles,) under a projection in the inside caravanserai passage—lots of donkeys close to us. We had a new dodge for a portable bed, simply a large canvas bag, to be filled with chopped straw at night. It made a remarkably good couch.

On the 27th, continuing our ride, we passed many more dry canals, and two with deep streams in them. The bridges over these were in good repair. At 1.30 P.M., having started at 8.30 A.M., we saw a large mound, so we cut across to get at it, but were stopped by a deep canal, up which we had to ride to find a bridge. After this we rode straight to the enormous hill-like mass, which we discovered to be the Majellibè of Rich. It was oblong, at least one hundred feet high, and from a distance appeared to be composed of dry mud, but on approaching and dismounting, we found a portion of it to be solid brick wall of stupendous thickness, and in other parts the material of which the mound was composed was perfectly friable, so that on pulling out one brick, a whole mass would tumble down. Here there were several large clay vases, cinerary urns; we pulled one out and thus discovered another just behind it. There was nothing but dry mould and bits of bone inside. We walked round the mass and got on to the top, where we saw many traces of excavations, as the Arabs freely pull out the bricks to build houses with.

We now sent on our guide with a letter to Kalif Aga, the governor of Hilleh, and rode across country, over dry canals—the plain full of mounds; —on the right a palm forest, which, from the top of the Majellibè we discovered, grew on the banks of the Euphrates. It was a lovely afternoon, and the river stole lazily along amongst the palms and long grass. We soon came to another enormous mound, the Kasr of Rich, on to which we rode, and found the remains of a stout brick building, apparently of rather more recent date than the Majellibè. Descending, we came to an Arab village. One of the inhabitants rushed out and asked whether we had seen a stone bull amongst the ruins. We had not, and so rode back to the Kasr, where, in an excavation, stood a black basalt hewn figure, more resembling a lion than a bull, and not unlike an enlarged edition of the lions frequently seen in Persian churchyards. The face was mutilated and the legs broken off; the sculpture very rude. It had been discovered a long time, we believe, though it is strange that more have not been found. We rode on, and soon got between mud walls enclosing palms, which extended for some two miles. When we reached the outskirts of Hilleh, a servant on horseback met us, saying that he had been commissioned by the European doctor of one of the regiments quartered here to offer us a room. We therefore rode through a mangy bazaar, (principally for corn,) to the doctor's house. He spoke French, and we discovered that our muleteer, who knew of his being in the town, had gone to him, and told him that we had seen the room appointed for us by the aga, but finding it not sufficiently good, had expressed our intention of going to the doctor. Of course we explained. Every article of furniture, as well as the house itself, was of palm-wood, even to the matting of shreds of palm.

On the 28th, at 11 A.M., we rode out to Birs Nimroud, the supposed tower of Babel (or Belus),

We crossed the Euphrates on a bridge of boats, which then presented an animated scene, as a long string of camels was crossing, attended by its Arab conductors, a swarthy set, tall, and with bright red and yellow silk kefyehs, kept on their heads by long skeins of camel's hair. A small toll is payable for crossing. Then we passed through a tolerable bazaar, and out of the town, when we immediately descried the Birs Nimroud at a distance, about seven miles out. We had to make several circuits, in order to avoid canals and to find bridges, before getting to the Birs.

We rode on to an enormous pile of earth and ruins, some fifty feet high and a quarter of a mile long by 300 yards broad; immense quantities of broken and valueless pottery scattered about; close beyond rose the tower, a gigantic mass of brickwork almost round in form, but broken up, and covered with *debris* at the bases. A, yet standing, massive piece of wall like a very thick column, and constructed of the most solid brick, rises about fifty feet above the main body of the edifice, forming a distinct landmark. We climbed up to this, and viewed the flat landscape. The river made a bend to within a mile of our standing point and was very wide, as if the inundations were beginning. On the south side of this mass huge pieces of brickwork have fallen down, as it were vitrified into slag by intense heat, perhaps that of lightning.

On returning we paid a visit to the vice-governor. He received us in a shabby room, where we had the usual Arab coffee without milk or sugar but with plenty of sediment. After dinner, the doctor Demetriades, a Greek, took us to the barracks; a square building in two storeys, with rooms round a large court, and a gallery round the upper storey. We went into the bandmaster's room, who presently came in as drunk as possible. He insisted on exchanging our wideawake for his "fez," which was miles too big for us. Luckily he soon fell asleep, and tumbled off his divan, upsetting his narghilè (Turkish for kaleoun). At 7 P.M., the hour of the "retraite," the band struck up in the court, and played polkas, and English and French song tunes very tolerably. When it was over, we slipped out, and recrossed the bridge beneath which the river flowed silently in the moonlight night. The coffees which were crammed at six were empty now. Their divans of palm branches with backs and sides seemed very rude and hard to lie upon.

On the 1st of March we started on our journey back to Bagdad. The vice-governor insisted upon sending two *very* irregular cavalry Bedouins as an escort, but we soon managed to get rid of them; just at sundown we reached the Khan of Bir Noos, where we halted for the night. A wild Arab insisted that our room (!) was engaged for some soldiers who had not yet arrived; but we observed in the vernacular, "first come, first served," and the sight of our whip effected the rest. Next day we reached Bagdad at 3 P.M., having to lead our horses through one small canal, whose waters had swollen since we crossed it, going.

On the 3rd we saw the Pasha riding in the bazaar. He paid a visit to the resident, bringing our firman for the road with him.

An export duty of four per cent. was charged upon many things in a box which we sent to

MISSIONARY SUCCESS! 347

England *via* Bombay (which by the way had not arrived eleven months afterwards !) Five years ago the duty was nine per cent., but the Turkish Government were induced to agree on lowering it to one per cent., by taking off one per cent. every year for eight years. Messrs. Bruhl and Eppstein, two missionaries from England to the Jews, with their English wives, were about to leave for England, having, during nine years' ministration, succeeded in converting two Jews, one of whom, we believe, soon relapsed. However, the schools that they instituted did much good.

4th.—We start to-morrow, and have already paid our horse hire for the first four stages. The letting of post-horses is in this country farmed out to different proprietors, who supply so many stations with horses. The man who farms the first distance supplies four stations, so these are prepaid.

CHAPTER XII.

On the 5th, the English dromedary post from Damascus came in, and we started on our long ride after breakfast. We rode two stages, and found a Mr. Weber, a merchant at Mosul, just going to start at the changing-station. Near Bagdad the road was rather bad, intersected by small watercourses with a very narrow bridge over each. We reached Yengiyeh early, doing thirty-nine miles in six hours, including the half-hour for stoppages; we travelled with only three horses—one for ourselves, one for Awa Baba, and one for the postilion. Our bed was strapped behind ourselves, our luggage (!) behind our servant, and saddle-bags carried our cooking utensils, &c., on the third horse.

The first station was on the left bank of the Tigris, then over a bad marsh. The post-house is a large square with stables all round, not more than ten feet high (we slept in a kind of guardroom);

it is only accessible by one door, so as to be easily defensible against any wandering Arabs, who sometimes are troublesome along the road; they are said to have been quiet lately, only having robbed the last Turkish post to Constantinople of many thousand pounds' worth of treasure and jewels—this notwithstanding a strong escort, which most likely connived at the robbery, although two of the number were killed and as many wounded, not being in the secret. The robbers of course instantly made for the Persian frontier. Palm trees still grow around the villages by the Tigris. The telegraph again adjoins our track as in Persia. This is the best season for travelling down here— neither too hot nor too cold. The air is delightful, and early spring flowers are beginning to blossom.

On the 6th the road led to a meandering river, at present just level with the plain; many kinds of shrubs grew about, and the banks were often occupied by the settlements of Eeliauts, here Kurds, we believe. After changing horses, we crossed a long and low ridge of the Hamaram hills. A few stones set up in the road marked the spot where the post was attacked. We reached Kara Teppah—fifty-four miles—in nine hours. The accommodation was of the vilest. The surreje, or postilion, generally rides a mare; the other two are horses; the charge is 2½d. per horse per mile—very little. The number of storks on their nests is almost ludicrous; every house has two or three of them upon it.

Starting early, we crossed a spur of the snow-covered mountains on the east, and were delayed three-quarters of an hour at the station, as there were no horses. After all only two were obtainable, so we took on one that we had come with. We rode along a low range of hills to Tooz Khurmati, where we were accommodated in a decent mud room. In this post-house there was a very pretty girl with large black eyes,—almost the only pretty face we had yet seen. Oranges were to be bought at all these stations, and good honey. Fifty-one miles in nine hours and three-quarters. We observed several crows with white backs and breasts, and crossed a broad but shallow river just before this station. During the night a bitumen light was burnt in our room, and by its glimmer we saw a man stealthily creeping about, groping for anything he could find. He found nothing, however, and a slight movement on our part induced him to crouch in a corner for half an hour, occasionally imitating the purr of a cat; then he crept away.

On the 8th we crossed another river, and reached Taough, the changing station, in three and a-half hours. A mounted horseman generally wished to ride with us as an escort, whose services we as generally declined; for if we were to be robbed one horseman would do no good, but rather make any stray marauders think that there was something worth getting in our possession. We reached Kirkook at 4 P.M. Eight and a-half hours, forty-eight miles. It is a prosperous town, with a large Turkish garrison. The barracks are the best house in it. The town is apparently divided into three quarters, one across a little rivulet with a wide channel, another on an elevated and isolated plateau, and the third around it, where the post-house was situated. The pomegranates were remarkably fine, as indeed we found them to be ever since Busheer. The proprietor of the post-horses here, who farmed a distance of 180 miles, was particularly anxious to impress upon us the advantages to be derived from paying him for the distance from Zab to Mosul. As his farm only extended to Zab, he wished to send his horses on thence with us, and to *do* the post-horse owner there, besides calling the distance three miles further than it really was.

On the 11th, as we were bound on one of our longest rides, it began to rain early, and continued without ceasing all day, making the roads bad; we found no horses at the next station, and had to take our old ones on, after baiting for an hour and a half; we reached Arbil at half-past nine, the last two hours and a half ride, in the dark—sixty-three miles, thirteen hours and a quarter. We passed two isolated mounds with flat tops, on which were the ruins of some houses, probably built there for security. Now, however, the road here is perfectly safe, and the district well cultivated, as the system of government has been changed. The Pashas receive a fixed salary, instead of paying so much for their office, and then grinding so much more out of their subjects. Arbil is built on a flat mountain, accessible only on one side; walls all round besides. The post-house is below amongst some other houses. Next day our surreje, a young boy, lost his way, and we rode over ploughed fields for some time, so that we reached the greater Zab late. We crossed in a rough ferry-boat, and then had to ford a smaller arm of the same river, which was rather deeper than we expected. We changed horses quickly, as we had to reach Mosul before sunset, and waded through certainly 200 yards of water up a stream by a ford.

The mountains of Kurdistan rose far to our right —the country was high and very undulating; at last we arrived in sight of Mosul, and rode through the ruins of Nineveh, which are nothing now but large mounds, not distinguishable from the natural hillocks. We passed a portion of suburbs on a low hill, with several mosques and minarets on it, the largest of them is called Nebbi Junas; the prophet

Jonas is reputed to be buried underneath. The room which contains his sepulchre is about sixteen feet square, the passage to it narrow, the walls of green glazed tiles. The sepulchre is raised from the ground and about eight feet long by half as broad; it may be of wood, but rich coverings and costly Persian rugs completely hide it. There is a bason in one corner of the room, and the attendant Mullah informed Mr. Rassam, that every Friday Jonah rises from his tomb to perform his ablutions, after which he quietly returns to his coffin! We think most people would hardly return having once got out. We reached the bridge of boats at half-past six o'clock; a stone bridge is built nearly half way across the river bed, but water only flows underneath it in spring; then the bridge of boats spans the main stream of the Tigris, here considerably shrunk from its dimensions at Bagdad. This bridge, as at Bagdad, is removed when the river rises.

Paying a small toll, we entered the gate, and passing through several squalid and filthy streets, we reached Mr. Rassam's, the vice-consul's house.

Mr. Weber, who had outstripped us, had informed him of our arrival, and we were shown into an excellent room. The house was entirely built of marble from the neighbouring mountains, of a sort of blue grey colour, streaked with white. Mr. Rassam and his wife were about starting for England in September, then he was going to return to Mosul to arrange his affairs, and give up his post.

He was actively engaged in translating portions of the Old Testament, especially the Prophet Isaiah, from the original into English, giving each word in Syriac, with his authorities for his interpretation in colloquial Arabic phrases.

On the 12th we went into the bazaars, and found them most intricate and badly constructed, but the stock in trade good. The jewellers congregated in a street without an arched roof. some portions of the bazaars were only arched in with branches. All fuel comes from the mountains on donkey-back. The ruins of Nemroud are about twenty miles down the river and those of Khorsabad fifteen miles on the opposite side.

Nothing is, however, to be seen at any of them. The excavations made by Mr. Layard are all covered up again.

13th. During the course of the day two Roman Catholic bishops, who had been educated at the Propaganda of Rome called, and stayed to tea, previously a Chaldean Catholic bishop looked in. They all three wore the common Turkish fez, with rolls of thick black cloth, about four inches broad, wrapped round it. The bishops had on black gabardines with red tunics and close-fitting sleeves. The Chaldean appeared to be a funny fellow, full of anecdotes, and with always a simile ready on all occasions. One of his anecdotes we remember:—" Some Arabs plundered a mosque dedicated to some great Mohammedan saint. On being remonstrated with by the dwellers around— who were too weak to attempt other measures—on the impiety of their proceedings, they said, ' Oh, never mind, we will make it all right with the saint,' so going into the mosque they had rifled, they ejaculated the following:—' Oh ! saint, if thou art indeed a believer, then what we have obtained from thy shrine is thy bounty unto us; but if thou art an unbeliever then we despoil thee rightly, and burn thy father!'"

14th. An Ullema, or doctor of the law, came in and smoked a chibouk. Soon after him came a Nestorian bishop with one attendant. The bishop wore a conical felt cap, with a long black calico handkerchief wrapped round it in disorderly folds. His beard was black, and his long uncombed flowing hair brown, altogether a shaggy-looking personage! Later the Pasha, a benevolent-looking old Greek, paid Mr. Rassam a visit, attended by his narghilé. The bowl of this is almost always of Bohemian glass, the receptacle for tobacco is about five inches above it—the Pasha's was of silver, shaped like a bunch of flowers. The whole is placed on the ground, and the smoke is inhaled through a leathern snake. We went on to the roof and surveyed the town. Nothing remarkable: mud-brick houses so close together that no streets were perceptible; flat roofs and parapets around them. There are sulphur springs near, which are said to be very healthsome. It was now just eight months since we left England. A Syrian Catholic bishop called in the evening. We had seen church dignitaries of every description here. This one was a Mosulee, educated at the Propaganda and a monsignore, as he wore a long black cloth garment doubled with purple; his tight sleeves and tunic were also purple. A handkerchief of black silk with a gold Maltese cross embroidered in front was on his head. At Mosul the last palm tree grows; it is carefully wrapped up with matting in the winter. Cucumbers grow to the length of six feet and two feet round! As the Pasha was collecting objects to be sent hence to the Paris Exhibition of 1867, we suggested that one of these cucumbers might be as wonderful as anything else! The underground portion of Mr. Rassam's house, whither he retires in summer, was very grand, resembling the crypt of some large church. Most of the good houses here are interiorly built of marble. The north part of the town rises gradually in hillocks. About two hundred yards down the river, we saw a square building with a high whitewashed wall pierced everywhere with windows, probably the barracks, or a sort of fort.

On the 15th we started again, the horsekeeper at first objected to the weight of our load, but soon gave in, not having a "locus standi." We recrossed the bridge, turning north; a small stream, here flowing into the Tigris, had its banks covered for some distance with—washerwomen! we rode over a very undulating country till sunset, crossing three little streams, and soon reached Ismael, a wretched little village with a still more wretched little post-house. We slept on the ground in a barn, whence we previously turned out two donkeys to make room for ourselves.

Next day, we rode over rough road to Zakoo, where an old castle on rising ground above the village contained the post-house; then we forded a large stream, and two others at intervals. At sunset we got amongst hills, when the surreje told us to ride on rapidly, as the road was in bad repute. Sure enough, we saw, down a ravine close to us, a lurid light, waving about in a cavern; however, the inmates, whoever they were, did not perceive us, and we reached the Tigris. Here we had to halloo across the stream for a kelek or raft. After a time one came over. It was about twelve feet square, of rough boards on inflated sheepskins. We left the horses to return without us, and were rowed across by two men. On the opposite side we found four horses and a man with a lantern awaiting us. In half an hour's walk we reached the post-house; it rained more or less all day, and the lighted fire there was grateful to us. The village was called Jezireh.

Leaving early, we mounted a little, and then came to an immense plain; the road was of the most appalling description, rendering any pace faster than a slow walk a moral and physical impossibility. It consisted of mud two feet or more in depth, with boulders scattered about so thickly, that there was only just room between them for the horses' hoofs to sink into the mire. This lasted, more or less, for thirty-six miles, a piercing north-easter blowing all the time. We passed the Turkish post, only two days late from Stamboul. Jezireh is under the government of a mudir—an officer inferior in rank to a Pasha and a Kaimacan—it is a telegraph station. The Indian traffic, for which a large sum was paid to the

Sultan's government, is sadly impeded by the trivial messages sent from one pasha or mudir to another. These are generally twenty words of compliments, then ten words of real business, and another twenty words of more compliments. We changed horses and rode along the same plain, but on a better road. The district appeared to us very populous, as there were a number of small isolated hills like large tumuli, scattered about at intervals of about three miles in every direction, and on the southern slope of each of them a Kurdish village was erected. However we were told that many of these were deserted, and formerly the whole region was devastated by Arab ghazus or forays, which still compel the post to make an immense circuit, as the whole road up to Zakoo is directly out of the straight direction to Diarbekir. We rode on another thirty-six miles after the change, till we crossed several branches of a stream on a causeway bridge without a parapet, and entered Nisibeen, where we slept.

20th. Still on the plain. We came to a ruined castle, which the surreje informed us was of early

Christian architecture, in reality dating from the Roman empire, having probably formed one of the frontier forts. We then turned off into a small by-path, to visit the great Roman fortress of Dara. It was built at the foot of a low rocky range of mountains, the first outskirts of the Antitaurus (?). The first impression conveyed to our minds was that we were approaching an immense ruined mass of hewn stones. We crossed a small stream just above a massive broken stone bridge, of thorough Roman solidity. Fifty yards higher up stood the remains of, probably, a dam, a wall some 100 feet high and 10 thick, of solid hewn stone facing, and rubble between; at the bottom were three arched openings, about eight feet across, probably sluices, as the holes for the hinges of the locks were still visible. Then the stream had broken through the wall, and in the portion on the left bank a miller had installed himself. Two hewn stone walls once formed a conduit on the bank to admit the water into the massive edifice, but now it enters by another aperture. This kind of mill is very common; for almost all the little streams are utilised in this way,—a portion of the water is carried along the bank in a conduit, till it is of sufficient height to allow of its pouring through the mill with sufficient force to turn the wheel. Fifty yards above the dam, another bridge of three arches spanned the stream, whose banks had been apparently confined by walls of hewn stones. From this bridge a magnificent road once wound up the eminence; now only a few traces remain to indicate its existence—a few steps here and there. Some columns were lying about, one standing some fifteen feet high and four round. Upon the low hill to which the road led, was a mass of buildings, something like a forum in shape. Some Corinthian capitals lay about.

Kurds have installed themselves in one part of the ruins, where a building with many fine broken arches is standing on the left bank of the stream. Some of the inhabitants now gathered around and offered to show us the principal remains. We acquiesced and followed one of them into an opening under the forum-shaped mass. This was a passage with sides of hewn stone. At the further end we turned to the right into a very dark passage where our conductor lighted a tallow candle. We soon came to some steps which led down along a hewn stone wall, a slight parapet was raised on the other side to prevent falling into a tremendous excavation that in Roman times was probably used as a granary. This formed a magnificent hall, supported by immense square pillars of hewn stone. The roof was arched, and a little light from the outer world just allowed the magnitude of the work to be seen. The hall appeared to be some 150 feet high, by 120 broad. At the sides little chambers were excavated, and walled with blocks of stone.

On emerging again, we purchased a quantity of copper coins, most of them of Justinian and Constantine. We now rode along the hills; where the quarries and catacombs in the rocks were distinctly visible. Sometimes one excavation had two little pillars and an arch cut in the rock for a doorway. In the quarries the stone was sometimes hewn in steps, presenting a very picturesque appearance.

Riding on, we gradually approached a high mountain, on which traces of houses were dimly discernible; as we drew nearer these became more distinct and we found them to constitute Mardeen, whither we were bound. The situation of this town was perhaps the most extraordinary we had ever seen. It was built more than half-way up a precipitous hill, along whose southern flank it extended for some mile or so, and up for half a mile—below the wall, a bleak rock to the plain. The houses rose one above the other, as it were in storeys, so that each possessed a view over the plain as far as the eye could stretch. The access to it was very difficult: we first went round a mountain below that on which stood the town, up a difficult path, until we came to a neck of land connecting the two hills, which we rode over, and entered the gate just an hour before sunset. The streets were ill-paved, and sometimes led over the roofs of the houses below.

Above the town the rocks rose quite perpendicularly, and a ruined fort was perched on the table-land at the top. We passed some fine Saracenic archways of friable stone, and after some trouble discovered Mr. Williams' house. This gentleman was a missionary of the American Presbyterian Church, whose head-quarters are in Boston, U.S. The society does a great deal of good amongst the Christian populations of Asia Minor. The Armenians are those who afford the greatest number of converts, the Jacobites and Nestorians also contributing. There is a congregation of these Protestants at Mosul, but that station is, with justice, deemed so unhealthy to Americans, that it is only occasionally visited, native preachers keeping the congregation together. Our host had to deplore the loss of three wives, each sacrificed to the climate in a very short time. His house contained an excellent classical and theological library; it was situated in the lower portion of the town. Having partaken of his hospitality for one night, we started again. The inhabitants, a turbulent set, amongst whom robbery and even murder is rife, boast that even the invincible Tamerlane had to turn from Mardeen without entering it. Now its walls are fast crumbling into ruins; indeed one need not go to a gate at all to get out; some of the mosques are very fine and solidly constructed. We rode along a bad rocky path, sometimes up, sometimes down, to Khanakee, twenty-four miles; no post-horses; so we baited our old ones for three hours. We had hardly proceeded half a dozen miles when darkness came upon us. We persevered for some time longer, and then, as the gates of Diarbekir are closed at sunset, and there is no admittance afterwards even on business, we put up in a wretched little village, Khan Achbar, in an outhouse boasting of a roof but not of very much more.

Next morning we rode gradually downwards over a road varying in badness, till we saw the Tigris again and rode along its right bank. Immediately above us, on our left, rose a high range. The snowclad Taurus loomed around us on the north-east and west. At length we came to where the road winds up to the gates of Diarbekir which stands on a flat hill overlooking the river. We passed by a good stone bridge, just before beginning to ascend; then the ruggedly paved road led us through gardens, in some of which stood Turkish villas, and in one the English Consulate.

Mr. Taylor has a somewhat extended field of usefulness as consul at Erzeroum and this place, and does not possess the gift of ubiquity; so being at Erzeroum he was not at Diarbekir! The road became very good for the last hundred yards, and passing a large graveyard on our left we entered the gate. The Tigris makes an immense bend just below the town; the portion of country included in the bend is most richly cultivated. We were most kindly received by Mr. Walker (to whom Mr. Williams had given us a letter) and introduced to his wife and a Miss West, a lady missionary, who had chosen this portion of Asia Minor as the field of her disinterested, and by no means thankless labours. The congregation, under Mr. Walker's charge numbered six hundred souls, and a third chapel was in course of construction, the two already in existence being too small to contain their increasing numbers. The members of the congregation, although generally very poor persons, supported their teachers and chapels to the utmost of their means; those who were too poor to contribute in money, worked at the construction of the new chapel.

We visited the chapels after breakfast on the 20th. One of them was in the shape of a cross, although not originally built for a place of worship. The larger was in the old Consulate and sadly in need of repairs. There was a separate room for the various books sent out by the English Bible Society, and those printed in New York in Armenian and Kurdish; the Bible was the first book ever printed in the Kurd tongue, which has properly no written language, the letters used for the purpose were Armenian. The principal languages employed were Caramanian, Turkish and Arabic, and many books, besides those of prayer, were translated into them. Amongst the rest, Bunyan's "Pilgrim's Progress" held the chief place. Whately's "Evidences," and other useful and instructive books came in for their share of popularity. A quantity of little children were at school near both the chapels. They were bright-looking little lads, worthy of Armenian parents, some of them were Jacobites. We entered the Jacobite church; it was a fast-day, and many women were worshipping—that is, going up to a money-box, putting a small coin inside, and having a large silver cylinder containing the hand of some saint rubbed over their heads and bodies. After this they went and knelt down in front of the centre shrine—a tawdry affair—whereupon the gates in front of it were closed by the attendant acolyte, and the women offered up prayers that they might be opened to them again, which after a short space they were! The church is a very old one. The patriarch's house is good, with hewn stone porticoes.

We then walked to the old walls, of massive hewn stone and immense solidity, containing within their thickness the rooms for the garrison and their stores in case of siege. They are said to date from the time of Constantius, and they have only four gates, one for each point of the compass. The stone of which they are built is dark; there are towers at stated intervals; crenelated parapets and a moat hewn in the rock all round; covered ways inside. We afterwards entered the courts of two mosques, both of stone. The first had a splendid portico in front of it, and on two sides of the court of the other, were columnar walls of great age and beautifully executed. This is said to have been an old Christian church in days when there were caliphs in Bagdad; the mosque was on one side. The appearance of the whole is equal to that of the best preserved Roman ruins. The pillars in the walls support arches, and over these there is another set of arches and pillars. Probably these two remaining walls formed those of some covered space— perhaps of a basilica—there are almost one hundred yards between the two. On the left some lower columns support the third wall. One of the mosques we passed reminded us, by its hexagonal form and alternate layers of black and white marble, of some churches in Milan. The minarets looked as like a gigantic candle with an extinguisher on the top as possible. The lower part was square, of stone, then a large tube-like concern was painted white, and the angular roof was of tin or iron. The superintendent of telegraphs here was an Englishman, married to an Italian wife. We visited them, and met there an Italian doctor M. Arrivabene, and the French consul, M. Pons. The sultan has ordered a road practicable for carriages to be made from Samsoun on the Black Sea (whither we are bound) to this place, each pashalick is to bear its share of the expenses and to construct its portion of the road. This order has had the effect of causing about two miles of road to be made outside Diarbekir—then it stops. One of the streets, leading to the northern gate, is broad and fairly paved. The houses being all built of stone, look much more decent than in any other town we had yet seen. Some of them have overhanging lattice windows. The bazaar is very intricate; the principal portion is of gridiron shape—several galleries parallel, and cross arcades—the stock pretty good. We saw two Circassians; they have come here in large numbers, flying from Russia, and are immediately sent down to colonise a ruined city on the border of the mountain land, where they will serve as a barrier against the Arabs. In this town telegraphic messages are received for transmission, in French, Italian, German, and English. The local Turkish and through-Indian lines were in separate rooms in the same building. A third wire had lately been put up to Constantinople; but as for the greater portion of the way it lacked insulators, of course it did not work! When we were there the communication with India was very perfect; a message only took twelve hours to Akyab, on the east coast of India.

On the 23rd we took a walk outside the Stamboul gate, and on our return, sat down on a low stool just outside—where an itinerant coffee and narghilè vendor had established himself—to indulge in a portion of his stock. Close at hand rose a wonderful contrivance for preserving ice during the whole of the intense summer heats: a hole is dug, not very deeply into the ground; in this ice in blocks is symmetrically arranged, rising some feet above the ground, then it is covered over with about five feet depth of chopped straw, and the thing is done; to get at it, the proprietor has only to poke a hole in the straw and take out as much ice as he requires.

An American story: a very fat man was hurrying to get into the gates of some city, which were closed at a certain hour. Fearful that he should be late, he asked of a passer-by whether he should be able to get into the gates in time? "Wall," quoth the addressed, "I guess you might; a load of hay passed through this morning!"

One of the missionaries that we met during our journey suggested that the best means of saving life in America would be to hang a few prominent Southerners!

On the 23rd, we started out of the Stamboul gate past an extensive cemetery, on a good road for two miles (the two made by way of going to Samsoun!) We rode over an elevated plateau for some thirty miles, and got amongst some low hills, when we soon saw Arganah, our changing-station, perched up on a projecting hill. Above rose another higher one, upon which a sort of large guardhouse was built some 2,000 feet over our heads. We found the post, by no means one of the lowest houses in the village. Having changed horses we had to get down the hill again only to mount another one, and yet another, till on reaching a crest of hills, a panorama of great wildness lay stretched out before us; a series of conical mountains, some seemingly below us, some as high, and all of the most varied colours, red and brown, black and yellow, in endless succession. After sunset we passed a smelting-furnace for copper. There were several mines of this metal near Maadan, a village of some extent, where we stopped in a tolerably clean post-house.

On the 24th we started at half-past 6 A.M., and rode up a very steep mountain, with much snow about; then a steeper descent. Indeed, now the road seemed to go up high mountains for the sole purpose of coming down again. Unfortunately there is no other road; the scenery was startlingly wild, the colouring magnificent. After some time we came to a lake some twenty-five miles in circumference, with very blue water reflecting the snow-covered mountains. We rode along the northern shore and up a hill. On arriving at the summit we looked down into a mountain-locked plain, much below the level of the lake, with several villages scattered over its surface. We descended, and rode across it, through three villages. Here civilisation first stared us in the face in the shape of a common cart, like the plaustra of Persia. We had seen nothing on wheels since leaving Teheran. We passed some decent whitewashed barracks, surrounded by a wall pierced with windows, and were in Mazrah. About six miles off to the right, we saw Kharpoot, situated somewhat like Mardeen on a hill. It is a great American missionary station, and we passed it with some qualms of conscience, as it was the only place in Asia which, containing civilised beings (one cannot call them Europeans!) we had not visited. There is a large seminary, where converts are educated to be native preachers and teachers. The streets of Mazrah betokened awakening civilisation, probably owing to the proximity of this station. Some of the houses had wooden arched doorways with windows on each side, evidently new, and resembling some streets in German villages. Indeed, over one shop we observed "Pharmacie" written up in French! We were constrained to stop here, as they would not give us horses, these being wanted for the post, which was expected to pass hourly. We slept in a stable some fifty yards long by twenty broad, the roof supported by stems of trees in two rows; some fifteen horses were tied to the wall on either side; a little raised platform of mud constituted our bedstead. During the night sleep was rather out of the question; we had long ceased to care about fleas, but the horses kept us awake by the noise they made. Five men also slept about the stables; they appeared to be up, more or less, all night, wrangling and fighting at intervals. In the morning we had a great squabble about the number of horses to be taken. The postman said four; we said three—our usual number. Eventually three were agreed upon, and we got off at half-past six, riding over picturesque mountainous country. We suddenly came upon another portion of the projected carriage-road, skirting a mountain above a brawling torrent. It was really very well Macadamized, and blasted through portions of rock, but ended abruptly; thus, of course, being of no possible use, except to accelerate the speed of horses over some four miles of ground; then a very bad bit of road, where a sort of pavement had been attempted, led us into Maadan Gunish, where there was a silver mine, whose produce certainly did not seem to flow into the pockets of the inhabitants, as there were many deserted and half ruined houses in the village. There was a good mosque, however, with a portico in front, and a dome covered with iron plates. The minaret was of hewn stone, and the balustrade from which the muezzins call the faithful to prayers, was adorned with carved pomegranates. The silver mine was not being worked when we passed; perhaps it was exhausted. Leaving this, after changing horses, we crossed the Euphrates in a rough ferry-boat. The river here made a bend, and the stream formed two backwaters, one at each bank, thus facilitating its crossing immensely. On again till sunset, when the surreje informed us that he had lost the way. We tried back, and then made for the first village that we could discover, where we got a guide to our station, Argooan Dagh, which, fortunately, was nigh at hand. Fifteen hours and sixty miles.

Next day we rode over the usual picturesque country, and on a good road. After changing our horses, and mounting some small ponies, we got into snowy districts; patches of snow lay on the ground, and the mountains covered with it gathered close around us. We reached Allaje Khan one hour after sunset, a baiting-station, where we stopped, as the road was very bad; fifty-seven miles, twelve hours and three quarters. Just before arriving we met another Turkish post, reduced to the commonest of walks by the badness of the road. It had no escort.

On the 27th, starting early, we rode over high ground with a good deal of snow here and there. After eighteen miles, we came to some that lay extended for the next nine miles, a narrow path serpentined through it, so that if the horse stepped off, he immediately sank into about three feet of snow. The glare of the sun was trying to the eyes. Reaching Delekli Dash, a wretchedly cold-looking village, we changed our ponies for capital horses, and soon got out of the snow by a rapid descent. Then we rode rapidly on over a good road, till half an hour before sunset, just after our horse had tumbled with us into the mud, we sighted Seevas, lying in a plain by the river Kizzil Irmak or Halys; we were on a high point, whence we could see it well. Thence descending, we crossed a long bridge, then two smaller ones, and got into the town as night fell. The river had much overflowed its banks, so that the road into the town was covered with water. After some search, we found Mr. West, the missionary physician's house. He himself had gone to Kaisaryeh to the S.W., but a Mr. Bryant and his wife were in the house, and Mrs. West most kindly put us up. This is also an American Presbyterian station, and three families live here.

In the morning we walked through the town with Mr. Bryant. We went to an old mosque, in front of which stood two magnificent Alhambresque gateways, richly carved in Saracenic ornamentation. Opposite these another sculptured gateway led into a court surrounded by massive hewn stone arched buildings. Under one of these there were some tombs. This town is supposed to be the Sebaste of Mithridates. An old citadel stands on an eminence above the town; the old town walls still partially stand; they were evidently built upon still older foundations, as bits of sculptured stone are promiscuously stuck into them. In the midst of the town stands a very strong stone gateway, with two iron folding doors at each end; in the space between there are some dark underground dungeons with loopholes for windows looking out into the street. We next walked into the bazaar. The principal products of Seevas are woollen stockings, carpets, and extremely pretty plaited straw-work, only used to ornament pipe-stems. Some of the shops were quite civilised; that is, had their stock exposed at windows, and were on each side of an uncovered street. Portions of the bazaar reminded us of the fair at Nijni Novgorod. Wooden porticoes ran in front of wooden shops. The arabas, or rough carts, in the streets, contribute to give the town the appearance of factitious civilisation. Seevas is 3700 feet above the level of the Black Sea. The population is considered to amount to 75,000, though returned at 50,000 for this reason—the number of inhabitants is always returned as low as possible, as the taxes vary according to the population. We called on the Italian superintendent of telegraphs, and he very kindly gave us a letter for the Russian Consul at Samsoun, where there is no English functionary.

We started again on the 20th, and rode up the hills on the N.W. The road took us over high ground and was rather bad; we stopped at Kakheen in a decent room, though the village seemed poor. Next day over a stony mountain; we met the weekly post to Seevas; this is sent on from post to post, without any special Tatar to accompany it, the sole escort being the surreje and one policeman. The latter came back with us, and left the post to its fate and the postilion. We saw the ruts made by many carts plainly on the road now, and rode on to Tokat by an abrupt descent. All the houses there, like most of those at Seevas, were covered with tiles, giving the village quite a Swiss appearance when seen from a distance. It is encircled by mountains excepting on the north side. As we descended, we emerged from winter into spring; the fruit-trees were in blossom and the grass growing; a rapid river ran by the town and then into a broad valley along which lay our road, where we met many Circassians going into the interior. We had to wait an hour for horses, as their proprietor had very properly gone to church, and very improperly left no one in charge of them. We passed two Saracenic portals and several ancient cut stone buildings in the village; the bridge over the river was of the same material and also very old. After about four hours' riding, we came to another portion of the carriage road, here on comparatively level ground; it only consisted of the mud dug out of two deep trenches about twenty-one yards apart, and flung in between them; an excellent khan with glass windows, and of two storeys, was built by its side. We could not stop there, however, as it was not the post-house; but continuing our ride we soon turned off abruptly, and reached Toorkal by a cross road, the regular track being inundated; we had to ford a considerable stream just before coming to the village, and found even the post-house yard covered with water; twelve hours and a quarter; fifty-one miles.

Starting at half-past five o'clock next morning, we made for the north, coming again upon the carriage road for about 100 yards. This portion of road may be some five miles long altogether. We now galloped up branching valleys; the mountain sides began to be covered with dwarf oak, birch, and a species of fir; up an abrupt ascent, and down more gradually into a widening valley. Here there were plenty of orchards, with each a villa possessing a tiled roof but otherwise in fearful *dis*-repair, as they were built of a wooden framework with unburnt mud bricks laid in between; these had generally crumbled away, leaving large gaps, and sometimes only the woodwork. The road now turned to the right up a valley; on both sides the mountains rose abruptly. We rode along another piece of good carriage road, with orchards between us and the hill on our right-hand and a rapid river on our left; orchards again on the other side of the river, reminded us forcibly of some roads in the mountainous parts of Germany. The variegated blossoms on the fruit trees and the spring flowers all around, with the tiled houses peeping out, gave the place an extra look of Europe. At length, bending round a corner, we entered Amasiyeh, where we observed several carved remains of antiquity, especially Saracenic gateways, and one massive square building with round towers at each corner. The first houses were in a sad state of decay. There is a flourishing German colony here, and we observed a cart with *spoked* wheels. Further on the houses were very good. The town is situated somewhat like Tiflis, with a rapid river running in the midst of it, but the hills are closer together, and higher on the west, where there are artificial caves sculptured in the rock, singularly carved in imitation of the front of a house and an old castle of stone on the summit. Here we had an adventure. We changed horses and started again, but had not got far when the postman came running after us, to say that we had got one wrong horse, and he must take it back; we, rather feebly, acquiesced. After waiting in the street for about twenty minutes, the man returned, bringing the very same horse back again, whereupon Awa attacked him with a heavy riding-whip and beat him severely, much to our dismay, as a crowd immediately gathered around us, and the head-postman, a tall powerful individual of about six feet three, coming up, endeavoured to pull Awa off his horse. In this he did not succeed, but a policeman who came up insisted that we should go before the Pasha; so we were ignominiously led across a wooden bridge to a large house consisting of three storeys, where we passed through a large hall crowded with Turks, up a double flight of stairs into an antechamber. After waiting here for about half an hour, we were ushered into the presence. The Pasha sat on a divan in a small room, with several other men. We handed him our bulti, or road-order and general certificate of respectability that the Pasha of Bagdad had given us, and, after hearing the aggrieved man and our servant, he said, very justly, that he thought the best plan would be to make the man a small present. This we accordingly did, whereupon the postman kissed Awa with effusion, and we rode on, having been detained one hour and a half. The good road wound through delicious orchards for about four miles, when we began to ascend a lofty hill. At the summit a thick mist, resembling the palmiest of London November fogs, gathered round us, and night came on. The road also became execrable as we sank in deep mud at every step. However, everything comes to an end, and we reached Eladick where we got a good room with glass windows. In the morning we observed a fine mosque in the village.

On the 1st of April we started for our last day's ride in Asia Minor. We rode along a mountainous country, through woods, where the ground was carpeted with primroses, anemones, violets, and every sort of wild flower. The road was perhaps the worst of our whole journey; it took us seven hours to accomplish the first twenty-four miles, and it rained torrents during four of them, thus rendering our last also one of our hardest days. At length we rode down into a little valley, through which flowed a stream that we could see emptied itself into the Black Sea; then ascending to the top of the opposite hill, we beheld long-looked-for Samsoun, and the Black Sea stretched calmly in front of the town. A steamer was at anchor in the roadstead.* Samsoun is delightfully situated on the slope of the green hill down which we were riding, but is terribly given to fevers in summer. There are many decent houses in it. We first attempted to discover some inn to put up at, but ineffectually, so we rode out to the Russian vice-consulate. This stands to the East of the town, outside, and near the other consulates. Although we neither belonged to his own nation nor to that for which he acted, Chevalier J. Cacaci received us most cordially. He was a Greek by birth, and his brother served as dragoman in the English army before Sebastopol.

In the morning we were intensely surprised by seeing, coming up the stairs, no other than Mr. Walton, our host of Ispahan. He was going home on sick leave, so we of course immediately

---

* For list of stations and distances from Bagdad to Samsoun see page 394.

booked a passage on board the "Neva," of the "Messageries Impériales," the ship in which he had come from Trebizond. We found that as far as ships went we were in luck, for she was a large vessel built for the Mediterranean passenger trade, and had first-class accommodation for about one hundred passengers; but, on the other hand, she had been ordered by telegraph to go back to Tireboli, a short distance from Trebizond, to take on board the passengers of a smaller ship, the "Orient," which had met with a misadventure. She would not call here on her way back, so we were constrained to make the extra trip with her, and to perform twenty-seven hours' longer sea journey than necessary. After all, she called at Samsoun to take up four passengers.

We coaled at Sinope, a magnificent harbour; a promontory juts out into the sea, forming a land-locked bay, protected from all but N.E. winds, which never blow hard. The town itself, surrounded by an old wall, is built on the neck of the promontory, so that after lying for some while in the bay, and then steaming out of it, on rounding the point we again saw the town on the other side. We called at Ineboli just in time to find that a Russian steamer had embarked sixty-five deck passengers destined for us. The fare on board was excellent and the prices a lesson to the English steamers in the East. Most of the deck passengers were taken on board by contract. Some man collects a quantity of poor labourers at the different ports, and then brings them on board, paying their passages, and accompanying them on the ship. These people generally have not even money to buy their scanty food, which is supplied by the contractor. On arriving at Stamboul, they are taken on shore and securely locked up. Then when any labour-owner wants workmen, he comes and chooses out of their number as many as he may require, paying the man who brought them over their passages and all other expenses, which he afterwards deducts from their pay by instalments—a sort of organized traffic in labour!

Our passage of three days and nights was perfectly calm; indeed the Black Sea is always more or less so from the months of April to

October, making up for it, however, in the winter.

At length we entered the far-famed Bosphorus. The weather was cold, and the sun did not shine brightly, but nothing is able entirely to efface from the mind the impression of extreme beauty left upon it by the scene, which fortunately has been oft described. We obtained our certificate of health at the quarantine office, near the entrance, and steamed through the twenty-three miles of green hills with villas dotted along them on both shores. We passed twenty magnificent palaces belonging to the Sultan. It is said that whenever he gets any spare cash into his hands, he immediately sets about building a new one, possibly thinking that the money thus laid out does him as an individual, more good than it would if diffused over a larger field, in improving his government.

After casting anchor in the magnificent harbour between Pera and Stamboul, we were rowed in a small boat to the custom-house, where everything was searched and nothing found. We, of course, made for Misseri's Hotel in the Grande

Rue de Pera, where we were soon comfortably installed. We observed that riding was the fashionable mode of transport; the streets were so badly paved that the few carriages we saw, resembling Lord Mayor's coaches as they might have been constructed two hundred years ago, had a hard time of it. Sedan chairs have found their last refuge in Pera! The view from the Galata tower is one of the most magnificent sights in the world. The Grande Rue was lighted with gas, and the adjoining streets were allowed the same lights to the length of one hundred yards, when utter darkness was only relieved by an occasional dim oil lamp. We crossed over to Stamboul on one of the two bridges of boats, and explored the bazaars. The number of windings in the arcades almost rendered Ariadne's twine necessary as a guide to find our way back. Some gauzes, embroidered with silk, were perfectly lovely; and every kind of embroidery was, of course, seen to great perfection there.

A very creditable Italian Opera company sang in one of the theatres at Pera whilst we were there. We occupied ourselves during ten days very pleasantly. The weather on the 12th of April was quite warm, with a southerly wind. However, having brought our reader again into Europe, we take leave of him, as our further journey, by Kustendje and the Danube to Vienna and London, presented nothing calling for special notice, and we stopped nowhere on our road, being glad to get back again to old England! Vale!

List referred to in page 388.

List of Stations and Distances from Bagdad to Samsoun, with occasional remarks for the use of any future travellers. Three miles are reckoned to the hour :—

NO.	STATIONS.	HOURS.	REMARKS.
	Bagdad:		
1	Jedida	7	
2	Yengiyeh	6	
3	Delli Abbas	9	
4	Kara Teppa	9	Crossing Hamaram ravines
5	Kifri	7	
6	Tooz Khurmati	10	
7	Taough	7	
8	Kirkook	9	
9	Altoon Kupri	9	
10	Arbil	12	
11	Zab	7	Boat ferry
12	Mosul	9	
		101 hours	
13	Ismael	12	
14	Zakoo	9	Two hours for pass
15	Jezireh	12	Tigris, raft ferry
16	Deroomah	12	
17	Nisibeen	12	
18	Mardeen	12	
19	Khanakee	8	Baiting station
20	Diarbekir	10	
		87 hours	

LIST OF STATIONS AND DISTANCES (*continued*).

NO.	STATIONS.	HOURS.	REMARKS.
21	Arganah.	12	
22	Maadan	4	Copper mines
23	Kharpoot	12	In reality Mazrah
24	Maadan Gunish	10	Euphrates, boat ferry, copper and silver mines
25	Argooan Dagh	10	
26	Hassan Killekee	12	
27	Delekli Dash	16	Bad road
28	Seevas	10	
29	Kakheen	9	
30	Tokat	9	
31	Toorkal	8	
32	Amasiyeh	12	Road branches to Scutari (Stamboul)
33	Eladick	8	
34	Kawak	6	
35	Samsoun	8	146 hours

Total hours, 334; miles, 1002. Steamers three times a week to Stamboul. Samsoun is the ancient Amisus.

INDEX.

Abada, p. 267
Accommodation at Khunsakh, 88
Achmedi, 315
Acquaintance, a casual, 106
Adventure, W.'s railway, 14
Agent, British, at Ispahan, 249
Allaje Khan, 379
Alexander's Bridge, 336
Alison, Mr., 206
Amasiyeh, 385
Ameenabad, 266
Amusements of Armenian pilgrims, 160
Ananoor, 122
Anecdote, an, 356
Antelope, 245
Aptarasseen, 208
Ararat, first glimpse of, 149·50; last, 173
Araxes river, 172
Arbil, 352
Arch of Chosrocs, 337
Architecture, Saracenic, 119; at Tiflis, 124; Alhambresque, 126
Ardon river, 106
Arganah, 374
Argooan Dagh, 378
Ark, the Shah's palace, 226
Armenia, King of, 161
Armenian character, 122; costume, 134; cunning, 145; pilgrims, 160; priest's dress, 156
Armenians, revolt of, 161;
Armour, Ispahan, 249
Arpachi river, 166
Artesh Goor, the, 262
Artillery, camel, 211
Ascent, an, 306
Asia Minor, 368; last day's ride in, 387; wonderful journey in, 294

Astrachan, 44—63
Awa Baba, our Persian servant, 135

Babylon, ruins of, 341—5
Baggage, trouble with, 75
Bagdad, 339
Bagh i No, 291; i Tacht, 292; Nazaar, 302
Bahren, Island of, 319
Bakers, German, in Tiflis, 134
Bakoo, naphtha springs, 51
Bakshish, 175
Ballroom, largest in Europe, 9
Banians, 319
Banks of Volga, 30
Barasgoon, 315
Bariatinsky, Prince, 83
Barjgar, 285
Barge, passenger on Volga, 63
Barracks, Turkish, 345
Bassora, 230—3
Bastinado, the, 259
Bazaar at Astrachan, 54
Beach at Petrovskoi, 66
Beedush, 243
"Bints," W.'s term for women, 30
Bir Noos, 346
Birs Nimroud, 344
Black Sea, 388—91
Bokhara lambskins, 54
Bosphorus, the, 391
Botlick, fever's home, 92—4
Boulevard, Tiflis, 129
Bread, Tartar, 81
Brewery, French, at Tiflis, 136
Bridge, Alexander's, 336; at Ispahan, 247; in Daghestan, 87; over Kur, 130
Brigands near Istibulleh, 143
Bug Meeanee, 184

INDEX.

Bund Ameer, 284
Busheer, 316—27
" Bust," taking, 239, 252

Caliphs, City of the, 339
Camelthorn, the, 244
Canauts in Persia, 180
Caravanserai, a ruined, 176
Cashan, copper bazaar, 240
Caspian Sea, distance from Nijui, 25 ; on the, 64 ; tame fish in the, 67
Cat at Preschiskaya, 116
Catholicos of Armenians, 155, 251
Caucasus, languages of, 86 ; mineral capabilities of, 85 ; first day's travelling in, 67 ; view in, 76
Cay, 186
Cazbek, 119 ; height of, 120
Cazveen, 201
Chaldean Catholic, bishop, 356 ; our servant, 150
Chappar Khanee, a, 264
Char Bagh, the, 246
Chatham Hotel, 1
Chehel Sittoon, Ispahan, 256
Chenarada, 295
Chodjakias, 189
Chosroes, Arch of, 337
Christmas Day, 1865, 275 ; Eve, 271
Church at Astrachan, 47 ; Etchmiadzcen. 157 ; Ispahan, 250
Churchyard at Tiflis, 133
Circassians on the Volga, 29
Coins, old, 294
Constantinople, 392
Constitution, the Polish, 17
Convention, telegraphic, 233
Corn thrashing in the Caucasus, 69
Cosmein, 339
Cossacks, various, in Russian army, 44
Cothul i Dochter, 299 ; i Gamarej, 309 ; i Mulloo, 312 ; i Pierazan, 297
Cotton trade, 295
Crown of Persia, 232
Ctesiphon, 337
Cuneiform inscriptions, 282
Cunning of Armenians, 145
Curiosity dealers at Ispahan, 252

Custom-house in Persia, 176 ; Russia, 174
Cyrus, tomb of, 273

Daghestan, 70 ; ancient name of, 70 ; governor of, 66 ; Niello work, 86 ; scenery in, 80
Dalachy, 314
Dam in Persia, 241
Danadgar, 189
Dantzick, 3, 4
Dara, ruins of, 362—4
Darahleglass, 149
Dariel, defile of, 119
Decorations of Shah's palace, Teheran, 223
Defence, a gallant, 321
Dehbeed, 269
Del Cason, an orange garden, 290
Delekli Dash, 379
Demavend, 205 ; height of, 217
Deria Caveer, great salt desert, 237
Deriehnoor, the Shah's diamond, 232
Derivation, a, 198
Descent, an abrupt, 299
Devil's Elbow, the, 334
Diarbekir, 367—73
Dijillah, the, 237
Dillijan, 143 ; detention at, 146
Dinner, a Russian, 19 ; at Teheran, 206, 226
Diplomatic difficulty, a, 210, 224
Don, champagne of the, 56
Drawback of Persian towns, 234
Drill at Astrachan, 46
Drunkenness, 17

Eagles in Caucasus, 80
Echo in chasm, 87
Ecclesiastical dignitaries, 356
Eden, Garden of, 333
Eeliaut encampment, 194
Eladick, 387
Elbrouz, Mount, 105—111 ; view of, 115
Elburz Mountains, 203
End, the, 393
English, company of Volga, 29 ; gathering at Ispahan, 253 ; products in Georgia, 121
Erivan, 152 ; leave, 164

Escort in the Caucasus, 74; in Georgia, 145; a singing, 75; new, 86
Etchmiadzeen, 154—163
Euphrates, the, 378
Export duty in Turkey, 347
Ezra, tomb of, 333

Fair at Nijni, 26
Fao, 329
Fatima the Immaculate, 238
Fire brigade, Astrachan, 48
Fireworks at Teheran, 206
Fish in Volga, 33
Fley Fley, romantic story of, 336
Ford, a, 313
Fort, old Georgian, 131
Fuel at Urmah, 77
Futteh Ali Shah, portraits of, 255; tomb, 238

Gaiamee, a female missionary, 162
Galata tower, 392
Gardens, public, at Tiflis, 137
Georgia, entrance into, 119
German colony at Amasiyeh, 385; at Tiflis, 128
German Bakers, 134
Gez, 254
Gezd, 245
Gooitcha lake, or Sievan, 148
Goolaheck, 218
Governor, the, of Astrachan, 49; his salary, 49; of Daghestan, 66
Gounib, 81; ascent of, 81; flora of, 84; Schamyl's defence of, 82; spot of surrender, 83; summit, 84
Grapes at Cazveen, 202
Grazzini, our servant, 28; his lament, 90, 96; his notion of geography, 79
Grosna, 100

Hadjala, 189
Hadjelmachi, 80; women's dress at, 80
Hafiz, tomb of, 191
Halys, the, 380
Hamadan wine, 237
Hamaram ravines, 349
Hare hunting, 244

Haroun al Rashid's wife's tomb, 340
Hasht Behesht, the, 263
Hassarkoobad, 203
Hats, Kalmuck, 58
Hens, ill-treatment of, 30
Hermitage at St. Petersburg, 5
Hilleh, 343
Hoopooids, 108
Hotel at Astrachan, 44; at Dantzick, 3; at Erivan, 152; at Moscow, 27; at Naxshivan, 168; at Nijni, 24; at St. Petersburg, 4; de l'Europe at Tiflis, 125; Misseri's, 391
Houses in Caucasian villages, 69, 70
Houssein, tomb of, 340
Housseinabad, 235
Houz i Sultaun, 237
Hulver, 254

Ibrahim, shrine of, 235
Ice at Diarbekir, 373
Ilandagh, 167
Illuminations at St. Petersburg, 10
Ineboli, 390
Insects in our room at Astrachan, 51
Interview, a ceremonial, 289
Invitation, a Persian, 226
Ismael, 359
Ispahan, 246—63
Issavodsk springs, 114
Istibulleh, 143; brigands, 143
Isvodskys, Russian drivers, drunken, 116
Italian opera in Tiflis, 125

Jacobite church, 370
Jellanook, dried fish, 148
Jetty at Petrovskoi, 65
Jewels, the crown, of Persia, 229—33
Jewellers at Tiflis, 135
Jews in Dantzick, 4
Jezireh, 360
Joolfa in Persia 247; in Russia, 173

Kabardians, 112
Kabobs, mutton, 90
Kahetic wine, 168
Kaisaryeh, 380

Kakheen, 382
Kalamdaun, Persian writing-case, 171
Kaleoun, water pipe, 176
Kalmucks, encampment of, 43; visit to, 58—63
Kara Teppa, 350
Karg or Karrick, 319
Kasan, 31
Kasr, the, 342
Kat Koder, a, 267
Kauzaroon, 302
Kefyeh, Arab headdress, 324
Kerbelah, 340
Kerman, 253
Kerstch, room in Hermitage, 6
Khanakee, 367
Khana Khora, 269
Khan al Hassan, 340
Kharpoot, 376
Khauna Zenyoon, 296
Khelaut Shah, 188
Khodabundeh, Mohammed Shah, 198—201
Khorsabad, ruins of, 355
Khunsakh, 87; lodgings at, 88
Kiare river, 107
Kinara, 279
Kirkook, 351
Kislovodsk, 113; springs, 114
Kizzil Irmak, the, 380
Kohrood, 242
Komishah, 265
Koom, the "abode of the pious," 238
Koorumderah, 201
Konar Tachta, 310
Kour Ab river, 284
Kremlin at Astrachan, 56; Moscow, 13; Nijni, 25
Kreuzberg, the, in Georgia, 121
Kumeenabad, 275
Kumuk, 70
Kunperkalieff, 68
Kur, the river, 123, 132
Kurdish encampment, 194
Kutellamara, 337
Kutishi, 78

Ladder, the great, of Persia, 298
Lake, small, in Caucasus, 94
Laziness, Oriental, 135
Lepers, 193
Lesghians, 83; their houses, 89

Library at Etchmiadzeen, 159
List of stations between Bagdad and Samsoun, 394
Locomotion, means of, in Persia, 189
London, leaving, 1
Louse market at Moscow, 19

Maadan, 375
Maadan Gunish, 378
Macdonald's, Sir J., tomb, 157
Madre e Suleiman, 278
Maidan at Ispahan, 248
Majellibè, 341
Malek el Most, 236
Marble, white, in Daghestan, 88
Mardeen, 365
Margil, 331
Mayar, 264
Mazrah, 376
Medressa at Ispahan, 248, 255
Meeanee, bug, 184; arrival at, 190
Melka, river, 107; tollgate, 109
Merand, first sleeping station in Persia, 177
Merdusht, plain of, 279
Meskeen, 201
Mian Cothul, 297
Minarets, shaking, 267
"Mineral Waters" at Petrovskoe, 10
Mirza, a Persian title, 288
Missionaries, Presbyterian, 366—8; success at Bagdad, 347
Mohammedan tombs, 68; mosque at Tiflis, 132
Mohammud, 329
Monastery, Troitza, 18
Money, Persian, 183
Montefick Arabs, 329
Moorchacoor, 244
Moorgaub, search for, 271
Moscow, 13—19
Mosque at Diarbekir, 371
Mosul, 353
Mountains near Piatigorsk, 112
Mujicks, 24, 30
Museum, Berlin, 2

Naclowzum, river, 195
Naksh i Rustam, 305
Names cut at Persepolis, 282
Nationalities, mixed, at Moscow, 21; at Nijni, 27

Natives near Vladikavkas, 118
Naxshivan, 167—70
Nazrah, 102
Nebbi Junas, 353
Neekbash, 194
Nestorian bishop, a, 357
New Year's Day, 293; Eve, 290
Niello work, 86
Nijni Novgorod, 24; the fair, 26
Nimroud, ruins of, 355
Nineveh, ruins of, 353
Nisibeen, 367
Norooz, Persian New Year's Day, 227
Numismatist, a, 294
"Nux" in Persia, 267

Oka, river, 24
Oman, sea of, 319
Ooch Killeasea, another name for Etchmiadzeen, 154; West church, 161; East church, 162
Ooroomeah, 192
Orange trees, 287
Orchards at Astrachan, 58
Ordy, 336

Padarojna, our, 22
Palace at Ispahan, 257
Palm trees, demanded by British public, 37; at Fao, 330
Pasagarda, ruins of, 272—3
Pasangoor, 240
Pasha of Amasiyeh, the, 386
Pavement, a spasmodic, 193
Pearls, 230, 319
Pedometer, 73; its last functions, 79
P**l's waterproof boots, 243
Pera, 392
Persepolis, pillars from, at Teheran, 222; first view of, 279; the platform, 282—4
Persia, first view of, 172; first sleeping station in, 177; farewell to, 327
Persian decorations, 171; excitability 325; executioners, 208; frontier, 173; insect powder, 38; painting on wood, 249; passenger on the Volga steamer, 33; scribes, 171

Peter the Great's statue, 6; his house, 8
Peterhoff palace, 7; fountains, 8
Petrovskoi, 64; landing at, 65; posthouse, 66; town, 65
Piatigorsk, 105; "Baden of the East," 109—13
Picturesqueness, why incompatible with cleanliness? 17
Pigs on Volga, 30
Pilgrims, Armenian, 156
Piratical junk, a, 324.
Ploughing in Armenia, 151
Plumpudding in Persia, 278
Policeman, a, 21
Polish constitution, 17
Poole Dullak, the barber's bridge, 237
Porcupine, taste of, 254
Post from England to Tiflis, 130; horses in Persia, 175
Prayers, Kalmuck, 60—1
Presbyterian missionaries, 366—8
Preschiskaya pheasants, 116
Priests, Kalmuck, 59; Russian, 20; procession of, 20
Printing press at Etchmiadzeen, 159
Prussian railways, 2
"Pylæ Caucasiæ," the, 120

Races in Teheran, 209—14
Railways in Russia, 14, 23; in Caucasus, 127
Ramadan, the, 330
Recsheer, 320
Religion of Kalmucks, 60
Religious toleration in Russia, 53
Repairs for palaces at Ispahan, 256
Repsimah, a female missionary, 162
Residency at Busheer, the, 317
Revolution at Abada, 267
Rhè, ruins of, 216
Riding, of Lesghians, 79
Riots in Tiflis, 138
Roads in Russia, 104—8
Romanoff House, 17
Room, our, on Christmas day 1865, 276
Royston, letters of Lord, 32

2 D

Ruins of Babylon, 341—5 ; Dara, 362 ; Pasagarda, 272—3 ; Shapoor, 303
Russian, Mission at Teheran, 209, querist, a, 114

Saadi, tomb of, 290
Sadarack, 165
Sadowa, 303
Salahlee, 142
Samara, 35
Samovar, Russian tea urn, 142
Samsoun, 388
Saracenic architecture, 119, 380
Saratoff, 38
Sarepta, German colony of, 42
Scenery in Daghestan, 80
Schamyl, songs in honour of, 75 ; a patriot, 81 ; prison of, 83 ; at Videne, 96
Schkootes, barges on the Volga, 36
Scorpion's bite, 295
Sculpture at Persepolis, 283 ; at Shapoor, 304
Seevas, ancient Sebaste, 380-2
Sein-Sein, 240
Sengarood river, 255
Sepah Salar, the commander in chief, 225
Serfs belonging to the Governor of Astrachan, 49
Servant, our Italian, 28 ; Joseph Seffer, 136
Shah, palace of, 207, 221—4 ; Nusreddin, 212 ; Abdulazeen, 216 ; Abbas, 257
Shapoor, 303
Sharshan, 194
Shat el Arab river, 328
Sheah heresy, the, 207
Shibookli, a station on lake, 148
Ships, decayed at Astrachan, 55
Shiraz, first view of, 285 ; height of, 262 ; tobacco, 176
Shoolgestaun, 266
Shrimps four inches long, 225
Sichau, animals, 194
Sievan Killeassa, on Lake Gooitcha, 148
Simonoff monastery, 15
Simon Stylites, a Caucasian, 107
Sinope, 389
Slipsowsky, 101

Smoking in Moscow, 20
Snoring fowl, a, 236
Soldatsky, why called so, 116
Songs of escort in the Caucasus, 75
Soofianeh, 178
Soormuck, 268
Sophiabad, 203
Springs, at Piatigorsk, 112 ; sulphurous in Persia, 315
Stables used as " Bust," 253
Stamboul, 392
Steamers, war screw, 64
Stories related to us, 140
St. Petersburg, Miss Benson's, 4 ; people of, 4 ; St. Isaac's, 7 ; winter palace at, 12 ;
Strachey " the beautiful," 255
Strauss, concert at Paulowsky, 12
Suganloo, 139
Sultan's palaces, 391
Sunday at Astrachan, 54
Sunset in Persia, 242
Sweetmeats, Persian, 254

Tabreez, 179—87
Tacht i Fernoun, 305 ; i Jumsheed, 280 ; i Rustam, 280—1 ; i Shahi, 300 ; i Taous, 279 ; i Timour, 301
Taough, 351
Tark Kesra, 337
Tartar, tombs, 140 ; khan, 170
Tchetchen dress, 101
Teheran, 205—34
Telega, a Russian cart, 66
Telegraph at Busheer, 320 ; at Fao, 369 ; at Shiraz, 286 ; in Russia, 127 ; in Teheran, 215 ; new line in Persia, 253
Telegraphic convention, 233
Telegraphy, expensive, 225
Temichanshura, 66, 71—3
Temperature near Kutishi, 79
Temple, Kalmuck, 60
Terek river, 103, 119
Theem, a royal palace, 241
Thiergarten, Berlin, 2
Tiflis, 124—39
Tigris, the, 335
Tireboli, 389
Tlock, our house there, 89
Tobacco plant, the, 240
Tokat, 382

Toleration, religious, 53 ; in Persia, 215
Tombs of Mohammedans, 69 ; of Mohammed Khodabundeh, 200; of Mr. Rich, 250
Toorkal, 383
Tooz Khurmati, 350
Torrida palace, 9
Trade, carrying, of Russia, 57
Translations of Scripture, 369
Travelling in the Caucasus, 67
Troglodytes, fit houses for, 141
Troikas, Russian carts, 68
Troitza, monastery of, 18
Tsaritzin, 40
Tsarkoe Seloe, palace of, 11,

Urmah, 77

Vegetation in Persia, 292
Venetian ironwork, 17
Versailles of Persia, 292
Videne, ball at, 97 ; reception at, 96 ; romantic gorge, 95
Visit in Persia, a, 186
Vladikavkas, 102—5
Volga, the, 26 ; length of navigable portion of, 56 ; villages on the banks of, 38 ; when frozen, 32

Walnut trees at Tlock, 90
Walpole collection of pictures, 7
Watch towers in Daghestan, 79
Water—melons, 41 ; supply, tenure of, in Persia, 219 ; tower, Moscow, 16
W., departure of, 318
Whist at Videne, 90
Wierzoboloff, Russian frontier, 4
Wine—at Astrachan, 54 ; in Daghestan, 81 ; at Shiraz, 288 ; skins in Tiflis, 134
Wodki, Russian brandy, 8
Women, Armenian, 144 ; pilgrims, 156 ; riding of, 145

Yengiyeh, 348
Yenitaieff, 41
Yezd, 253, 269
Yogunarshic, 152

Zakoo, 359
Zakuska before dinner, 9
Zengan, 195
Zengi, river, 149
Zengutai, 76
Zirgoon, 285
Zobeide, tomb of, 340
Zoog, 243
Zoological gardens at Teheran, 217

THE END.

J. SWIFT, REGENT PRESS, KING STREET, W.

www.ingramcontent.com/pod-product-compliance
Lightning Source LLC
Chambersburg PA
CBHW022120290426
44112CB00008B/743